Ecclesiological Investigations

Series Editor
Gerard Mannion

Volume: 14

Perpetually Reforming:
A Theology of Church Reform and Renewal

Other titles in the series:

Perpetually Reforming:
A Theology of Church Reform
and Renewal

John P. Bradbury

BLOOMSBURY

LONDON · NEW DELHI · NEW YORK · SYDNEY

Bloomsbury T&T Clark

An imprint of Bloomsbury Publishing Plc

50 Bedford Square	1385 Broadway
London	New York
WC1B 3DP	NY 10018
UK	USA

www.bloomsbury.com

Bloomsbury is a registered trade mark of Bloomsbury Publishing Plc

First published 2013
Paperback edition first published 2014

British Library Cataloguing-in-Publication Data
A catalogue record for this book is available from the British Library.

ISBN:	HB:	978-0-567-64409-1
	PB:	978-0-567-65689-6
	ePDF:	978-0-567-36333-6
	ePub:	978-0-567-38879-7

Library of Congress Cataloging-in-Publication Data
A catalog record for this book is available from the Library of Congress

Typeset by Deanta Global Publishing Services, Chennai, India

In memory of Daniel W. Hardy

Contents

Acknowledgements

Extracts from the *Basis of Union of the United Reformed Church* (London: United Reformed Church, 2000) reproduced by kind permission of the United Reformed Church.

All biblical references are (unless otherwise indicated) from the New Revised Standard Version. New Revised Standard Version Bible, copyright 1989, Division of Christian Education of the National Council of the Churches of Christ in the United States of America. Used by permission. All rights reserved.

Abbreviations

CD Karl Barth, *Church Dogmatics* (Edinburgh: T&T Clark, in 4 volumes, 1936–77).

1536 John Calvin, *Institutes of the Christian Religion.*1536 edition (Battles, Ford Lewis (trans.), Grand Rapids: Eerdmans, 1995).

1559 John Calvin, *Institutes of the Christian Religion.* 1559 edition (McNeill, John T. (ed.), Philadelphia: The Westminster Press, 1960).

LW Martin Luther, *Luther's Works, American Edition* (Lehmann, Helmut T. (ed.), 55 volumes, Philadelphia: Fortress Press, 1958–1986).

Foreword

'I have a love-hate relationship with the church'. When I spoke those words at my ordination to the Ministry of Word and Sacraments, they were much commented upon. It was considered a very unusual thing for a minister to say in public. The response was overwhelming. I was engaged by many people saying things like, 'I didn't know other people felt like that too', and, 'maybe if a minister feels like that, it is all right for me to feel that way too'. I suspect many people within the life of the churches feel this way. The church is 'home'. It is the place where we find our orientation in life. It is a place we come to know ourselves as loved in the sight of God and God's people. Yet, also, it is a place that drives us up the wall. It lacks integrity as it never seems to live up to its own standards, and at its worst, can be deeply abusive and damaging. We love it. We hate it. Particularly, perhaps, at this moment in history, the people of the church feel this way. The church has meant and means so much to us. It is indeed that place where we are loved and cherished by God and God's people, and yet that is deeply under threat. For those of us who have always been members of the church in traditional denominations, there is a sense of fear that soon they may not exist. The things we love about them are the things that are seemingly entirely ignored by the world. In that context, all too often panic sets in, and we flounder around, attempting anything in sight that might just help.

This book emerges in great part through my own love-hate relationship with the church, and as someone who often feels that he does not know what to do in the midst of a small, dying denomination within the nations of England, Wales and Scotland. It cannot offer complete answers, but it can, perhaps, reframe questions and shine some light in corners of hope. That is the intention.

This work has come into being over a very long period of time. My initial interest in the topic of 'the church' came to academic birth during my undergraduate studies at the University of Edinburgh. At that point, my interest was primarily ecumenical: what would an ecumenical ecclesiology look like?

As I began to work on this, I began to realize that my own reformed tradition did not seem to produce the volume of work on 'the church' that our Catholic, Orthodox or even Anglican friends did. To be ecumenical means to engage, but what I began to find was that I was not quite sure what my own tradition was wanting to offer into that engagement. My attention was then caught up in the project of reformed ecclesiology. The danger in that, though, is that it can end up hardening identities through attempting to have something to define oneself by in engagement with the other. One of the reasons, I concluded, why the reformed tradition lacks the quantity of ecclesiology that other traditions have is precisely that we are quite an open and porous tradition. Any tradition that claims to be 'perpetually reforming' will find it difficult to pin down exactly how it wants to define itself. These reflections came together through my experience of local ecumenical life, ecumenical dialogue on behalf of the United Reformed Church and in my academic studies. Eventually, this all found its way into my interest in what it meant to talk about being 'perpetually reforming'. This book is part of that journey.

This work began life as a PhD thesis at the University of Cambridge. It was my intention for some years to make substantial revisions to it before seeking to publish. As is perhaps often the case, that process began to take on a life of its own and has turned into something a little different. In the light of that, I have returned to the original thesis and have made more modest revisions in preparation for publication (though 'minor revisions' have become rather more extensive than I originally planned!).

Throughout this journey, there have been many amazing people who have supported me, stimulated my thinking, guided me in the ways of theology and ministry and without whom this project would never have seen the light of day. I owe a particularly large debt of gratitude to the late Rev Prof Daniel W. Hardy who was my doctoral supervisor. Dan's wisdom was phenomenal. He was a deeply gifted teacher, theologian and priest, who saw the academic theological project as encompassing the whole of life. Theology could never be engaged with outside the joy and struggle of life in the world because theology concerned itself with the entirety of life in the world. Dan always knew how to ask the right questions and always sought to allow me to find my own theological voice within my own tradition. He is greatly missed.

My initial research was made possible by a University of Cambridge Award that funded my PhD, and I'm also grateful to Prof Eberhard Jüngel for making possible a research term at the Evangelische Stift at the University of Tübingen. I'm also very grateful to Rev Dr. Philip Luscombe and Prof Michael Welker for offering their suggestions and insights during the examination of the thesis.

There have been many other people who have been very significant through the years that have led to this book. Others who have supervised me and engaged with me academically and within the life of the church particularly include Rev Dr David Cornick, Rev Prof David Thompson and Prof David Ford. The academic staff of Westminster College were amazingly supportive to me when I was a student, particularly Rev Dr. Janet Tollington as tutor (and proofreader!), and also Rev. John Proctor, Rev Dr. Lance Stone, Rev Dr. Peter McEnhill and Rev Prof. Stephen Orchard. Janet and John have also been wonderful colleagues as I returned to Westminster as part of the teaching staff a few years ago, along with the Principal, Rev Dr. Susan Durber and the Revd. Neil Thorogood. Without all their wisdom, guidance, vision, friendship and enthusiasm, Westminster College would not be the creative and vibrant place it is. I am also very grateful to Westminster College and the United Reformed Church for making sabbatical time available to me and generously funding that. Equally, the folk I studied with myself at Westminster have been very important over my years in ministry, particularly the Revs Sarah Moore and Janet Sutton-Webb. The students I've been privileged to teach and journey with at Westminster have also been the source of great theological stimulation. Particular thanks must go to Phil Wall for his careful reading of the original dissertation and his penetrating questions and insights. Colleagues within the wider Cambridge Theological Federation have also been significant to me; it is a highly encouraging and diverse context out of which to engage with the practice of theology. The joy of teaching a course on the Church and Sacraments to an ecumenical group of students with my Roman Catholic colleague, Dr. Oonagh O'Brien, has been particularly significant.

My years in Liverpool in ministry were also deeply formative of many of the themes which have emerged within this book. I owe particular thanks to the folk of Earle Road United Reformed Church, who taught me so much about what being church is about, and the members of the City Centre Ecumenical Team who provided wonderful colleagueship. Particular thanks must go to

Rev Dr. Barbara Glasson, whose wisdom and sense of fun taught me a huge amount about what really matters in ministry. The community she ministered with, 'Somewhere Else', which gathered around the baking of bread, equally taught me a great deal about what church really could be.

My engagement with ecumenical dialogue and faith and order issues has also been massively formative of my own theological work. I must thank all those who I have had the privilege of working with, particularly the members of the URC's Faith and Order Reference group, the URC-Roman Catholic ecumenical dialogue, the Community of Protestant Churches in Europe dialogue groups I've been privileged to be part of, and the United Reformed Church's Human Sexuality Task Group.

Over the years, there have been many, many people with whom I've enjoyed theological conversation which is the engine that powers the whole theological project. Theology can never be done in isolation. Many have been members of the Society for the Study of Theology which has been a very significant place for such conversation to happen. There are far too many people who have been great conversationalists to name them all, but some of those who have been significant include Rachel Muers, Chad Pecknold, Jon K. Cooley, Julie Gittoes, Giles Waller, Sophie Lunn-Rockcliffe, Matthew Prevett, Paul Nimmo, Nigel Uden, Tom Greggs, Tony Bottoms and Mike Higton. There are many other friends from over the years who have been a wonderful source of inspiration and support. A particular note of thanks must go to Romilly Micklem whose careful (and trenchant!) engagement with the original dissertation led to some of the more significant revisions.

The church is an amazing place. It can also be a very difficult place, and thanks are due to all of those people who have helped me cope with some of the difficulties the maddening institution of the church throws at us from time to time. Most of all, I want to thank my parents, whose love and support have been incredible over the years, and who have taught me most of all what it means to be the church in the cradle of the 'domestic church', the family. Thank you.

Introduction

The problem with 'Church'

The church exists. This fact is one that is most inconvenient for anyone attempting to engage with the theology of the church. Throughout the world, people gather to worship, to engage with preaching and teaching, to celebrate the Lord's Supper, to take part in sacramental practices and to witness and serve within their communities in the name of Jesus Christ. Church buildings litter the landscape and clergy appear in the media to comment on the matters of the day. There are structures – councils and gatherings of people who claim to be the church. These range from a local church meeting to international gatherings of the ecumenical movement. There are organizations that call themselves church, ranging from independent local congregations meeting in borrowed rooms to the worldwide institution and structures of the Roman Catholic Church. All claim the title 'church', all are recognized as such by society, often formally so through legal recognition of their status.

Just to restrict our reflection to local groups of people within Britain who claim the title 'church', we find those for whom true worship takes place only in silence and those for whom worship is a very noisy experience; those for whom formalized and ancient rituals are essential to their self-understanding as church and those for whom the planning and preparation of worship is anathema. Yet, somehow, whether one walks into a great and ancient cathedral at worship or into the gathering of a black Pentecostal community, we will recognize something which we term 'church'.

If we assume (and it may not be a correct assumption) that in engaging with the theology of the church, in the activity we call 'ecclesiology', we are in some way defining the word 'church', we begin to realize, right at the outset, that this is no easy task. Whatever we say about the church, it will be possible to point to some group of people who claim the title whose existence flatly contradicts whatever definition we might offer. Indeed, the attempt to define 'church' is one which is not just a theological enterprise. Various possibilities present themselves. A historian may offer a definition based on the history of such institutions that claim the title, or equally (and here, there may be considerable overlap with the work of a historical theologian), may offer a definition based on the history of ideas. A sociologist may well wish to attempt to define 'church' on the basis of enquiry into the formation of social groups. An anthropologist may attempt the matter through discussion of concepts such as 'culture'. Someone engaged in the field of the study of religion may attempt a definition based upon the notion of a 'religious phenomenon'. These are just a small number of examples of how we might go about defining 'church'. These, however, come from recognizable academic disciplines. We must also remember that within western society, most individuals would have some understanding of what they might mean by 'church': often, it might be a building or a place. Equally, one can ask the various bodies and organizations who define themselves as 'church' and they would give many and varied possible definitions.

Perhaps, one should not be surprised at such diversity within the bodies who claim the name 'church'. Paul Minear, in his work *Images of the Church in the New Testament* delineates approximately 100 different 'images' used within the canon of the New Testament to speak of the church.[1] Only a few of these images Minear identifies as seminal; namely, *the People of God*, *the Body of Christ* and *the New Creation*, but the existence within the New Testament of such a variety of images is highly significant. It is a very simple observation to note that the diversity of images within the New Testament correlates with the enormous diversity of expressions of the life of the church that we have noted above. In such a situation, one cannot but draw the conclusion that no one definition of 'church' will be possible. Given this, any ecclesiology that is attempting to engage with the church must offer no easy definitions and must avoid the temptation to devise a neat and tidy conclusion. If we reflect on the fact that the images Minear identifies are only from the New Testament, one can only wonder at the number of images that would emerge if a similar study were to identify all of the images used for the people of God, of Israel, in the Hebrew scriptures. To say this simply underlines the point that the church will

---

[1] Paul S. Minear, *Images of the Church in the New Testament* (London: Lutterworth Press, 1960).

neither permit definition nor systemization. Neither will scripture. Any attempt at ecclesiology that seeks to maintain its integrity in the face of scripture and the concrete reality of the church must attempt to avoid the pitfalls of simple definitions or neat systemization.

Nicholas Healy, in his work *Church, World and the Christian Life* has issued a call for ecclesiology to respond to some of the challenges outlined above. Healy states the issue this way:

> To the extent that modern ecclesiology is governed by an abstract, rationalistic and overly theoretical approach, it makes it difficult for theologians to acknowledge the realities of the church's concrete identity. Ecclesiology is misguided if it attempts to construct, on the basis of a single model or principle, a systematic blueprint for the church that applies normatively always and everywhere. Such a blueprint can be very powerful and replete with profound theological language. Yet it may well prove to be a harmful presence to the ecclesiological context and thus practically and prophetically false. Ecclesiology is not a doctrinal theology that can be worked out without close attention to the concrete life of the Church.[2]

Here, some of the methodological issues that emerge for the discipline of ecclesiology become very apparent. How does one simultaneously pay close attention to the concrete life of the church and say anything at all when the manifestations of the life of the church are so diverse and multifarious? Healy begins almost immediately to narrow down his definitions when he restricts his enquiry to 'all those diverse Christian groups who accept what is sometimes cumbersomely called the Niceno-Constantinopolitan creed'.[3] This immediately excludes some historic, and many new, manifestations of church and already is applying something of a 'principle' in the definition of 'church'. Despite this, he has offered a highly generative account of some of the problems that emerge within what he terms 'blueprint ecclesiologies'. These he identifies as having five key methodological elements:

> One is the attempt to encapsulate in a single word or phrase the most essential characteristic of the church; another is to construe the church as having a bipartite structure. These two elements are often combined, third,

---

[2] Nicholas M. Healy, *Church, World and the Christian Life: Practical-Prophetic Ecclesiology* (Cambridge: Cambridge University Press, 2000), p. 50.

[3] Healy, *Church, World*, p. 6.

into a systematic and theoretical form of normative ecclesiology. A fourth element is a tendency to reflect upon the church in abstraction from its concrete identity. And one consequence of this is, fifth, a tendency to present idealized accounts of the church.[4]

This kind of account of how ecclesiology frequently functions begins to explain some of the difficulties it encounters in offering a helpful account, or constructive understanding, of the reform and renewal of the life of the church. Such idealized accounts of the church that function as a blueprint, end up offering what I term an 'eternalized' account of the life of the church. In the reformed tradition, from which I work, this has frequently emerged within accounts of a bipartite structure of the church in terms of its visible and invisible realities. As we shall see, while this is originally rooted in an understanding of the need to protect the sovereignty of God, what too often can end up happening is that an abstracted notion of the invisible church ends up functioning as an almost platonic ideal of the church, which the real historical church must attempt to emulate. This runs a very real risk of stating that the church, as we experience it within historical reality, is not actually the church at all. It turns the church which, in the creedal formula, 'We believe', into an abstracted, idealized one, rather than any church in which we worship or practice our faith and grow.

The methodological problem becomes very apparent when one extends these lines of thinking. Given the shear diversity, and even, at times contradictory nature of the historical reality of the church, how can one take it seriously in its concrete reality? Even if one can find an appropriate way of doing this, one might wish to stand back and then ask whether any theology of the church that emerged was truly a theology of the church, or was a mere description of historical realities that call themselves the 'church'? How might one then test, theologically, whether they are indeed the church or not? A theology of the church cannot remain only at the descriptive level, but rather, must also challenge the church to become ever more faithful to its vocation, ever more fully 'the church'. How does that happen unless there is some kind of idea of what the church is, which then runs the risk of abstraction or functioning as a blueprint? The task becomes even more complex when one stops to consider

[4]   Ibid., p. 26.

that the empirical church is equally not simply static. Put simply; it changes and develops. The church, as we live and experience it today, is in both continuity and discontinuity with the earliest church. The church is a dynamic movement and institution. While it is a slogan particularly of the reformed tradition, it is reasonable at a basic descriptive level to state that the church is always perpetually reforming. How are we to account for that? What, theologically, can we say about how that happens? This requires close attention not only to the concrete reality of the church, but also to how it is that the church exists, both in continuity and discontinuity.

The account that Healy offers of the dynamic of the concrete church pays close attention to the historical context of the church, and the practical and prophetic task of theology as it addresses the church. However, Gary Badcock has questioned the assertion that only a *praxis*-driven approach to ecclesiology has a significant impact upon the life of the church. Reflecting on the role played within Roman Catholic ecclesiology and beyond by Karl Rahner in the twentieth century, Badcock states that 'highly theoretical accounts of the being of the church have had, and can thus presumably still have, a massive impact on the concrete reality of the church. Therefore what one *thinks* would appear to make a great deal of difference to what one *does,* how one *acts,* what one concretely *is*'.[5] In terms of the theologies of the church that Badcock is addressing at this point – namely, Karl Rahner and Karl Barth – this is undoubtedly the case and is realized through close attention to historical reality (not least the impact of Rahner's thought on Vatican II).

Badcock's defence of more theoretical attempts at ecclesiology is helpful, and causes us to think about the nature of theology itself. Praxis approaches to theology, as often set out in terms of Practical or Pastoral theology, often revolve around the notion of a 'cycle', which relates practice to reflection on that practice that, in turn, then informs the renewal of that practice.[6] There is no doubt that such 'cycles' have had a considerable impact upon the theological life of the church, particularly in the preparation of students for ministry. They are, however, based upon a number of assumptions that should not go

---

[5] Gary D. Badcock, *The House Where God Lives: Renewing the Doctrine of the Church for Today* (Grand Rapids/Cambridge: Eerdmans, 2009), p. 6.

[6] For a classic account of such a cycle, which has had considerable impact in the formation of clergy for ministry, see Laurie Green, *Let's do Theology: A Pastoral Cycle Resource Book* (London: Mowbray, 1990), pp. 24–41.

wholly unchallenged. First, they accept a broad division of the *practical* from
the *theoretical,* which is not always easy to sustain. To theorize is actually a
practice. Theology can (and indeed, I will argue, should) be understood as
one of the fundamental practices of the church. The practice of theology is
itself inherently practical, rather than simply being able to be understood
solely as *theory.* Secondly, this notion of a pastoral theological cycle returns
us to the question of how one might recognize the church as church, from
mere description. It inherently runs the danger that reflection on practice ends
up being reflection on *bad* practice, unless appropriate reparative theological
critique is offered. There is also a tendency for the working assumption to
be that the locus of theological thought is always the individual. While this
is clearly, in some ways, simply common sense, this is by no means always
the case. Theology is also a practice of the church that makes itself manifest
in creedal and confessional statements, the results of ecumenical dialogues,
reports of Synods and commissions and so on. At their worst, these could
perhaps be written off as 'theology by committee'; at their best, however, they
are a vital way in which it becomes possible to hear the voice of the church
speaking collectively as it reflects on the self-identity of itself as what, in
Bonhoeffer's terms, we might speak of as a 'collective person'.[7] Ways need to be
found that allow the concrete reality of the church to truly be taken seriously
(which Pastoral theologies do) as the church, but that also takes seriously the
nature of theology as a practice of the church (often a reparative practice) that
does, at times, work precisely by holding a vision of the church before the life
of the church that calls it to reformation and renewal.

Another recent attempt to engage precisely with the concrete reality of the
life of the church as well as take very seriously the theological voice of the
church itself has been the significant three-volume project of Roger Haight, S.J.,
Christian Community in History.[8] Haight distinguishes between ecclesiology
'from above'[9] and ecclesiology 'from below'.[10] Seeking to develop an ecclesiology

[7] Dietrich Bonhoeffer, *Sacntorum Communio: A Theological Study of the Sociology of the Church*
    (Glifford J. Green (ed.), Reinhard Krauss and Nancy Lukens (trans.), Dietrich Bonhoeffer Works,
    Volume 1, Minneapolis: Fortress Press, 1996), pp. 118–21.
[8] Roger Haight, S. J., *Christian Community in History* (3 vols, New York/London: Continuum), 2004,
    2005, 2008.
[9] Roger Haight, S. J., *Christian Community in History: Historical Ecclesiology* (New York/London:
    Continuum, 2004), pp. 18–25.
[10] Roger Haight, S. J., *Historical Ecclesiology*, pp. 26–66.

'from below', he concerns himself with many of the methodological questions that have detained us. He is concerned, above all else, to take seriously the historical reality of the life of the churches, in a similar way to Healy's concern with the concrete reality of the church. As such, he is concerned with the empirical reality of the church. This, however, is far from restricted to the investigation of the empirical reality of the present church, but is concerned with the life of the church throughout its history. He begins with a volume on the church till the time of the reformation, continues with a comparative study in the second volume of the reality of the church from the reformation period to the present, and then in the third volume, attempts to distil the ecclesiological results of this into an account of what ecclesial existence might mean and what its contours are. His approach is helpful precisely because it attempts both to take seriously the empirical reality and also the theological self-understanding and expression of the identity of the church historically. This is not simply a study of institutions, but of the self-understanding of those institutions. One might note that even such close attention to the historical and comparative reality of the church results in an account of ecclesial existence which one might be able to categorize, with Healy's notion of a 'blueprint ecclesiology'. What is so immensely helpful in this account, however, is that the historical reality of the church is accounted for in terms of change and development. Haight states that, 'The language of belief, doctrine itself, takes on new meanings in new situations. How is the church to measure its identity and continuity with its past in history?'[11] This is to raise the question of change and continuity. How is it that the church both remains the church, and yet is always, in reality, changing?

Haight's response to the question of ecclesial change and continuity is in many ways highly successful. He offers a 'transdenominational'[12] ecclesiology, which leads to an exploration of major issues that, taken together, begin to offer an account of the church which covers the nature and mission of the church, the organization of the church, the membership of the church, the activities of the church and the church in relation to the world. The argument is, in essence, that there are continuities within these aspects of the life of the

---

[11] Ibid., p. 54.
[12] Roger Haight, S. J., *Christian Community in History: Ecclesial Existence* (London/New York: Continuum, 2008), pp. 5–12.

church that become historically contingently expressed in different forms in different times and places. The supporting of this account by such a historical reading of the concrete reality of the life of the churches is massively helpful, and in certain respects could be taken as supplying the background to this present work. What concerns this book, however, is not the church as a whole in broad terms, but the more focused question of the processes of the formation of the identity of the church within history. What happens, or what is it that the church does (or should do), that reforms and renews the life of the church, while it simultaneously remains the church?

The Church in the twenty-first century context

The question of the reformation and renewal of the church is one which has become particularly pressing within Western Europe because of the massive rates of decline in church membership and attendance. There is considerable debate as to whether this decline is simply a European phenomenon or not. In 1999, Michael Jinkins published his *The Church Faces Death: Ecclesiology in a Post-Modern Context*, which emerged from the North American context and the decline of the mainstream churches there. He quoted startling figures based on research by the Presbyterian Church in the United States of America (PCUSA), which show that the traditions that make up that church lost 28 per cent of their membership between 1965 and 1985, and that similar mainstream denominations had faced other major losses (American Baptists, 37%, Disciples of Christ, 42%, the Episcopal Church, 20%, the United Church of Christ, 19% and the Methodist Church, 17%).[13] He quotes the PCUSA membership in 1996 as standing at 2,631,446. The figures for 2010 stand at 2,016,091.[14] This decline is one that Jinkins seeks to treat with theological seriousness, as he asks what this means for the mainstream churches in the United States of America. One cannot also ignore the reality that overall, the United States of America is still very religiously active when viewed from a European perspective. Some of this decline of the mainstream churches is not so much decline, but rather

---

[13] Michael Jinkins, *The Church Faces Death: Ecclesiology in a Post-Modern Context* (New York/Oxford: Oxford University Press, 1999), p. 10.

[14] http://www.pcusa.org/media/uploads/oga/pdf/2010-comparative-summaries-stats.pdf, accessed, 12th April, 2012.

'switching' to other, often independent, conservative forms of Christianity.[15] As such, sociologists of religion such as Grace Davie, Peter Berger and Effie Fokas, note a fundamental difference in the patterns of religious observance and belief between Europe and other parts of the world, notably in terms of discussions surrounding the relationship between modernity and secularization in North America.[16] Something of the seriousness with which Jinkins takes the demise of the church, even in North America, would be supported by another sociologist of religion, Steve Bruce, who has mounted a strong defence of the secularization theory, arguing that, with careful interrogation of the figures, religious observance is not what it might first appear, and that secularization has happened both in terms of the decline in influence in public policy, and also in terms of the secularization of the church itself.[17]

While for our purposes, we do not need to take a position on how one understands the relative patterns of church attendance within North America, what is clear is that even if attendance is taken to have been relatively stable, and relatively high compared with Europe, the nature of that churchgoing has shifted drastically away from traditional mainstream (particularly Protestant) traditions in the last 50 years. This, in and of itself, is causing churches to re-evaluate what being a church might mean, and out of this context new approaches to church life have emerged.

The European case is far more stark than that of the United States of America. Grace Davie quotes figures from 1999/2000, which suggest that just over 31 per cent of Europeans attend church once a week or once a month, with attendance in historically Roman Catholic countries being significantly higher than in historically Lutheran countries. At that point in time, in Great Britain (the context out of which this author is writing) attendance once a week or once a month stood at about 20 per cent.[18] Davie cites these statistics as coming from the European Values survey. It is interesting to compare them with the results of the English Church Census, which takes place roughly

---

[15] Grace Davie, *Europe: The Exceptional Case: Parameters of Faith in the Modern World* (London: Darton, Longman and Todd, 2002), pp. 29–30.

[16] See Peter Berger, Grace Davie and Efflie Fokas, *Religious America, Secular Europe? A Theme and Variations* (Farnham/Burlington: Ashgate, 2008) and Grace Davie, *Europe*.

[17] Steve Bruce, *God is Dead: Secularization in the West* (Oxford: Blackwell, 2002), pp. 204–28, and Steve Bruce, *Secularization: In Defence of an Unfashionable Theory* (Oxford: Oxford University Press, 2011), pp. 157–76.

[18] Grace Davie, *Europe: The Exceptional Case*, p. 6.

once a decade and asks a significant representative sample of congregations to literally count and report on the number of people in church on a given Sunday. This gives the result that in 1998 (just before the European Values Survey findings), 7.5 per cent of the English (note, not the population of Great Britain as a whole in this case) population were actually in church. In 2005, that had reduced to 6.3 per cent.[19] This author's own church, the United Reformed Church (which is found in England, Scotland and Wales) has suffered an extraordinary decline since its formation in 1972, initially from a Union of the Presbyterian and Congregational traditions in England. In 1973/4 (the first Yearbook to be published of the new denomination), its membership stood at 192,241 members in 2,080 churches.[20] In 2012 (after further unions in 1981 with the Churches of Christ, and 2000 with the Scottish Congregational Church, which increased numbers twice by union between 1972 and 2012), the figures stood at 63,680 across 1529 churches.[21] The English Church Census marks the United Reformed Church as the fastest declining mainstream church in England (down 53 per cent between 1979 and 1998), but in the same period other mainstream churches suffered a massive decline too, the Church of England by 24 per cent, the Roman Catholics by 32 per cent and the Methodists by 26 per cent.[22] The fact of the numbers themselves suggests that this has been a massive period of change within church life in Great Britain, even before one begins to ask more probing questions as to how this might be explained. What theological resources do we have to help us understand what it is for the church to experience such a change (not just this kind, but any)? By what processes and practices does the identity of the church undergo reformation and renewal in the midst of such fast-paced change? This work attempts to offer some theological ways of approaching the nature of the social identity formation of the church that might help the church understand what is to be re-formed in this context.

How we are to understand the processes that have led to this fundamental shift in the place that the church has in the Western world is a vital question, and one that merits far fuller investigation than it can receive here. This work

---

[19] Peter Brierley, *Pulling out of the Nose Dive: A Contemporary Picture of Churchgoing: What the 2005 English Church Census Reveals* (London: Christian Research, 2006), p. 12.

[20] The United Reformed Church, *Year Book 1973/4* (London: United Reformed Church, 1974).

[21] The United Reformed Church, *Year Book 2012* (London: United Reformed Church, 2012).

[22] Peter Brierley, *Pulling out of the Nose Dive*, pp. 26–31.

is not seeking to answer the question as to how the church responds to the social, intellectual and economic context in which it finds itself, but rather to a question at one removed from that: about the practices of church life that enable the formation of the social identity of the church. Clearly, one cannot entirely remove that question from the particular context in which we do find ourselves.

Attempts to understand what has happened in the Western culture that has led to secularization vary. Steve Bruce is the sociologist who most clearly stands within a classical position regarding secularization theory, which argues that one of the key origins of secularization is the Protestant reformation.[23] While the detail of the argument need not detain us, the broad sweep of it should give any theologian working broadly within one of the Protestant traditions pause for thought. In various forms, that work their way out in intellectual, social and economic forms, there is a line running from the Protestant reformation and its sense of the individual relating directly to God, and being responsible for the interpretation of scripture themselves, through to economic growth and social differentiation, which leads ultimately in the direction of a strong sense of individualism. This also leads to a cultural and intellectual relativity that ultimately undermines the fundamental premises of any collective institutionalized expression of 'religion'.[24] This thought has been explored and developed in a more explicitly theological direction by Gerald W. Schlabach, a former Mennonite who has converted to the Roman Catholic Church. He speaks of 'the Protestant Dilemma', which is essentially that intrinsic to Protestantism is the need to be always offering critique to all forms of community; always to be prophetic and faithful anew in the present moment.[25] As Schlabach states:

> The problem with the Protestant Principle is this: however right and proper are the corrective reflexes it names, once we elevate impulses to 'protest' into identity markers for entire Christian communities, those impulses tend to undermine the very bonds of Christian community. If the Protestant

---

[23] For a classic account of secularization theory, see Steve Bruce, *God is Dead*, pp. 1–44.
[24] We need to be careful of the term 'religion'. It is one that theology must not automatically assume is 'good' in the context of debates concerning secularization. For an outstanding account of the relationship of theology to the concept of 'religion', see Tom Greggs, *Theology Against Religion* (London: T&T Clark, 2011).
[25] Gerald W. Schlabach, *Unlearning Protestantism: Sustaining Christian Community in an Unstable Age* (Grand Rapids: Brazos Press, 2010), p. 24.

Principle is not just one principle among many – though quite near to the core of Protestant identity itself – then Protestantism will tend to undo itself.[26]

Schlabach is not, here, trying to make a cheap point against the Protestant position; in fact, he is at pains to point out that continual protest and self-examination is a vital part of healthy church life, but is pointing to something very significant about what it is that holds the community together, as the community enables the holding of the faith of individuals.[27]

Another major account of how we arrived at 'A Secular Age' has been offered by Charles Taylor in his monumental work of that title. His fundamental question concerns how Western society has moved 'from a society in which it was virtually impossible not to believe in God, to one in which faith, even for the staunchest believer, is one human possibility among others.[28] This, he maintains, cannot be understood simply by asking about belief itself, but, rather, by asking about the 'conditions of belief'. This concerns 'the whole context of understanding in which our moral, spiritual or religious experience and search takes place'.[29] Taylor goes on to examine the historical processes by which the 'conditions of belief' have fundamentally shifted, and he too places the Reformation in a particular place within this story. One of the key shifts that he identifies is the shift from an 'enchanted universe', to an 'unenchanted universe'. By these terms Taylor means a universe where the supernatural is ordinarily considered to be present to life in the world. He sees this as shifted through the reformation by a move away from 'various "sacramentals", or locations of sacred power which we can draw on', to 'our inner transformation, our throwing ourselves on God's mercy in faith'.[30] This shift moves the locus of action away from the practices of the community, into the realm of the thought and experience of the individual human being, and thus marks an intrinsic movement in the direction of humanism. This movement also moved us towards what Taylor calls the 'Disciplinary Society', the sense that what came to expression in Calvinism's desire to order society and to maintain personal and social discipline was something that leads in the

---

[26] Schlabach, *Unlearning Protestantism*, p. 33.
[27] Ibid., p. 31.
[28] Charles Taylor, *A Secular Age* (Cambridge, MA and London, England: The Belknap Press of Harvard University Press, 2007), p. 3.
[29] Taylor, *A Secular Age*, p. 3.
[30] Ibid., p. 79.

direction of the sense that humanity itself controls the giving of order.[31] Intrinsic to Taylor's account throughout is that the beliefs and practices of society as a whole, as they have developed historically, have led to a situation where belief has become one of the range of possibilities. Fundamentally, human beings have now understood that this is a choice that they can make, and that some developments of the church – both theologically and in terms of the relationship of the church to society as a whole – have led to this situation.

There are two primary issues that we need to take into consideration as we begin to explore the theological resources for understanding the reformation and renewal of the church. First, that Western society is now one where fundamentally individual human beings construe themselves as autonomous, and we determine our identity for ourselves, rather than our identity being formed primarily by the social group(s) to which we belong. This poses the most massive challenge to the church. Fundamental to Christian life is to be baptized into the body of Christ, which relativizes all human identities and brings us into a fundamental relationship with Christ through our relationships within the community of the church. This does not, in a world where we construe our own identities and 'opt-in' to human groups, make sense. Responses to this fundamental issue divide the church quite considerably at the moment. While this work is not setting out to primarily address this question (which hopefully can be addressed more directly in future work), it is one we must not lose sight of. If the processes of reformation and renewal within the life of the church are to be understood truly within the context of life in the world, as we are experiencing it in the West today, we need to offer some kind of account of the way in which Christian sociality is meaningfully formed within this primarily individualistic culture. Secondly, we also need to carry with us the intrinsic warning that has been sounded about the reformation of the life of the church. As someone who stands in the reformed tradition, and who remains convinced that the notion of the perpetual reformation of the church is of value, it still cannot be ignored that within this idea rests the possibility of the 'undoing' of any form of community that results. We cannot ignore the reality that the reformation itself has indeed been seminal in leading to what is now being experienced as secularization.

We must be wary of making too many assumptions and placing value judgements on our current condition; the church being a small one in Western

---

[31] Ibid., pp. 119–21.

Europe does not necessarily mean that it is a bad church (though of course, it might be). Neither should we necessarily assume that the church is meant to be large and thriving. In reality, that may not be the case. What we must be wary of are the understandings and practices of church life that are not sustainable because they suffer from an over-emphasis on reformation for its own sake.

Within this context there are various movements emerging, which are seeking to engage with the question of the reformation and renewal of the life of the church. A recent study by the Community of Protestant Churches in Europe on reform and renewal processes within Europe has demonstrated that structural reform (usually involving reducing the number of 'layers' of church structures between the local church and national church bodies), liturgical reform and experiments with new forms of church life are taking place across the continent.[32] The statistical evidence that we have already examined suggests that this is, at least as yet, making no discernible difference to the life of the churches in terms of numbers. Within the English-speaking world, of particular note are the Emerging Church and Fresh Expressions of Church movements. The Emerging Church movement is primarily rooted within the North American context, and Fresh Expressions is an initiative that arose initially out of the Church of England, but has been taken up by the Methodist and United Reformed Churches too.[33] Taking the Fresh Expressions initiative as an example, it is possible to illustrate how the question of the renewal and reformation of the church is taken up in some of these initiatives and movements. There is a fascinating definition offered to the term 'Fresh Expressions':

> The phrase **fresh expressions of church** is used in this report. The Preface to the Declaration of Assent, which Church of England ministers make at their licensing, states 'The Church of England . . . professes the faith uniquely revealed in the Holy Scriptures and set forth in the catholic creeds, which faith the Church is called upon to proclaim afresh in each generation.' The

---

[32] *Ecclesia Semper Reformanda*, a study of the Community of Protestant Churches in Europe. Adopted by the 2012 General Assembly of the CPCE. Available at: http://www.cpce-assembly.eu/media/pdf/ Unterlagen/11%20Ecclesia%20semper%20reformanda.pdf , accessed on 21st November, 2012.

[33] Literature abounds concerning these movements. It is unnecessary to offer a full review of all the available literature, but it is helpful to cite a few examples. See Brain D. McLaren, *Church on the Other Side: Exploring the Radical Future of the Local Congregation* (Grand Rapids: Zondervan, 2006); Brian D. McLaren, *Everything Must Change: Jesus, Global Crises, and a Revolution of Hope* (Nashville: Thomas Nelson, 2007); Dan Kimball, *The Emerging Church: Vintage Christianity for New Generations* (Grand Rapids: Zondervan, 2003); Eddie Gibbs and Ryan K. Bolger, *Emerging Churches: Creating Christian Community in Postmodern Cultures* (London: SPCK, 2006).

term 'fresh expressions' echoes these words. It suggests something new or enlivened is happening, but also suggests connection to history and the developing story of God's work in the Church. The phrase also embraces two realities: existing churches that are seeking to renew or redirect what they already have, and others who are intentionally sending out planting groups to discover what will emerge when the gospel is immersed in the mission context.[34]

Here we see something of the logic of *semper reformanda* at work. The church is called to 'proclaim afresh' in every generation. There is a distinction between the content of the faith and the way in which it is expressed within the life of the church. The former, it is presumed, does not change, while the latter is called to embody it differently according to the contexts in which it finds itself. The report goes on to outline the different forms in which Fresh Expressions might be found from café churches, to network churches, to churches that gather around specific special interests. The thesis is that these new forms of church life respond to a shifting cultural context, which the report analyses. It offers similar reflections on the nature of contemporary society that we have outlined above, but does so through categories such as changes in employment and housing patterns, new forms of family life and the increase of divorce, the rise of 'networks' over and above people being located in one particular geographical space and the rise of consumer culture.[35] It goes on to offer methodologies for missionary churches, which pay close attention to the context, and particular attention is placed on the idea of whom the church plant is for. There is a strong sense in which Fresh Expressions are aimed at a target audience. This is rooted in Donald McGavron's theory of the Homogenous Unit Principle, which suggests that people 'prefer to remain who they are culturally while changing to being Christian. Culturally they remain the same, and tend to gather with others from the same culture who share their faith'.[36] The report indicates that this is a controversial notion, but quickly dismisses objections to it, on the basis that the logic of incarnation is that the church should be contextually formed.

---

[34] Church House Publishing, *Mission-Shaped Church: Church Planting and Fresh Expressions of Church in a Changing Context* (London: Church House Publishing, 2004), p. 34.
[35] *Mission Shaped Church*, pp. 1–15.
[36] Ibid., p. 108.

There is no doubt that Fresh Expressions has gained much momentum within church life within the United Kingdom in recent years, but it has not been uncontroversial, and many of the presuppositions embedded within the movement have been criticized. From one side, criticism has come from John Hull, in a brief pamphlet, *Mission-Shaped Church: A Theological Response*.[37] Hull makes many criticisms, but key among them are that there is a confusion in the report between mission, the church and the kingdom. Hull suggests that far from being a 'Mission-Shaped Church', there is a considerable danger that, in reality, what is proposed ends up being a 'Church-shaped mission'. Hull suggests that, 'The purpose or function of mission is to bring in the Kingdom. In order to do this effectively the mission has (among other things) a church'.[38] The kingdom is the goal of the mission, whereas the church is the instrument. Hull fears that what is, in reality, going on in the movement is a centring on the church and the desire to create new churches. He goes so far as to call this attempt the 're-establishing' of Christendom.[39] This criticism is linked to a perceived lack of ecumenicity that sees the Church of England as, effectively, the only church called to minister within England. Hull sees a lack of commitment to the creation of the kingdom, both in terms of the report's reliance on the Homogenous Unit Principle, which he sees as ignoring the gospel call to the inclusion of diversity within one church, and through its lack of attention to the diversity of the world in which the church is situated. He particularly notes the report's failure to perceive the need to challenge the structures of the society which keep alive unjust divisions: 'The poor are empowered not by having their own poor churches but by escaping from poverty'.[40]

From a different perspective, the Fresh Expressions movement has been critiqued by Andrew Davison and Alison Milbank, in *For the Parish: A Critique of Fresh Expressions*.[41] Coming from firmly within the Church of England, and its more Catholic wing, this raises concerns of a related – but different – nature to those raised by John Hull. In fact, to some extent Davison and Milbank strongly criticize Hull, particularly in terms of his understanding

[37] John M. Hull, *Mission-Shaped Church: A Theological Response* (London: SCM, 2006).
[38] Hull, *Mission-Shaped Church*, p. 2.
[39] Hull, *Theological Response*, p. 20.
[40] Ibid., p. 33.
[41] Andrew Davison and Alison Millbank, *For the Parish: A Critique of Fresh Expressions* (London: SCM, 2010).

of the relationship between the church and the kingdom. They wish to see a far closer relationship between the church and the kingdom than in the *Mission-Shaped Church* report, rather than seeing the one as the instrument for the realization of the other. In following the logic that the church is the body of Christ, as Christ is himself, the church becomes both the agent and the objective of the mission[42]; 'The form of the Church here and now begins to live out the reconciliation that she promises in her message of salvation.'[43] They then go on to offer a biblical account of the diversity of the body of Christ image, with which they (more along the lines of Hull) critique the Homogenous Unit Principle and make the case for the traditional diversity contained within the territorial parish.[44]

Fundamental to the account that Davison and Milbank offer is an observation that they make at the start of their work about the relatedness of form and content, something they maintain that Fresh Expressions has lost sight of. 'They are bound together: the content is in the form; the meaning is in the practices. Change the form and we change how we understand the content; change the practices and we at least risk changing the meaning.'[45] They then go on to identify what they term the 'communal turn' in post-liberal theology, particularly in the work of George Lindbeck.[46] The Christian faith is not a set of propositional statements (as they suggest it is fundamentally understood within the *Mission-Shaped Church* report), but rather a set of embedded and lived communal practices. This works itself out in their account in a very high value being placed upon tradition. In the context of an exploration of postmodernity and consumer society, Davison and Milbank make the case for the significance of the 'givenness' of tradition as that which forms us, in comparison with the 'chosenness' of consumer society. Arguing that the church should exist in the former, whereas Fresh Expressions tends to the latter, they suggest that, '. . .this tradition comes to us in the structure of the church's life and in the liturgy as it unfolds week by week. These are accepted as the gifts they are. The question is not so much what we will make of the tradition, as what the tradition will make of us.'[47]

---

[42] Davison and Milbank, *For the Parish*, p. 61.
[43] Ibid., p. 63.
[44] Ibid., pp. 64–92.
[45] Ibid., p. 2.
[46] Ibid., p. 19.
[47] Ibid., p. 104.

This very brief overview (particularly of Davison and Milbank, whose work is a considerable and considered response to the Fresh Expressions movement) begins to open up some of the issues that the church has to grapple with as it considers the questions which surround the reformation and renewal of the life of the church. The question of how the church relates to its context is never far behind. All acknowledge that the context in which the church finds itself has shifted radically, yet two different strands of thinking are essentially at work in terms of responding to this. The Fresh Expressions movement seeks to find forms of church life that are more relevant and engaging within the context of late-modern, or postmodern society, whereas Davison and Milbank are seeking a re-engagement with traditional and embodied forms of Christian life as a means of relocating identity within contemporary culture. Within this, differences of perspective emerge (even within the critics of Fresh Expressions) over the way in which the church is related to the kingdom. Is the church fundamentally the beginning of the realization of the kingdom, or is there a more radical rupture between the church and the kingdom that is cosmic in scope, and in Hull's account, in its fullness, will not require the church? Such questions will need to concern us as we begin to develop a theology of reformation and renewal.

This book upholds a very fundamental interest in the practices of church life. In this sense, it recognizes the great significance of some of the observations on the relationship between form and content, practice and identity, which Davison and Milbank open up. However, it is also very concerned about being attentive to the wider context of life in the world, which opens up many of the questions that are motivating the Fresh Expressions movement, in terms of what it means to be church within a cultural context radically removed from many of the inherited expressions of church life we inhabit. The practices of church life do indeed uphold the social identity of the church which in turn upholds our individual identities as Christians. The practices of church life, however, do undoubtedly shift. While certain practices (baptism and the Eucharist, for example) remain constant in terms of the fact that these rites have been practiced since the earliest moment in the life of the church, many other practices of church life have shifted (even within the Orthodox and Catholic traditions) since the earliest days of the church. Even those sacramental practices that have remained constant within most expressions of the church have changed form considerably. All of this returns us to the fundamental question of the relationship between change and continuity within the life of the church. What does it mean, and how does it happen that the church is indeed perpetually being renewed and reformed, and yet it remains the church and some of its practices, and the beliefs embedded within them, remain constant? What, in over-simplistic terms, we require in a theological account of reform and renewal is precisely a theological account of change and continuity.

This book is not seeking to be in any way a practical handbook in terms of 'how-to' reform and renew churches. In that sense, its aim is very different from that of many other books on the subject, as might be typified by the *Mission-Shaped Church* report (or even, to some extent, Davison and Milbank's concern with encouraging the renewal of local parish life). Rather, it is extensively seeking to develop a theological account of how the social identity of the church is formed, re-formed and renewed. It will seek theological resources from scripture and the tradition, in an attempt to offer an account of change and continuity, reformation and renewal within the life of the church. It is hoped that this may provide theological sustenance to those seeking to help the church live out its ecclesial vocation in the midst of life in the world. What it is not presuming to do is to tell them how precisely to do that.

The Church, theology and the theologian

One cannot set out attempting to engage in the practice of theology, particularly concerning the theology of the church, without reflecting briefly on the relationship between the individual theologian and the church. For, particularly when engaging with ecclesiology, one does so not in relationship to something that one can legitimately understand as outside oneself (as a theologian might speak of the Trinity, for example), but one is speaking of, from, and to something of which one is a part. As an individual theologian, I am a member of the church through my baptism into Christ. My membership of the church is membership of a particular tradition of the church – in my case, the reformed tradition – and more tightly defined than that, I am a member of one particular church, the United Reformed Church. This reality inevitably shapes the way in which one engages with the practice of theology. As Healy acknowledges that his own Roman Catholic tradition forms his 'pre-understandings – sets of beliefs, questions, concerns, aesthetic judgments...',[48] the same list could effectively be applied to this author too, speaking of my own reformed tradition. The counterpart to this is that not only are we formed by the church which for us is 'home', but equally, in some senses we are seeking, in the practice of theology, to assist the reformation and renewal of the church. Healy notes that in the practice of ecclesiology, one is seeking to 'affect present Christian discourse and practice so that it more fully accords with their judgement about Christian identity and/or more adequately responds to the present context as they construe it. A specifically ecclesiological agenda will be especially concerned to alter the self-understanding of the church in order to bring about an appropriate change in the community's concrete identity'.[49] There is something of a dialectical relationship that emerges between the individual theologian and the church. One is formed by the church, one speaks from the church and one speaks to the church in a bid to form the church. Even in this statement, we can begin to see that the very practice of theology is one of the practices that forms, re-forms and renews the life of the church.

Theology, however, is not simply one of the practices of the church; it is also informed by other contexts from which it emerges, particularly perhaps that of the academy. Most often, the theology that emerges from the academy is seen as being fundamentally in conflict with that emerging from the church. Brain Gerrish characterizes something of this division as he reflects upon the relationship between university and seminary theology in the American context:

> On the one side, the seminaries are suspicious of what they call the 'academic theology' of the university. They perceive it as addressed to the wrong audience and the wrong situation; namely, to supposedly enlightened colleagues in other departments of the university for whom theology has become a quaint anachronism. A vital theology will not trouble itself with apologetics for the cultured despisers but will rather address the oppression, injustice, racism, discrimination, and exploitation that threaten to tear the human community apart and make our planet uninhabitable. A university

[48]   Healy, *Church, World*..., p. 2.
[49]   Ibid., p. 40.

theology, by contrast, is remote, philosophical, scholastic, inaccessible, and – from the church's viewpoint – insular, irrelevant and uninteresting. It is a theology that has lost touch with the things that really matter.

On the other side, the universities, when they notice theology at all, gladly turn it over to the seminaries because it is not a serious intellectual discipline: it lacks rigorous norms of argument and inquiry, is helplessly captive to passing fads and fashions, and trades critical reflection for mere ideology – to underwrite whatever case is currently or locally in vogue.[50]

While the context of this is clearly specific to North America with its concern for the university and the seminary, it accurately describes what all too often is the relationship between the church and academic theology (wherever it may originate from, all too often those who teach in theological colleges and seminaries are presumed to be all of the things that Gerrish lists as pertaining to university departments!). However, while this is often perceived to be the case, these categories of 'church' and 'academic' theology very quickly break down. In some respects the present author represents this. I received my theological education in the academy but was, during part of that education, also in formation for ordained Christian ministry within a theological college. I have ministered in local pastorate contexts, and also in ecumenical contexts that some might describe as 'Fresh Expressions'. I now teach in a theological college that teaches university degrees conferred by 'secular' universities, preparing women and men for ordained ministry. This particular work of theology is consciously and indivisibly of an academic theologian, trained within and working within an academic university context, and simultaneously a church practitioner who works within the context of the church. As such, this work will draw upon a range of academic disciplines that find their home within the university, not only theology, but subjects such as sociology and cultural studies too. It will also draw upon a range of sources that are far more ecclesial in origin and orientation too, such as confessional and ecumenical statements that churches make through their councils and hierarchies, as well as the worship of the church, and observation of the practices of church life.

---

[50] Brian Gerrish, "Tradition in the Modern World: The Reformed Habit of Mind", in David Willis and Michael Welker (eds), *Toward the Future of Reformed Theology: Tasks, Topics, Traditions* (Grand Rapids: Eerdmans, 1999), pp. 3–4.

As has already been made clear, theology does not arise simply from 'the church' generically, but rather from particular forms and expressions of the life of the church. Gerrish notes that, 'There are many churches and many ways of doing theology, not all of which are options for myself. If it is not permitted to do constructive theology out of a tradition, I don't know how else I could do it'.[51] This work situates itself particularly within the reformed tradition. That is not to say that it will not draw on sources within the wider Christian tradition outside of that, but it is the reformed tradition that has shaped and formed my own practice of theology. I have also been deeply influenced by other traditions (I have never exercised my ministry other than in overtly ecumenical contexts, working with Anglicans, Roman Catholics and Methodists throughout, and presently, also with Orthodox colleagues.), but that does not alter the fact that the reformed tradition is 'home'. This will be reflected in the choice of dialogue partners at times, and also perhaps in some of the presuppositions that the work makes. The very title of this book 'Perpetually Reforming' is indeed one of the 'slogans' of the tradition, and in some ways one which I am setting out to develop into a constructive theology.

It will be helpful to say something about the reformed tradition as it is being understood, worked within and from in this book. There are many different ways in which the reformed tradition finds expression, in terms of polity (Presbyterian through to Congregationalist, and even with the occasional bishop!), ethos and theological style. For some, the reformed tradition is one that holds to one of the classical reformed confessions of faith, normally the Heidelberg Catechism or the Westminster Confession. These can, at times, lead to a rather doctrinaire approach to theology and church life. However, in a tradition that has proclaimed itself to be *churches reformed according to the Word of God*, there is a strong sense in which it is never a tradition that is static, but rather, is one that is always seeking reformation through that Word. That Word is fundamentally Jesus Christ, the revelation of God in human form, revealed to us within scripture. The reformed tradition is, therefore, always a tradition that reads and re-reads scripture as part of the way it is continually formed. This mark of perpetual reformation is the most significant one that Gerrish lists as he is articulating what he calls the 'Reformed Habit of Mind'.[52] Following

---

[51] Willis/Welker, *Towards the Future*, p. 10.
[52] Ibid., p. 19.

that, this present work will seek to engage clearly with scripture, seeking to uncover the resources within scripture that help us understand the processes and practices of reformation and renewal within the life of the church.

The other reformed habits Gerrish lists are helpful in articulating the vision of the reformed tradition within which I am working. Gerrish points out that it is a *deferential* tradition, taking seriously those who have gone before us in the faith and the wisdom they have inhabited as Christ's body.[53] This work will seek to take seriously the voice of the tradition from the past, engaging with some of the classic reformed scholars and church folk who have been handed on to us. At the same time, Gerrish notes that the tradition is *critical*, in that it does not simply accept those voices as authoritative, but engages with them in such a way that we have a '*conversation* with the past: neither going in our own separate ways nor merely listening and absorbing passively . . . without criticism of tradition, there would be no reformation of the church.'[54] At times we need to accept that things we have received from those who have gone before us, despite their faithfulness, have had unforeseen consequences, or have ultimately led to undesirable places. We must not be scared of working through those issues in conversation with tradition. Gerrish also portrays the tradition as '*open:* open to wisdom and insight wherever they can be found.'[55] For this reason, we will also not be scared of seeking wisdom and understanding from fields outside the immediately theological ones. If, as Calvin insisted, creation is the 'theatre of God's glory',[56] insight can come, viewed through the lens of revelation, from anywhere within that 'theatre'. Therefore, we will at times pay attention to learning that comes from elsewhere in the academy, outside the faculties of theology and divinity, as we seek to understand the practices and processes through which the collective social identity of the church is formed. Gerrish's other 'habit' is that the reformed tradition is *practical*, by which he means that the tradition seeks always to form 'piety', but also has concerned itself massively with the transformation of life in the wider world.[57] This work too betrays its practical element in its concern to engage with the concrete historical church, and to offer theological resources by which the church might

---

[53] Ibid., pp. 13–14.
[54] Ibid., p. 15.
[55] Ibid., p. 16.
[56] See Calvin, *1559*, p. 72.
[57] Willis/Welker, *Towards the Future*, pp. 17–19.

better understand the processes and practices by which its very identity as the church is formed and reformed. While this book is not a handbook on what to do, it certainly seeks to be rooted in practical reality.

Jürgen Moltmann is another theologian who has reflected carefully on what it is to do reformed theology. He speaks about the fact that reformed theology is precisely at the service of the church, which is always reforming. It is easy to see the 'family resemblance' between Gerrish and Moltmann, when the latter offers the following definition of reformed theology as reformatory theology:

> Reformatory theology is theology in the service of reformation; reformation is its historical principle. Therefore, Reformed theology is *reforming theology*. . . It is not specifically known who invented this formula, but it accurately describes the principle of the church and theology reformed according to God's Word: *ecclesia reformata et semper reformanda,* and therefore also *theologia reformata et semper reformanda.* Tradition and innovation are one process. According to this principle, 'reformation' is not a onetime act to which a confessionalist could appeal and upon whose events a traditionalist could rest. In essence, 'reformation according to God's Word' is 'permanent reformation'; one might say, adapting Trotsky's call to revolution, it is 'an event that keeps church and theology breathless with suspense, an event that infuses church and theology with the breath of life, a story that is constantly making history, an event that cannot be concluded in this world, a process that will come to fulfilment and to rest only in the Parousia of Christ'. . .[58]

This set of ideas helpfully returns us to the reality that the practice of theology itself is part of the process of the reformation and renewal of the life of the church. It is precisely that practice which seeks to enable the church to reflect and act in ways that enable it to continue in every moment to more truly seek to be the church of Christ. A book such as this, therefore, must recognize that it is part of the very process that it is simultaneously attempting to understand and to offer a constructive theology of.

Within the reformed approach we have just outlined, this work is an attempt to move theological discussion from questions of descriptions or models of the church in the direction of attempting to understand the dynamic processes

---

[58] Jürgen Moltmann, 'Theologia Reformata et Semper Reformanda', inDavid Willis and Michael Welker (eds), *Toward the Future of Reformed Theology: Tasks, Topics, Traditions* (Grand Rapids: Eerdmans, 1999), pp. 120–1.

through which the identity of the church is perpetually re-formed. As such, it seeks not to offer a systematic presentation of doctrine concerning the church, but to highlight and examine the processes by which the church continually comes to be in any one moment and time. If there is any one particular 'methodology' underlying this project, one might term it 'realistic theology'. This notion is one which Michael Welker, another Reformed theologian, has developed. In the Preface to his work *God the Spirit,* Welker states:

> The procedure chosen here is, to be sure, not yet common in systematic theology. If one is seeking an academic label for this procedure, one could call it a 'realistic theology'.
>
> A realistic theology is a theology that is related to various structural patterns of experience and that cultivates a sensitivity to the differences of those various patterns. It is precisely in this diverse and complex relation to God's reality and to creaturely reality as intended by God that realistic theology seeks to performs [*sic*] its task. We try to squeeze God's reality into simple systematizations and forms of experience. As finite and limited human beings, we necessarily make this reductionist attempt. A realistic theology makes clear that God's reality is much richer than the forms into which we attempt to make it fit. A realistic theology makes clear that our experiences, our worldviews, our moral systems, and our value structures must be enlightened and changed in order to correspond to creaturely reality. A realistic theology also makes clear the way in which this must transpire.[59]

Welker's notion of realistic theology in this context relates particularly to the way he addresses the question of the Spirit of God. Much of what he states here, though, is valuable in addressing the question of the church. The church exists in a complex series of 'structural patterns' which, as we have noted, defy easy systematization. Beyond this lies the reality that the church is a social entity, and such entities themselves (which obviously occur in all spheres of human existence, not simply within the Christian church) have structural patterns intrinsically, both part of and bound together with 'creaturely reality' in the world. The church is, perhaps, the place where 'God's reality' and 'creaturely reality' collide most obviously. In suggesting that a realistic theology seeks to enlighten and change our worldviews, moral structures and value systems, this thesis attempts to enlighten these aspects of creaturely existence as they impact

---

[59] Michael Welker, *God the Spirit* (Minneapolis: Fortress Press, 1994), pp. x–xi.

on the dynamic process of the formation of the identity of the church. Equally, this book attempts to go some length in demonstrating the way in which this happens, both in terms of how the identity of the church is continually being formed, and in terms of the way in which the church can more consciously, and therefore effectively, understand the orientations required in church life to continually be reforming itself 'to God's reality and to creaturely reality as intended by God'.

The systematizing of theology, in the fashion Welker wishes to move away from, leads in the field of ecclesiology to what Healy terms 'blueprint ecclesiologies'. Such systematization inherently concerns itself primarily with questions of ontology: how is it that we can present a coherent system to understand what the church *is*? A realistic theology of the church, however, will stand in contrast to this by engaging with complex structures, orientations and practices to understand the church in the light of 'God's reality' and 'creaturely reality as intended by God'. The ontological question concerning what the church *is* becomes relativized within this kind of methodology. Such an approach, however, results in a theological understanding of the church that accords more accurately with the complex (and oftentimes messy) concrete historical reality of the life of the churches.

It has been suggested to me (by Michael Welker) that one could offer a typology of six thematic pairs that are brought into relationship with one another throughout this work: classical and contemporary theological thought; doctrinal theology and confessional evolution; systematic thought and biblical engagement; the church and Israel; theology and cultural studies and systematic and practical theology. These specific dialectical pairs are brought into relationship with one another in an attempt to develop a complex texture of interdisciplinary thought concerning the question of the identity of the church. These particular dialogue partners and disciplines offer, it is hoped, a wide enough range of engagement to form a picture of the dynamic process of ecclesial identity formation. However, this typology is not in and of itself definitive, and to it one could add a range of other dialogue partners and material that would extend and deepen the overall argument. What this typology suggests is that it is in bringing distinct and differentiated contributions to the debate into creative dialogue that a more satisfying understanding can be offered of the complexity that reflects the reality of the church. It is hoped that through this a constructive theological understanding of the processes and practices that reform and renew the church can be offered.

An outline of the work as a whole

Chapter 2 explores the origins of blueprint ecclesiologies identified by Healy as they find particular expression within the reformed tradition in the doctrine of the invisible church. The origins of this lie in an Augustinian doctrine of election, which, in its form as double-predestination, necessarily leads logically to a doctrine of the invisible church. In turn, the historical significance of the visible church becomes relativized and it becomes hard to offer the kind of account of change and continuity that a theology of reformation and renewal requires. Through engagement primarily with Calvin, Karl Barth and Colin Gunton, this chapter seeks to find the space within the received tradition to open up a more effective account of the historical reality of the visible church. In doing so, it offers a reparative account of the church's relationship to history, through a reading of Karl Barth's relocation of the doctrine of election in Christ and the community. This chapter begins to demonstrate how doctrinal development itself is one of the theological practices that reforms and renews the church. This chapter is perhaps the most technically doctrinal in approach and difficult to engage with. Readers interested in the argument of the book overall should not be scared of moving more quickly through this chapter to some of the material which follows.

Chapter 3 seeks to offer an account of the church and its reformation and renewal as this emerges in confessional statements, which are understood to be the voice of the church reflecting itself upon its own reality. It seeks to show what is implicit about the reformation and renewal of the church from the process of the development of confessional texts themselves. It then engages with one particular text in particular to tease out how one particular church, the United Reformed Church, understands its identity. Through this examination, various key themes emerge, which begin to open up the way in which the church is always open to renewal through a continued re-reading of scripture, and through the orientation it finds, both to God and the world in which it is situated. Throughout this, the themes of election and covenant remain a central concern, as they were for the more directly doctrinal approaches examined in the previous chapter.

Chapter 4 examines the process of the re-formation of the church, again through the examination of confessional texts. This time, it is through the examination of one particular issue: the church and Israel. Through a comparison of historic and contemporary confessional texts, it is immediately clear that the way the church understands Israel and Judaism has changed radically since the time of the Reformation. This chapter seeks to identify the dynamic that is at work within such confessional development, and notes various factors that are key. The impact of historical life in the world, in the form of the tragedy of the *Shoah*, is identified. Alongside this, one can see the centrality of the re-reading of scripture. From this, and the reality of the new confessional position of the churches that God's covenant with the Jewish people is ongoing, the ecclesiological questions that this raises are identified. It is suggested, through engagement with George Lindbeck, that this causes the church to re-engage with its 'Old' testament and also with contemporary Jewish understandings of what it means to be the People of God. Both of these become an ecclesiological resource for the church. These resources continue to point us in the direction of the significance of election and covenant as themes to be explored.

Chapter 5 begins the more directly constructive part of the book. Following the acknowledgement in Chapter 4 that it is necessary for the Old Testament to be reclaimed in ecclesiology, Chapter 5 explores the issue of covenant within the Hebrew scriptures. It offers a canonical survey of the theme of covenant, with particular reference to the way the covenant is presented as being *re-formed* at various points within the Old Testament history of Israel. It is argued that the covenant is re-formed, not that there is a succession of different individual covenants. Within this, the particular emphasis on memory and anticipation emerges. Throughout this chapter (and the next), I engage significantly with Jewish thinking regarding social identity and the processes of identity formation of Israel and Judaism. This opens up an alternative approach to the construal of the church and offers us an understanding of the significance of *practice* as the primary means of the maintenance and re-formation of the social identity of the people of God. The centrality of the re-appropriation of the covenant through the re-reading of scripture is also explored with reference to the way texts within the canon of scripture themselves offer re-readings and re-appropriations of earlier texts within the canon.

Chapter 6 continues to explore the theme of covenant – more specifically, the notion of the new covenant in Christ. It is argued that this too must be seen as a form of covenantal renewal and re-formation rather than a total break with the 'old' covenant. The life, ministry, death and resurrection of Christ become the central focus of the collective memory of the church. It is suggested that this memory can be best understood in the light of the way memory functions within the Old Testament, as outlined in Chapter 5. The central difference between the Jewish social identity as the people of God and the social identity of the church as the people of God rests with the orientation to the world. In contrast to Judaism, through the centrality of Christ, the church has an open and inclusive orientation to the world as opposed to an orientation of separation. The way in which the sociality of the church is presented within the New Testament opens up a historically contingent account of the life of the church, which is relativized through a particular eschatological perspective. The impact of this is explored in terms of the significance of accounts of the doctrine of election that see salvation as a hope for the whole of creation, rather than a possession of the church for the sake of its members. An account begins to emerge of the reformation and renewal of the church being suspended between the triadic relationship of the church to God and the world, and also in the triadic relationship of the past made present through memory, the future made present in anticipation, and the present worldly context of the life of the church.

Chapter 7 engages with the centrality of the practices of the church in mediating the orientations to the past, to the future and to the world which, it has been argued, are the fundamental orientations that energize the dynamic process of ecclesial re-formation. Building on the understanding of social and collective memory as elucidated within the social sciences, the centrality of *practice* as the mediator of both memory (*anamnesis*), anticipation (*prolepsis*) and orientation to the world, are explored. Practice is seen to function in this way in the specific practices of the law, particularly when it is understood as upholding and re-forming the covenantal social identity of the people of God. From this basis, an understanding of the worshiping practices of the Christian church is elucidated.

The conclusion, Chapter 8, seeks to draw together the strands of the work, and returns us again to the question of the contemporary life of the church in the world, and offers some suggestions as to how the reformation and renewal of the church might happen within contemporary society.

2

Visible and Invisible?

The contours of a problem

Any theology of the reform and renewal of the church is inherently a theology of change and continuity. It must be a theology of the historical church, and how the church, throughout history, is renewed within the contexts of shifting social, intellectual and institutional realities. This implies that the church is always in a particular concrete historical context, and therefore is always in relationship with the world. This chapter engages with some classical doctrinal theological approaches to the nature of the church, particularly within the reformed tradition, to examine how they handle the question of the church's relationship to its historical context. We will particularly examine two related doctrinal notions that have been particularly significant within the reformed tradition. First, the relationship between the doctrine of election and the doctrinal understanding of the church, and secondly, the way in which this informs the understandings of the church that speak of the church as both visible and invisible, even to the extent at times of suggesting that there are two churches.

We have already noted that there is a complex relationship between theology and the church, and as we begin to engage in the examination of some classical doctrinal understandings of the church, we need to remember that it is not necessarily self-evident that the church is, in and of itself, an appropriate locus for doctrinal theology. Wolfhart Pannenberg suggests such a cautionary note when he points out:

> It is not self evident that the concept of the church should be a separate dogmatic theme. This was not the case either in the early church or in the Latin Middle Ages. Accepted as the content of faith and Christian teaching

were the Trinitarian God, the creation of the world, its reconciliation by Jesus Christ, and the sacraments. The church did not form a separate theme in the systematic presentation of Christian doctrine until the 15th century.[1]

While this is the case in the sense that the church was not treated as a specific doctrinal theme in its own right with particular emphasis until the time of the Reformation, clearly, doctrinal thinking did engage with the question of the church at times. It is interesting to note that at the moments the church has appeared as a separate theological theme, it generally speaking, is at moments of the division of the church (and therefore, pre-eminently becomes such at the time of the reformation). For example, Cyprian engages the topic of the church in his tract, *The Unity of the Catholic Church*, at a time of schism when an alternative bishop, Novation, has been set up.[2] Jan Huss writes a tract on the nature of the church at the time of his schism with the church.[3] In a sense, both of these works are concerning themselves with the question of how one recognizes the true church at a moment when it would appear that there is more than one church on offer. It is notable that there is relatively little concern with the church as a locus of doctrine in pre-reformation medieval Christendom in Western Europe. Aquinas, for example, does not concern himself with the question of the nature of the church in the *summa*. This suggests that if doctrine is understood as the content of the faith, then the church is that which embodies and holds the whole of that teaching, rather than simply being one part of a theoretical doctrinal system. Since the time of the Reformation, the church has clearly been a doctrinal theme in its own right, but we must not simply accept this in an unquestioning way. How is it that the church embodies the whole of doctrine while at the same time being a part of the doctrinal schema itself? In some senses, this book attempts to offer a response to this question, but this chapter seeks first of all to pay particular attention to some of the resources that classical doctrinal approaches to the church offer us in terms of an understanding of the nature of the reform and renewal of the church.

[1]   Wolfhart Pannenberg, *Systematic Theology, Volume 3* (Grand Rapids: Eerdmans, 1989), p. 21.
[2]   St Cyprian of Carthage, 'The Unity of the Catholic Church', in Allen Brent (ed.), *On the Church: Select Treatises* (Popular Patristics Series, Nr. 32, Crestwood, New York: St. Vladimir's Seminary Press, 2006), pp. 145–82.
[3]   Jan Huss, *De Ecclesia* (D. S. Schaff (ed.), London: Charles Scribner's Sons, 1915).

In his guide to the reformed tradition, *Introducing the Reformed Faith,*[4] Donald McKim sketches the contours of the doctrine of the church. Following his outline of various biblical models of the church,[5] he turns his attention to specifically reformed understandings. At this point, he states that 'The church is both visible and invisible. As the universal fellowship of believers, the church is "open and known to God's eyes alone". . . . The outward "visible" church is a "mixed body" of true believers and those who may profess belief in Jesus Christ but do not genuinely enact it'.[6]

McKim is offering in his work an understanding of the reformed tradition which operates on what one might term a more closed model, which allows him to make such precise statements about the tradition. This stands somewhat in contrast to models of the tradition which are more open and concerned with the process of reformation itself. Here, however, he is outlining a commonly held perception of the doctrine of the church within the tradition. This poses some significant issues for the development of a theology of reform and renewal of the church because of the way in which the concrete, historical church with which we are concerned, becomes relativized in the light of the 'invisible' church, which all too quickly comes to function in the way Healy identifies ecclesiological dualisms within blueprint ecclesiologies.[7]

The reformed tradition cannot alone lay claim to the notion of the visible and the invisible church. In reality, it is a notion which concerns Luther more than Calvin. The notion goes considerably further back than this. It can certainly be traced to Augustine, primarily in his *The City of God,*[8] where he is concerned with the two cities, the earthly and the heavenly. For Augustine, the church is ultimately a mixed community. He states that, 'In this situation many reprobates are mingled in the Church with the good, and both sorts are collected as it were in the dragnet of the gospel'.[9] While Augustine is not specifically using the terms visible and 'invisible', his notion of the two cities clearly paves the way for this. The true members of the church (and therefore

---

[4] Donald K. McKim, *Introducing the Reformed Faith: Biblical Revelation, Christian Tradition, Contemporary Significance* (Louisville: Westminster John Knox, 2001).
[5] McKim, *Reformed Faith,* pp. 119–22.
[6] Ibid., p. 126.
[7] See above, p. 33.
[8] Augustine, *City of God* (Henry Bettenson (trans.), London: Penguin Books, 1984).
[9] Augustine, *City of God,* p. 831.

the city of God) are known only to God Godself[10] and the church, as we see it within concrete historical reality, is a mixed community. Here, we begin to see a classical Augustinian outworking of the doctrine of election which becomes so influential within the reformed tradition. There is clearly a dualistic notion at work, which perhaps also betrays the influence of neoPlatonism within Augustine's thought.[11]

Bound up with the idea of the two cities and the visible/invisible divide is a particular notion of the relationship between salvation, the kingdom of God and the church. For Augustine, the city of God is the eternalized eschatological city, and the earthly city, where the church is situated, contains both the saved and those not saved. This relationship between the church and salvation is one which can be traced further back, and finds a particularly influential formulation in Cyprian. His famous passage from his treatise on the church states:

> It is not possible for the bride of Christ to be counterfeited, there has been no tampering with her, and she is chaste. She knows one home, she guards the sanctity of one bedchamber with a chaste modesty. She watches over us for God, she seals her sons, to whom she has given birth, for the kingdom. Whoever dissociates himself from the Church is joined to a counterfeit paramour, he is cut off from the promises of Christ, and neither will he who abandons Christ's Church attain to Christ's rewards. He is a foreigner, he is deconsecrated, and he is an enemy. He cannot have God as his Father who does not have the Church as his Mother.[12]

It is from this particular form of thought that the highly influential notion that there is no salvation outside of the church (*extra ecclesiam nulla salas*) arises. There are various theological consequences to this statement. First, within this notion resides a conflation of the church and the kingdom which places eschatology and ecclesiology side by side. The saved are those who inherit the kingdom, and the saved are also necessarily the church. The church, therefore, is the community of the saved, a statement that assimilates the church to

---

[10] See Augustine, *On Baptism, Against the Donatists* (M. Dodds (ed.), Edinburgh: T&T Clark, 1872), p. 97.

[11] There is no scope for an examination of the influence of Platonic dualism on Augustine's ecclesiological thinking. For the general contours of the Platonic influence, see Gerard Watson, *Greek Philosophy and the Christian Notion of God* (Blackrock: The Columbia Press, 1994); Peter Brown, *Augustine of Hippo: A Biography* (Berkeley and Los Angeles: University of California Press, 1969); Henry Chadwick, *Augustine* (Oxford: Oxford University Press, 1986); Christopher Kirwan, *Augustine* (London: Routledge, 1989).

[12] Cyprian, *On the Church*, pp. 156–7.

soteriology: to ask what the church is, is to ask first who is saved. The reality of the concrete historical church is that it does appear to be a mixed community: it is historically fallible and sinful. If the true church is the saved, and yet the visible church is clearly not perfect, this logical dilemma apparently demands a logical doctrinal answer. From this situation, it is not difficult to see precisely how a doctrine of the invisible church arises. The dualism arising from Augustine's thought, coupled with the strong assertion that outside of the church there is no salvation leads to the conclusion that there is a true church of the saved (which is a correlate of the kingdom) and there is the historical visible church which is indeed a mixed community. This introduces a specific understanding of the relationship between history and eternity; the historical correlates with the visible church, and the eternal correlates with the invisible. From within this framework of thinking, to engage in ecclesiology becomes necessarily to speak not solely, or even primarily, of the concrete historical church, but rather to speak of an eternalized and idealized understanding of the church which then functions in the way Healy understands a 'blueprint'.[13] The move which has essentially been made is to prioritize an idealized ontology within doctrine when addressing the question of the church. This notion, as we shall see, becomes developed in Reformation theological thinking and still shapes much ecclesiological reflection today.

It is worth posing a historical question at this point. The notion that 'outside the church is no salvation', as it emerges within Cyprian's thought, is clearly aimed first at those who have divided the church and set up an alternative episcopate. Its primary referent is not the mass of people outside the church, but those who have denied one particular concrete expression of the church in favour of another. In this sense, it is not making a doctrinal claim which originates in an attempt to frame the relationship between the church and the world more generally. It is also worth pointing out that the clear logical sense of the assimilation of ecclesiology and soteriology is not one which much more recent reformed theology, notable Barth (but clearly noticeable in Schleiermacher too) has upheld. This calls into question the timeless authority of this particular claim as an ecclesiological truth, and opens up a new space in which the doctrine of the church can be considered and through which the relationship of the church, election and salvation, and the world can be

---

[13] Healy, *Church, World*, pp. 25–51.

reconceived in ways that make it possible to move beyond the dualisms and blueprints that Healy has noted.[14]

We turn now to an examination of major reformed theologians and their handling of these issues. The selection of John Calvin and Karl Barth as the primary examples is based simply on the fact that they are two of the most influential figures within the tradition, the one often being considered the 'father figure', the other being the most influential theological figure of the twentieth century. Our concern is not to provide a detailed study of the ecclesiology of either Calvin or Barth, but rather to explore how the issues outlined above take their place in their theological presentations of ecclesiology. Our concern is to receive from these doctrinal accounts the resources that will enable us to discern the theological space in which an account of the reform and renewal of the church within history can be developed. In doing so, we will take particular note of the classic issues we have already identified: the doctrine of election and the idea of the visible and the invisible church. From this, we will identify some of the ways in which classical accounts need to be received, and at times repaired, in order to enable us to understand how it is that the church exhibits change and continuity within history. This will open up a space to consider theologically the doctrinal, liturgical and ethical practices which uphold the process of the reform and renewal of the church.

John Calvin: The dualism of election

The context of the wider Reformation movement obviously colours Calvin's thoughts regarding the church. Part of this background is Luther, a theologian and pastor who, as his thinking progresses, becomes more and more committed to the notion of the invisible church. Luther's early thinking shows the beginnings of a move in this direction. His lectures on the Psalms from 1513 to 1515 refer to the church as being invisible: 'her entire structure is

---

[14] For a comparison of the way in which Barth and Schleiermacher understand the doctrine of election and the way in which this leads both thinkers in a universalist direction, see Matthias Gockel, *Barth & Schleiermacher on the Doctrine of Election: A Systematic-Theological Comparison* (Oxford: Oxford University Press, 2006). For discussion of Barth and the universalism implicit within his understanding of the doctrine of election, see Tom Greggs, *Barth, Origen and Universal Salvation: Restoring Particularity* (Oxford: Oxford University Press, 2009).

inward in the presence of God'.[15] This work is from a period of his life when he was particularly immersed in the work of Augustine and whose influence can doubtless be seen in this statement.[16] Later influences on Luther come from a surprising source, Jan Huss. Luther writes in a letter of February 14, 1520 that he had previously held all the teachings of Huss, but had not realized it;[17] Luther had received a copy of Huss's *De Ecclesia* the previous October.[18] Huss himself had developed a notion of the invisible church, referring to the church as 'Christ's mystical body, that is, hidden body . . .'[19] and this would appear to have influenced Luther in his writing *On the Papacy* later in 1520 where he says that '. . . we shall call the two churches by two distinct names. The first, which is natural, basic, essential and true, we shall call "spiritual, internal Christendom". The second, which is man made and external, we shall call "physical, external Christendom" '.[20] Here, we have a clear delineation of a visible and an invisible church – the invisible church being characterized as a holy Christian community, the visible being a mixed institution of the elect and the reprobate. Later, in 1539 when writing *On the Councils*, he would go on to demonstrate a dislike for the word 'church' altogether, preferring to speak of a 'Holy Christian People'[21] to make clearer the invisible nature of the true church over mistaken understandings of the word 'church', which refer to visible things. The notion of the invisible church is central to Luther, and one that influences the Lutheran theological tradition considerably. From within the reformed tradition, it is important to realize that this formulation of the visible/invisible doctrine emerges in this form in Huss and Luther and cannot simply be classed as 'reformed doctrine'. Calvin, in his presentation of the matter, actually deals with it in a rather different fashion.

We have noted that for Luther, the theme of the invisible church continues throughout his lifetime, intensifying as his thinking develops to the point that the very word 'church' becomes something Luther will not use. For Calvin, we see something of the reverse happening. Calvin, in the letter of dedication of the 1536 edition of his *Institutes* to Francis, King of the French, states at one point that

---

[15] LW 11, p. 30.
[16] Bernhard Lohse, *Martin Luther's Theology* (Edinburgh: T&T Clark, 1999), p. 45ff.
[17] LW 48, p. 153.
[18] Ibid.
[19] Huss, *De Ecclesia*, p. 17.
[20] LW 39, p. 71.
[21] LW 41, p. 143.

> Our controversy turns on these hinges: first, they contend that the form of
> the church is always apparent and observable. Secondly, they set this form
> in the see of the Roman Church and its hierarchy. We, on the contrary,
> affirm that the church can exist without any visible appearance, and that
> its appearance is not contained within that outward magnificence which
> they foolishly admire. Rather, it has quite another mark, namely, the pure
> preaching of God's Word and the lawful administration of the sacraments.[22]

This is an early writing of Calvin's and we see here a very clear and distinct
doctrine of the invisible church as the true church. If we compare this with the
1559 edition of the *Institutes*, we see that the position has changed (although
the dedicatory letter remains unchanged). Calvin begins Book Four of the
1559 *Institutes* (the whole book concerns the church and the sacraments) with
a passage that is startlingly similar to the passage quoted above from Cyprian.[23]
He states:

> I shall start, then, with the church, into whose bosom God is pleased to gather
> his sons, not only that they may be nourished by her help and ministry as
> long as they are infants and children, but also that they may be guided by her
> motherly care until they mature and at last reach the goal of faith. "For what
> God has joined together, let no man put asunder" (Mark 10:9), so that, for
> those to whom he is Father the church may also be Mother.[24]

Here, the theme of the church as the Mother of believers is taken (from Cyprian)
and utilized. He is not referring solely to the invisible church but states that
'The article in the Creed in which we profess to "believe the church" refers
not only to the visible church (our present topic) but also to all God's elect,
in whose number are also included the dead'.[25] The invisible church certainly
is that which is confessed in faith, but by 1559, the certainty of the church
as being only truly the invisible church has been laid aside for an extensive
practical and concrete ecclesiology of the visible church. For Calvin, it is
that visible church which is the 'Mother of all believers'. The invisible church
remains necessary to comprehend the church fully, but unlike Luther, Calvin
appears to wish to concentrate more, rather than less, on the significance of

---

[22] Calvin, *1536*, p. 9.
[23] See above, p. 30.
[24] Calvin, *1559*, p. 1012
[25] Ibid., p. 1013.

the visible church as his career progresses. To answer the question as to why this is the case, and to develop a critique of the theological tradition which will assist in understanding why the ecclesiology of the concrete historical church (which Calvin is attempting in Book Four of the 1559 *Institutes*) has been so problematic, it is necessary to examine how the church fits in with Calvin's wider theological scheme.

Calvin's systematic presentation of his theological scheme begins, both in the 1536 and the 1559 *Institutes*, from an essentially anthropological perspective. The first major section of the 1536 *Institutes* deals with the issue of the law. He uses the law to reveal his conception of the human condition. Through an extensive examination of the Ten Commandments, he sets out an understanding of the law as being an impossibility for humanity to attain. For Calvin, the starting point in the presentation of his system is essentially sin. It is the reality of the sinful human condition which demonstrates that salvation comes from God alone. He states:

> Therefore if we look merely to the law, we can only be despondent, confused, and despairing in mind, since from it all of us are condemned and accursed [Gal. 3.10]. That is, as Paul says, all those under the law are accursed. And the law cannot do anything else than to accuse and blame all to a man, to convict, and, as it were, apprehend them; in fine, to condemn them in God's judgement: that God alone may justify, that all flesh may keep silence before him. [Rom. 3:19f.][26]

In comparison, the 1559 *Institutes*, begins in a somewhat different place; it concerns the 'Knowledge of God and That of Ourselves Are Connected'. This shift in Calvin's thinking, away from a starting point of the law to the starting point of the knowledge of God does not, however, remove Calvin from a starting place concerned with the human condition. Whereas in the 1536 edition, it is the law which reveals the unrighteousness of the human condition, in the 1559 edition, it is the knowledge of God which performs this function. Calvin states:

> Again, it is certain that man never achieves a clear knowledge of himself unless he has first looked upon God's face, and then descends from contemplating him to scrutinize himself. For we always seem to ourselves

---

[26] Calvin, *1536*, p. 30.

righteous and upright and wise and holy – this pride is innate in all of us – unless by clear proofs we stand convinced of our own unrighteousness, foulness, folly, and impurity.[27]

The logical progression for Calvin begins at the point of human sinfulness. It is only in the comprehension of the human condition, be it through contemplation of the law, or the knowledge of God Godself, that humanity becomes aware of its sinfulness. It is on the basis of this sinfulness that the grace of God can then become apparent. What Calvin is doing is not so much constructing a particular logical order, rather, seeking to demonstrate and protect the sovereignty of God over salvation. The emphasis on the human condition is to make clear that salvation can only possibly be the work of God. Having laid out this precondition for the readers' understanding, Calvin is then able to move forward to an explication of the work of Christ.

In the 1536 edition of the *Institutes*, Calvin moves from a discussion of the law and the human condition to a discussion of justification. He states:

> Is it that Jesus Christ was the beginning of our salvation? Is it that he opened the way when he merited for us occasion for meriting? Certainly not. But, it is that "he has chosen us in him" from eternity "before the foundation of the world" through no merit of our own, "but according to the purpose of divine good pleasure"[Eph. 1:4–5, cf. Vg.]. and freed from ruin [cf. Col. 1:14, 20]. It is that we have been adopted unto him as sons and heirs by the Father [cf. Rom. 8:17; Gal. 4:5–7]. It is that we have been reconciled to the Father through his blood [Rom. 8:17; Gal. 4:5–7]. It is that, by the Father given unto his protection, we may never perish . . . In brief, because all his things are ours and we have all things in him, in us there is nothing. Upon this foundation we must be built if we would grow into a holy temple to the Lord.[28]

It is because of the stress on humanity's incapability to enact salvation, that Calvin is then able to locate salvation so firmly in Christ. It is here that we see his doctrine of election beginning to emerge. This election is one which is eternal, from 'before the foundation of the world'. This move, from the human condition to justification, is one which is followed in the 1559 *Institutes*, where a far fuller understanding of justification and predestination is worked out.

---

[27] Calvin, *1559*, p. 37.
[28] Ibid.

In the section concerning the doctrine of predestination in Book Three of the 1559 *Institutes*, Calvin states:

> In actual fact, the covenant of life is not preached equally among all men, and among those to whom it is preached, it does not gain the same acceptance constantly or in equal degree. In this diversity the wonderful depth of God's judgement is made known.[29]

It is the question of eternal election to salvation which is of interest to us here, particularly as it works itself out in Calvin's ecclesiology, for it is eternal election for Calvin which requires the existence of the invisible church. Calvin makes clear that it is impossible to determine who has been eternally chosen and who not. At the same time, Calvin is at pains to stress that '. . . outside this church and this communion of saints there is no salvation'.[30] This theme continues in the 1559 edition of the *Institutes*, as we saw above. It is here that the issue is located: if the church is synonymous with those who are saved, and it is impossible to know who is saved and who is not, then it is impossible to know who is the church and who not, therefore the church must necessarily be invisible. Where does this leave the concrete historical church? As with Luther, it must necessarily be a mixed community, even if, for Calvin, his very high ecclesiology leads him to the position that outside the visible church there is no salvation. It must be noted that both in the 1536 and the 1559 editions of the Institutes the position is not totally clear, particularly with regard to those who have been subject to the discipline of the church. Calvin is keen to point out that it is only for God to know who exactly the elect are, even in cases where the discipline of the church has been invoked.[31] This leads to the possibility (which Calvin has to acknowledge theoretically, although in practice he would have probably considered it highly unlikely) that someone who has been excommunicated, and is therefore no longer a member of the visible church, is nonetheless a member of the invisible church by virtue of election.[32]

What becomes clear in this analysis of Calvin's theological presentation is that, given his pre-suppositions, the invisible church is a logical necessity. If one is attempting to hold onto the fact that there is no salvation outside

---

[29] Calvin, *1559*, pp. 920–1.
[30] Calvin, *1536*, p. 63.
[31] See Calvin, *1536*, pp. 61–2, and *1559*, p. 1237.
[32] Calvin, *1559*, p. 1237.

of the church, and equally, if one wishes to uphold the sovereignty of God over salvation, it becomes logically impossible to maintain a doctrine of the church which is primarily visible, concrete and historical. This leads to Calvin's position on the marks of the church: the Word proclaimed and the sacraments lawfully administered.[33] It is not possible to state who the church is, but by its marks one may know that it is present. It is Calvin's particular ontology of the church which roots the essential being of the church in the gathering of the elect which necessitates the doctrine of the invisibility of the church.

The problem can be stated in different terms, as the eternalizing of the church. In creating a theology in which the invisible church becomes necessary, the true church becomes therefore an eternal entity, not an historical one. It is, therefore, only insofar as a historical body contains 'marks' of the eternal body that it may be known as church. Calvin, in dedicating such a huge proportion of his entire 1559 edition of the *Institutes* to the church is seeking actively to move away from the position which Luther was moving towards at the end of his life; one which makes it impossible to speak of the church at all. In seeking to write a practical ecclesiology concerning the ordering of the church, its sacraments and its ministry, Calvin places an extremely high value on the visible church, to the extent that he will say that it is the 'mother of all believers', outside of which there is no salvation (even if the logical caveat concerning church discipline has been added). To this extent, Calvin is a helpful guide to how it is that one might engage with the questions that surround the reform and renewal of the church. For him, it was primarily about offering a reading of scripture and the 'Fathers' of the early church to provide insight into how the church might be structured within the present context.[34]

Ultimately, although Calvin seeks to produce an ecclesiology of the concrete historical church, there is a sense of a lingering inherent dualism that prevents a clear understanding of the relationship between change and continuity within the historical life of the church. Despite the fact that Calvin is a theologian totally rooted in the day-to-day life of church organization,

---

[33] See Calvin, *1536*, p. 9, and *1559*, p. 1023.

[34] Calvin provides an interesting example of this when he engages the question of the form of the ministry of the church. Here, attention to scripture and the tradition allows him to develop his four-fold model of ministry, which meets the needs of the church in Geneva. At the same time, he is willing to allow that other forms of church government might be appropriate elsewhere. This offers an interesting example of the interplay between scripture and context. See Calvin, *1559*, pp. 1053–84.

worship, preaching, pastoral care and discipline, ultimately his ecclesiology struggles to be one which can adequately deal with the historical reality of the church because the true church is only eternal by virtue of its dependence upon his particular understanding of election which is rooted in the election of the individual. The question of the reformation and renewal of the church becomes then too easily a question of the order and structures of church life in their approximation to the eternalized ideal of the church.

Karl Barth: The dualism of time and eternity

Barth's famous statement, 'The community is the earthly-historical form of existence of the one living Lord Jesus Christ'[35] would appear to suggest that Barth is concerned with the concrete, historical church in a sense that might open up space for an account of the reform and renewal of the church within history. Certainly, Barth re-receives Calvin's account of the doctrine of election such that the logical doctrinal necessity for an account of the invisible church is removed. In this way, Barth opens up a new theological space in which it is possible to re-conceive the relationship between God, the church and the world in ways other than the election of individuals. While Barth does this through his radical re-centring of the doctrine of election in Christ, from which the election of the community becomes prior to the election of individuals, it is interesting (and, for our purposes, perhaps problematic) that Barth still retains the language of the visible and the invisible. This, however, rests more on his understanding of the relationship of time to eternity than it does on his doctrine of election.

For Barth, the doctrine of election begins in Jesus Christ 'electing and elected'.[36] This highly Chalcedonian account of Christology places Christ as both fully divine, the fully electing God and fully human, the fully elected human being. It is in the relationship between Christ as human, and the fullness of his humanity such that he represents all humanity, that his election encompasses, as many people would argue, all humanity. Tom Greggs puts it this way, '. . . the relationship between Christ as elected human and all other

---

[35] CD IV.I, p. 669.
[36] CD II:2, p. 94.

humans is, for Barth, an actual understanding of election in Christ. Rather than instrumentalizing the "in", election is actual both in terms of the self-determination of God in His act in Jesus Christ and in the resultant identity of Christ with each member of humanity."[37]

Barth then goes on to make the move towards understanding the impact of this election of Christ upon the life of the Christian community and the individual. It is telling that, for Barth, the community must come first. Barth notes that to follow a scriptural line of thinking, '... starting from the election of Jesus Christ it does not immediately envisage the election of the individual believer ... but in the first place a mediate and mediating election."[38] For Barth, this mediating election is the election of the community, which he understands to be the communities of Israel and the church. The question of the place of Israel in understanding the nature of the church is one we will return to at length.[39] For now, what interests us is the impact that Barth's re-centring of the doctrine of election has on his ability to engage the church as a concrete historical reality and to offer a theological account of change and continuity within the life of the church.

Barth is clear that received doctrines of election have concentrated too simplistically upon the election or rejection of individual human beings: 'The traditional doctrine of predestination of every school and shade has always begun with this problem, and has made no essential progress beyond it.'[40] Instead, Barth moves from Christ to the place of the community. This radically turns on its head Calvin's doctrine of election and therefore his doctrine of the church. The (true, invisible) church is no longer made up of elect individuals; rather, the election of the church is rooted in the election of Christ and is prior to the election of individuals. The church becomes the mediator of the election of Christ within the world, the mediator of election to humanity, which has been elected in the election of the fully human Christ who is the electing God. In speaking of the election of the community, Barth states:

> The honour of its election can never be anything but the honour of Jesus Christ, the selfless honour of witnessing to Him. If the community tries to be more than His environment, to do something more than mediate, it has

[37] Greggs, *Barth, Origen*, p. 29.
[38] CD II:2, p. 195.
[39] See below, pp. 87–116.
[40] CDII:2, p. 306.

forgotten and forfeited its election. Again, the existence of the community cannot be regarded as an end in itself with respect to the world. It has been chosen out of the world for the very purpose of performing for the world the service which it most needs and which consists simply in giving it the testimony of Jesus Christ and summoning it to faith in Him. It has forgotten and forfeited its election if it is found existing for itself only and omitting this service, if it is no longer really mediating. The inner circle is nothing apart from the relation to the outer circle of the election which has taken place (and takes place) in Jesus Christ.[41]

The church, in this view, is not formed primarily out of individual elect human beings, but is itself an elect community that mediates and witnesses the work of God in Christ of election to the whole of the world. As Greggs puts it, '"being for" is an existence orientated on those outside the walls of the church, in a manner which breaks the introverted and communally egotistical self-imaged idols of the church's creating. Being for the world involves the church prioritizing the serving of others over its own benefits, even to the point of cost to itself or self-sacrifice.'[42] This is a seemingly highly historical account of the vocation of the church, as an electing community within world history that witnesses the electing work of Christ.

Barth has overthrown the primary theological reason why Calvin (himself following the earlier tradition from Augustine) requires a doctrine of the invisible church in that his account of the church is not one rooted in an invisible election of individuals. It is, therefore, perhaps surprising that Barth ends up upholding some kind of account of a church that is visible and invisible. This results from his account of time and eternity, rather than his account of election. The result poses an issue that needs addressing before the full creative power of Barth's theology for our understanding of the reform and renewal of the church within history can be harnessed. There is still a concern that, in the form of the visible/invisible divide that Barth upholds, it becomes very difficult to account for change and continuity within the life of the church, largely because of the kind of account of history that Barth offers.

---

[41] Ibid., pp. 196–7.
[42] Tom Greggs, *Theology Against Religion: Constructive Dialogues with Bonhoeffer and Barth* (London/New York: T&T Clark, 2011).

Barth develops a unitary model of the visible and invisible church. He states that

> . . . the visible and the invisible Church are not two Churches – an earthly-historical fellowship and above and behind a supra-naturally spiritual fellowship. As we have already seen, the one is the form and the other the mystery of one and the self-same Church. The mystery is hidden in the form, but represented and to be sought out in it. The visible lives wholly by the invisible. The invisible is only represented and to be sought out in the visible. But neither can be separated from the other. Both in their unity are the body, the earthly-historical form of existence of the one living Lord Jesus Christ.[43]

What then, for Barth, is the difference and relationship between the visible and the invisible? The whole of his ecclesiological reflection takes place in the context of his thinking regarding the work of the Holy Spirit,[44] and the church becomes visible by the activity of the Spirit; 'For the work of the Holy Spirit as the awakening power of Jesus Christ would not take place at all if the invisible did not become visible . . .'[45] This happens for Barth in event; 'The Church *is* when it takes place, and it takes place in the form of a sequence and nexus of definite human activities.'[46] So, the church *is*, for example, when the people of the church subject themselves to the law of the gospel, when the people of the church 'receive the verdict on the whole world of men . . .' or when there is a common hearing and obeying.[47] So, the church *happens* in a series of events. It is very unclear in what way these events are related other than by the fact that they are all the work of the Spirit. There is little sense in Barth's presentation that the church is in historical continuity.

In the second book of Volume Four of the *Church Dogmatics*, Barth introduces the notion of the 'true' church, and of the 'perceived' church that is only the 'semblance' of a church.[48] He states:

> Thus, to see the true Church, we cannot look abstractly at what human work seems to be in itself. This would not be a genuine phenomenon but a false. The real result of the divine operation, the human action which takes

---

[43] CD IV.I, p. 669.
[44] Ibid., pp. 643–50.
[45] Ibid., p. 653.
[46] Ibid., p. 652.
[47] Ibid., p. 651.
[48] Ibid., p. 617.

place in the true Church as occasioned and fashioned by God, will never try to be anything in itself, but only the divine operation, the divine work of sanctification, the upbuilding of Christianity by the Holy Spirit of Jesus the Lord, by which it is inaugurated and controlled and supported. To the extent that it is anything in itself, it is the phenomenon of the mere semblance of a Church, it is only this semblance, and not the true Church, that we shall see when we consider this phenomenon.[49]

Thus, it would appear that for Barth, any attempt at an ecclesiology that engages the concrete historical church would be perceived as a false project, for that would only be to seek after the semblance of something, not the real thing itself.[50] So, the church, in this doctrinal construction, is something essentially invisible, as it is the work of the Spirit and divinely initiated, and it becomes visible in a series of events, the primary one being the event of worship.[51]

For Barth, unlike Calvin, the invisibility of the church does not seemingly arise out of soteriological necessity, but rather because it is fundamentally a divine activity, and therefore essentially invisible other than in the moments of divine event. This poses a number of questions, but the most pressing one concerns the relationship of the church to time and eternity. Here, it is necessary to examine Barth's understanding of time and eternity to begin to see how, for him, the church happens. For Barth, the discussion of time takes place in the context of revelation. When he states that it 'will be always in the revelation of God that the true church is visible,'[52] we are required to ask after Barth's conception of time, both the time in which the church exists, and the time of revelation.

For Barth, the discussion of time in Volume One of the *Dogmatics* provides the means to comprehend at once the otherness of God (which he is at pains to protect at all costs: God must remain the subject, and creation the object, bringing with it the sharp dualism of the subject/object dichotomy). For Barth, the question of history and of time is bound up with his fundamental question concerning revelation. In Volume One of the Dogmatics, Barth makes a clear distinction between human time and God's time (or the time of God's revelation). He states:

49   CD IV.II, pp. 616–17.
50   See CD IV.I, p. 668.
51   CD IV.II, pp. 638–9.
52   Ibid., p. 619.

> Of course God is the Creator of time also. But the time we think we know and possess, "our" time, is by no means the time God created. Between our time and God-created time as between our existence and the existence created by God there lies the Fall . . .
>
> If God's revelation has a time also, if God has time for us, if we really (really, in a theologically relevant sense) know and possess time, it must be a different time, a third time, created alongside of our time and the time originally created by God.[53]

For Barth, the fall makes it impossible for God to be revealed in human time; human time is, as it were, human, and not Godly. In this sense, creation as the external ground of the covenant is, in the post-lapsarian context, not as it was intended to be, and therefore cannot be the true space of revelation. Humanity, in its fallen sinfulness, and human time, 'our' time, is not the place of revelation, or even of the covenant of grace. Rather, God's time, which is made for us, is that location, it is a third time, a time of revelation.

Given Barth's understanding of time, one has to ask how humanity, in its fallen time, can ever be subject to revelation. For Barth, this is the function of the Holy Spirit, which is the subjective side of God's revelation. In the summary at the head of his discussion of the subjective work of the Spirit, he writes:

> According to Holy Scripture God's revelation occurs in our enlightenment by the Holy Spirit of God to a knowledge of His Word. The outpouring of the Holy Spirit is God's revelation. In the reality of this event consists our freedom to be the children of God and to know and love and praise Him in His revelation.[54]

The appropriation of revelation, indeed, the appropriation of the covenant of grace, is the work of God in God's mode of being as Holy Spirit. The pouring out of the Spirit is that which enables the subjective reception of revelation, and therefore the Holy Spirit itself is the gift of the time of revelation, the time of the covenant of grace.

The question of history is, for Barth, bound up intrinsically with his understanding of creation and covenant. For Barth, there is a fundamental distance between God and creation, summed up in the simple statement

---

[53] CD I/II, p. 47.
[54] Ibid., p. 203.

towards the beginning of his discussion of creation and covenant: 'God could be alone; the world cannot'.[55] The world depends for its very existence on God, whereas God can exist without the world. The world becomes the external form of the covenant, and the space for the *history* of the covenant is intrinsic to creation; hence: 'The creation is the setting up of the space for the history of the covenant of grace' (my translation).[56] Barth goes so far as to say that the very reason for creation was the covenant: 'The covenant whose history had still to commence was the covenant which, as the goal appointed for creation and the creature, made necessary and possible, and determined and limited the creature'.[57]

This is to suggest that the very nature of creation, and therefore the very nature of God's creative intent, is the covenant. The covenant becomes almost an ontological necessity of creation. Were this a statement simply concerning the revelation of God's nature through God's historical engagement with creation, it would not be so problematic. Barth is concerned, on one level, to do just this. He is concerned to show the nature of God's historical engagement within time as an essential component of the creative order. Hence, he states that, 'The aim of creation is history. This follows decisively from the fact that God the Creator is the triune God who acts and who reveals Himself in history'.[58] As such, the creative intent is historical: God, through creation, demonstrates the intention to be actively historical within creation itself, and that the covenant is the concrete manifestation of this intention. This, however, seems to be in contradiction to the statement concerning the essential relatedness of creation and covenant discussed above. To what extent is God actually historically handling the world if the covenant is not ultimately a historical action but the intention of creation itself and therefore something which could be more accurately conceived of as eternalistic? Barth would appear to be constructing an image of creation that is multilayered, allowing only for full divine activity within particular layers within the scheme. However, the space for the covenant simply *is*, it is the creative intention, it comes into being with the very act of creation itself. Therefore, it is not something which ultimately

---

55 CD III/1, p. 7.
56 Original: KD III/1, p. 46. 'Die Schöpfung ist die Erstellung des Raumes für die Geschichte des Gnadenbunds'. In CD III/1, p. 44 the English translation fails to offer the precise connotation of the German. It is rendered: 'Creation sets the stage for the story of the covenant of grace'.
57 CD III/I, p. 231. 'limited the created' might be a better translation.
58 Ibid., p. 59.

can be construed as historical, at least in the sense that we might normally use the term. It is historical only in the sense that it is the space for human history, not the history of God, as, after the Fall, the place of creation is not the place of God, rather, the interaction between God and human space and history happens in the 'third time' of revelation.

We noted above that for Barth, the visible church, as seen by the world, is in fact only the semblance of the church, not the true church itself. It is now possible to recognize that, whereas in Calvin, it is a soteriological necessity which drives the dogmatic need for the invisible church, in Barth, it is the conception of Divine and human time which drives this need. The church as it is seen exists within human history, which, in the light of the Fall, cannot be the place for the revelation of God. Rather, the introduction of a third time is necessary for Barth to maintain the subject/object divide between God and the world necessary for his system of thought. Therefore, the church, as it exists in human time, can never be the true church. The work of the Spirit is that which functions, as the time of revelation, in bringing the true church into visible form. This, however, is essentially an ahistorical process. There is no sense of God accompanying history. Rather, God breaks into history through the work of the Spirit in any one particular moment.

When Barth addresses the question of the time of the church, he begins the discussion in what appears to locate a linear view of history as central, as he states that, 'The time of the community is the time between the first *parousia* of Jesus Christ and the second'.[59] This time is not a historical time in the sense of God accompanying history. Rather, into this time, the church comes into being in the form of the events and happenings which, as we have already noted, are central for Barth's understanding of the formation of the Christian community. This notion of event is highly significant. It is the event of Jesus Christ which is the primal event and opens to us an understanding of the events which form the life of the church. So, to consider the reality of the church, both visible and invisible, it is necessary to view history as a series of events. Hence, Barth contends that, '. . . we must not neglect to consider its actual condition at every momentary situation between the beginning and the end, between the resurrection of Jesus Christ and His return'.[60] It is the

---

[59] CD IV/2, p. 725.
[60] Ibid., p. 732.

individual moments as the time of revelation enters history which create the church; the true church is not something historical at all.

The critique I am advancing here is not dissimilar to that advanced by Richard Roberts in his essay, *Karl Barth's Doctrine of Time*. In a penetrating analysis, he examines the roots of Barth's conceptions of time and eternity within idealism, and particularly Hegalian thought. Roberts finds Barth's concept of time fundamentally ambiguous. He states that

> . . . the vast and complete temporal system that emerges in the *Church Dogmatics* must never coincide with non-theological temporal categories in identity, only in the so-called dialectic of transcendence. Can, however, the 'time' that emerges be the time of the world of experience and the cosmos if it is systematically at one remove from it, as what Barth will term the 'true time' of revelation?[61]

This critique is disputed. Greggs offers a response to this kind of argument and suggests that it fails to take into full account the importance of simultaneity within Barth's thought.[62] Greggs approaches this from three angles: first, that for Barth, perfect simultaneity within eternity does not mean there is a lack of integrity within any one particular moment; secondly, that God is co-temporal with the world, and thirdly, that there is 'time in the very eternity of God'.[63] Essentially, Greggs is arguing that Barth's conception of eternity does not dissolve time into history, but rather history retains its integrity within Barth's account as fully encompassed within the eternal, and within God.

This book is not fundamentally concerned with Barth's account of time and eternity, and ultimately is not in a position to take a definitive position within this debate. It does seem, however, that our exploration of Barth's understanding of the visible and invisible church leads to a situation where it is very hard to account for the visible church as being anything other than a 'semblance' of a church, the 'real' church occurring only in the in-breaking of the eternal in momentary events. This would suggest that the concrete ecclesiological outworking of Barth's understanding of time and eternity means that Roberts' critique has substance and needs to be taken very seriously.

---

[61] Richard H. Roberts, 'Karl Barth's Doctrine of Time', in *A Theology on its Way?* (Edinburgh: T&T Clark, 1991), p. 26.

[62] Greggs, *Barth, Origen*, pp. 38–41.

[63] Ibid., p. 39

Greggs uses, appropriately when dealing with Barth, a musical image. He suggests that the matter might be thought of like a chord which 'comprises notes which are ordered and can be played in succession, yet which when played simultaneously do not cease to be what they are in themselves, but become something more in their simultaneity while still retaining their distinctiveness and order.'[64] This is a helpful analogy, one that would be interesting to extend further. If the issue we are encountering within Barth's theology concerns the inability to account for the visible church within history (we might speak of the historic succession of the church, but we would not mean anything to do with particular forms of episcopalianism as we did so), this would require the musical analogy to be extended further from a simple chord, to the interplay of melody and harmony. A chord represents a vertical reading of the musical score, where indeed each individual note has integrity in itself but yet together form a coherent and complete whole. However, if each of those notes in a chord is also related to the note which preceded it and the note which follows it, then one needs to be able to offer a horizontal, melodic, account of the musical score, as well as the vertical, harmonic, account.

In some senses, whether Roberts is right that in Barth history is ultimately dissolved into eternity and hence, the visible church is dissolved into the eternal moments of the visible, or Greggs is right that within Barth's scheme history maintains its integrity within the threefold structure of Barth's conception of eternity, does not matter (for our purposes, at least). What we need to take note of is that any account of the reform and renewal of the church needs to be able to account for the horizontal line in our musical analogy. We must be able to account for the relationship of the church to both God and the world in what we might construe analogically as the vertical line within our metaphor of a chord, but we must also offer an account (which may or may not stack up within Barth's own conception of time and eternity) which can account for the 'melodic' line of history, which itself impacts upon harmonic progression, but is what will allow us to offer an account of change and continuity within the concrete historical church, and thereby begin to offer an account of reform and renewal.

Barth offers us interesting constructive material with which to move forward. His relocation of the doctrine of election opens up new theological space in

---

[64] Ibid.

which it becomes possible to account for the concrete historical church as that which mediates the election that is in Christ to the whole of the world. This removes the logical necessity for the church to be truly invisible because it consists only of the elect who are known only to God. However, Barth still operates within a scheme that holds to an account of a visible and an invisible church, and this is related to his understanding of time and eternity. The danger of this account is that it operates an ecclesiological dualism which ultimately functions rather like Calvin's in that the visible, concrete historical church becomes that which somehow mirrors imperfectly the real church, which breaks in upon history only in moments where eternity breaks into time.

Locating the 'Problem' of ecclesiological dualisms

In Calvin and Barth, we have seen how McKim's statement that the church is visible and invisible within the reformed tradition manifests itself in two of the tradition's key theologians. We must note, however, that the inherent dualism within the notion of the visible and invisible church is not solely a product of the reformed tradition, even if it finds its most explicit outworking in the specific notions of the invisible and visible church here. Nicholas Healy perceives ecclesiological dualisms as being generally notable in contemporary ecclesiology across a broad range of denominational traditions.[65] Healy construes the move as one which seeks to develop a 'twofold ontological structure'.[66] He neatly explains this in the following way:

> One of its aspects, the primary one, is spiritual and invisible, often described as the church's "true nature" or its "essence". The other aspect is the everyday, empirical reality of the church, its institutions and activities. The relation between the two aspects is often described by saying that the primary one "realizes" or "manifests" itself in the subsequent one, or that the visible church is the "expression" of its invisible aspect.[67]

His conclusions in this matter correspond well to what we have identified as happening within the thought of Calvin and Barth. Healy has identified

---

[65] Healy, *Church, World* . . . pp. 26–31.
[66] Ibid., p. 28.
[67] Ibid.

carefully the reality of much ecclesiology, but leaves us with the question as
to why this is the case. Why is it that attempts to reflect on the theology of the
church leave us so often with what Healy terms a 'blueprint', rather than one
which can and does engage the concrete, historical church and therefore one
which can account for change and continuity within the life of the church?

To begin to answer this question, it has been necessary to extend the range
of the enquiry wider than Healy does. A simple examination of the ecclesiology
of Calvin and Barth might have revealed the issue as Healy presents it, but
it has only been possible to isolate the more deep rooted issues at work in
the case of Calvin and Barth by placing their ecclesiological accounts in the
context of their wider doctrinal schemes, and to a certain extent, within the
history of the development of doctrine itself. This has revealed that the issues
of the relationship between time and eternity, and the place in the doctrinal
system occupied by soteriological concerns, lie at the root of the persistence
of ontologically dualistic notions of the church as invisible and visible. This
demonstrates the interrelated nature of the doctrinal enterprise. No one part
of a doctrinal system can be addressed without paying adequate attention to
the whole; it functions as what one might term a doctrinal matrix. We have
also noted that the very nature of doctrine itself struggles to comprehend
the church by virtue of its relationship to and reliance on the church for its
existence. These observations lead us in two possible directions, which are not
necessarily mutually exclusive. First, one can conclude that there is a more deep-
rooted problem still within doctrinal theology than the issues of time, eternity
and salvation, which needs to be addressed before an ecclesiology engaging
the concrete historical reality of the church becomes possible. The second
issue is perhaps more radical, which is to suggest that doctrinal systems, when
they offer only post-rationalizations of the existence of communities of faith
(i.e. the church), and objectify the church from which doctrine emerges, are
incapable of dealing adequately with the reality of the church alone. This is to
say that by virtue of being reflection 'after the event', such doctrinal approaches
fail with regard to the church because the event is ongoing in the continued life
of the church in all the myriad and contradictory forms which we identified
in Chapter 1.

One theologian who has grappled with some of the issues surrounding the
origins of dualistic understandings of the church is Colin Gunton. Gunton,

who was a minister of Word and Sacrament in the United Reformed Church, was another mainstream academic and reformed theologian and someone for whom the distinctions of 'academic' theologian and 'church' theologian break down. Gunton takes what one might describe as the first route we outlined above; he seeks to locate at a more fundamental level the doctrinal issues that lead to a dualistic understanding of the church. He does this both in terms of the interconnecting web of the doctrine itself, and in terms of the historical development of doctrine.

Gunton traces the weakness in ecclesiology back to Augustine, whose impact we have already noted. Gunton suggests that the dualistic ontology of the church, which results in the emergence of the doctrine of the invisible church, lies not simply in a general philosophical dualism, as we noted at the beginning of this chapter, but locates it as being more deeply rooted in weaknesses in Augustine's doctrine of God. Gunton states that

> . . . we shall find that the problems with the theology of the church run in parallel with some of the chief weaknesses of Augustine's theology of the trinity, among which lies his failure to establish adequate distinctions between the modes of action of Father, Son and Spirit. Because the differences between the persons become effectively redundant, they no longer bear upon the shape of thought about the realities of life in the world, and in this case are not able to shape ecclesiological thinking.[68]

Here, we see Gunton engaged in the activity of doctrinal theology, attempting to engage the whole matrix of doctrine in a search for a more adequate ecclesiological expression. Gunton compares Augustine's understanding of the Trinity with that of the Cappodocian Fathers, suggesting that in the Cappodocian Fathers, the understanding of the ontology of the trinity which emerges is based on the notion of three persons – concrete particulars – whose ontological unity lies in their relations with one another.[69] In contrast, Gunton suspects that the neo-platonic influence on Augustine leaves his Trinitarian theology dangerously close to a form of Monism where the underlying being of God rests in something other than the persons themselves.[70] Gunton argues

---

[68] Colin Gunton, *The Promise of Trinitarian Theology* (Edinburgh: T&T Clark, 2003), p. 57.
[69] Gunton, *Trinitarian Theology*, p. 39.
[70] Ibid., p. 42.

for this thesis through an examination of Augustine's analogies, particularly the analogy of memory, understanding and will – all of which Gunton sees as deriving from the being of the mind.[71] Gunton then goes on to critique the place of the Spirit in Augustine's understanding.[72] Gunton's argument is that such a Trinitarian conception does two things: first, it introduces an inherent dualism into the doctrine of God: that God is other than God as made known in the economy of the persons of the Trinity[73]; and secondly, it fails to comprehend the ontology of God as persons in relation and leads to a failure to comprehend the church in a truly Trinitarian fashion.[74] From this position, and coupled with the impact the Constantinian settlement had on the life of the church, Gunton notes the effect on the doctrine of the church:

> This in turn led to two developments: the first a strong stress on the institutional nature of the church, which fostered a tendency, with us to this day, to see the clergy as the *real* church. The church does not have its being from the congregating of the faithful – because not all of the faithful *are* faithful! – but from its relation to a hierarchical head. The mixed nature of the church necessitates in turn an imposed, platonising distinction between the visible and invisible church. The real church – represented by the clergy? – is the invisible church, those known only to God, the elect.[75]

What Gunton is pointing to is the relationship between the doctrine of God and the doctrine of the church. In attempting to correct what he sees as fundamental doctrinal errors emerging from the thought of Augustine, he seeks to overcome these through relating a Cappodocian model of the Trinity to the ontology of the church.[76] Gunton suggests that the church is to be an 'echo' of the divine communion of persons of the Trinity in the finite visible world.[77] Gunton concludes his reflection by stating:

> To return to where we began, with an attack on the monism of the church and its dominance by an ontology of the invisible, it must be said that there is no invisible church – at least not in the sense in which it has usually

---

[71] Ibid., pp. 45–8.
[72] Ibid., pp. 48–55.
[73] Ibid., p. 54.
[74] Gunton, *Trinitarian Theology*, p. 59.
[75] Ibid.
[76] Gunton, *Trinitarian Theology*, p. 74.
[77] Ibid., p. 80.

been understood – not because the church is perfect, but because to be in communion with those who are ordered to Jesus by the Spirit is to be the church.[78]

The question then arises as to how this happens. How is it that the church becomes a visible and historical 'echo' of the communion of the persons of the Trinity? Gunton gives us a brief indication:

> The concrete means by which the church becomes an echo of the life of the Godhead are all such as to direct the church away from self-glorification to the source of its life in the creative and recreative presence of God to the world. The activity of proclamation and the celebration of the Gospel sacraments are temporal ways of orienting the community to the being of God. Proclamation turns the community to the Word whose echo it is called to be; baptism and eucharist, the sacraments of incorporation and *koinonia*, to the love of God the Father towards his world as it is mediated by the Son and Spirit. Thus there is no timeless church: only a church then and now and to be, as the Spirit ever and again incorporates people into Christ and in the same action brings them into and maintains them in community with one another.[79]

This passage is illuminating, both for methodological and substantive reasons. We noted above that there were two possible responses to the doctrinal difficulties of the church, as this chapter has outlined them. Gunton illustrates the first alternative, which is to return to the doctrinal matrix in search of the systematic problem that underlies the presenting issue, which in this case is the problem of the invisible church and its failure to articulate a theology of the concrete, historical church. Through his critique of Augustine, Gunton achieves this end with some considerable success. In offering a remedy to the doctrine of the Trinity, he creates the space for an understanding of the nature of the church, which removes the necessity for the invisible church and allows for theological engagement with the concrete, historical church. However, it is in the question, *How?* that we meet the second issue. Gunton states in the passage above that it is in the proclamation of the Word and the celebration of the sacraments that the church becomes the 'echo' he speaks of.

There is an interesting relationship to note between Calvin and Gunton at this point. Calvin notes that the marks of the true church are the proclamation

---

[78] Ibid., p. 82.
[79] Ibid., pp. 81–2.

of the Word and the lawful administration of the sacraments, and here, Gunton is referring to the same activities. This is in itself indicative of an important stream within, but not confined to, the reformed tradition which places these two activities as fundamental to the life of the church. We should note that the two are functioning rather differently. In Calvin, preaching and the sacraments are the marks by which one might know that a true church exists in this visible community. For Gunton, their role has developed into something which has to happen for the church to exist. In this sense, Gunton is offering a theology of the church which succeeds far more than does Calvin in engaging with the reality of the concrete historical church and in explaining how the church is perpetually reformed and renewed by these scriptural and sacramental practices.

It is interesting that, following such detailed doctrinal investigations, Gunton presents such a cursory account of preaching and the sacraments. This is perhaps the point at which an approach other than the doctrinal becomes necessary. The doctrinal approach is perhaps then, best understood as one of the practices by which the identity of the church is formed. It seeks out ideas and notions which influence our understanding and articulation of the reality of the concrete historical church, which may be hindering a helpful theological enterprise which seeks to engage with the church as it actually is. Continuing along the trajectory of Gunton's doctrinal 'corrections', we are left needing to ask the *how* question. Identity is not formed and reformed simply in the act of stating, or subscribing, to doctrinal statements. Rather, doctrine, as a practice, intersects with other practices of the church. One anecdotal example might be the way the doctrine of the invisible church, so prevalent as it has been in the reformed tradition, tends to lead to schism. The reformed tradition is the most schismatic of all the major Christian traditions to have emerged from the reformation period. These two things are not unrelated. The doctrine upholds the ability to leave the 'visible' church and divide it, without leaving or 'dividing' the invisible church. That process of division both upholds the doctrine and forms identity in other ways too. The practice of doctrine, as the church engages with it, is one formative practice alongside (and embedded within) others. This understanding allows for the church to be taken seriously as it is, its practices understood as reformatory, and for doctrine to be understood as precisely one of the reformatory practices that calls the church back, and on, to reformation 'according to the Word'.

Doctrinal moves are one way in which creative space is created to remedy this situation, as we've seen in Barth's relocation of the doctrine of election, and Gunton's re-conception of ecclesiology in the light of a renewed Trinitarian theology. Alongside this, it becomes clear that we need to ask after a wider range of practices of the church as they form and reform the identity of the church. What is required is a more 'realistic' theology, as we noted in the Introduction. Such a theology will not allow itself to be driven primarily by a need for internal consistency or the promise of an idealized vision. Rather, it will itself be a reformatory practice, which seeks to articulate the content of the faith the church embodies in the service of the continued embodiment of that faith.

3

Confessional Identities

The practice of confessing

The practice of Christian doctrine is one of the ways by which the identity of the church is renewed. In the previous chapter, we looked at examples of doctrinal understandings of the church, and the way in which the theological tradition develops and acts as one of the motors of renewal. This chapter continues to develop this theme, but does so with reference to the practice of confessing – the writing of confessional statements. There is much in the practice of confessing which is very closely related to the kind of doctrinal enterprise that individual theologians engage with on behalf of the church. One of the key differences is that in the development and adoption of confessional statements, it is the church itself which is acting – councils and synods of the church develop and adopt such statements. As such, they represent a more directly ecclesial example of the statement of the content of the faith.

There are two primary levels on which examining such statements is helpful to our project. First, for what the statements themselves reveal about the self-understanding of the church about its own concrete historical identity – what is embedded within such statements that can help us understand the way the church considers itself to be open to reform and renewal? Secondly, there is the level of confessing as a practice of church life, which itself takes its part in informing the process of identity formation and reformation within the life of the church.

This chapter works very specifically within the reformed theological tradition. This continues the line of thinking that opened up with the choice of dialogue partners within the last chapter, and continues to reflect the confessional position of the author. It is worth noting that while the reformed tradition particularly understands itself as a confessional tradition, and has a long history of the development and adoption of confessional statements, one could develop similar arguments from within other church traditions. For example, one could look at the place that conciliar or pontifical statements have within the development of doctrine and practice within the Roman Catholic tradition, or the part the bilateral ecumenical statements have more recently come to play within the development of ecclesial identity within the Anglican tradition.

Within reformed worship and liturgy, confessions play a relatively small part. In more traditional 'catholic' worship, the confessing of the faith through the use of historic creeds plays a central role. In the reformed tradition, however, it is unusual to hear a confession of faith, or indeed a historic creed, said collectively by the gathered congregation. Taking the United Reformed Church as an example, the *Statement of Nature, Faith and Order of the United Reformed Church* would only generally be publicly used at services of ordination or induction of Elders of Ministers of Word and Sacrament. Despite this, the reformed tradition, more than any other, has produced new confessions of faith and confessional documents. What status do such confessions have in presenting the theological reflection of reformed churches? To answer this question, it is necessary to examine how confessions have arisen historically within the life of the reformed churches.

There is no one confession of faith within the reformed tradition. Some confessions are given greater weight than others; for example, the *Heidelberg Catechism* is held in a prominent position by the reformed churches of continental Europe. Within Scotland and North America, the *Westminster Confession* predominates. These two examples of historic confessions of faith are but two of a huge number. The index to the English edition of Karl Barth's *The Theology of the Reformed Confessions*[1] lists 70 different confessional texts – many historic, some more recent – and this only represents confessions in existence (and known by Barth) in 1923. In 1982, Lukas Vischer edited a collection of confessions and statements of faith from reformed churches which runs to 28 different texts, all from the second half of the twentieth century; and it is by no means exhaustive of the texts adopted by churches in

---

[1] Karl Barth, *The Theology of the Reformed Confessions* (Louisville: Westminster John Knox Press, London, 2002).

this period.[2] This gives us an overall impression of the proliferation of such texts within the tradition. But why is this so, and what does this practice of producing confessional texts tell us in and of itself?

A frequent starting point in beginning the meaning of such a multiplicity of confessions within the reformed tradition is by means of a comparison with Lutheranism. Jan Rohls, in the introduction to his *Reformed Confessions: Theology from Zurich to Barmen*,[3] suggests that, 'In Lutheranism the process of confessional development came to a conclusion with the *Formula of Concord* (1557) and the *Book of Concord* (1580). On the reformed side there is nothing that corresponds to this conclusion.'[4] This point is fundamental. There is no closure within the reformed tradition regarding confessions. Confessional texts arise in different situations and contexts as the need is perceived.

Barth notes five essential differences between the Lutheran position regarding the *Book of Concord* and the reformed approach to confessions (and the language of Lutheran position compared with reformed approach is in itself significant). First, he notes that the Lutheran *Augsburg Confession* is intended to be an ecumenical confession.[5] This is to use the term 'ecumenical' in a very specific sense. The *Augsburg Confession* is seen within Lutheranism as holding the same status as the ecumenical creeds arising from the ecumenical councils of the early church. The *Augsburg Confession* was presented to the Holy Roman Emperor in 1530, in a way that was never attempted for a single reformed confession. Barth notes that reformed confessions, rather than being understood as universal (i.e., ecumenical), were particular to countries or regions.[6] This is related to his second point that reformed confessions are not understood as intended to be a single unifying principle[7] in the same way that the *Augsburg Confession* is.[8] The third point Barth makes is that the Lutheran documents are conceived as a symbol, in the same way that the

---

[2]   Lukas Vischer (ed.), *Reformed Witness Today: A Collection of Confessions and Statements of Faith Issued by Reformed Churches* (Bern: Evangelische Arbeitsstellle Oekumene Schweiz, 1982).
[3]   Jan Rohls, *Reformed Confessions: Theology from Zurich to Barmen* (Louisville: Westminster John Knox Press, 1998).
[4]   Rohls, *Reformed Confessions*, p. 9.
[5]   Barth, *Reformed Confessions*, p. 1.
[6]   Ibid., p. 8.
[7]   Ibid., p. 12.
[8]   Ibid., p. 2.

ancient creeds are conceived,[9] whereas the reformed confessions are explicitly not understood in this fashion.[10] Fourthly, reformed confessions do not have the authority that the *Augsburg Confession* has.[11] Speaking of reformed confessions in comparison with the *Augsburg Confession*, Barth states that:

> . . . regardless of how seriously they were meant, how powerfully and resistant to all contradictions their propositions were, and how widespread the general acknowledgment of their content might be, these confessions were fundamentally intended as merely *provisional*, improvable and replaceable *offerings*, never as an authority, as the 'form and rule'. . . that the Formula of Concord found in the Augsburg confession.[12]

Reformed confessions are not intended to be eternal statements of truth. Rather, they seek to make provisional statements concerning the gospel *as is deemed necessary in one time and place*. In some sense, the fact that historic confessions such as the *Westminster Confession* and the *Heidelberg Catechism* are still held in authoritative esteem in parts of the church, not only as a historical record of how it was deemed necessary to confess the faith at a particular period, is something idiosyncratic within the tradition. At the very least, it serves to remind us that, just as the tradition has produced multifarious confessional statements, it is multifarious in other ways too; some parts pay higher regard to historic confessions, other parts emphasize the continual need to confess through the writing of new confessional statements. Following Barth's analysis of the subject, the rewriting of confessions would seem to embody the idea of the reformed tradition as understood at its inception.

Barth's fifth distinction between the Lutheran and the reformed position concerns the commitment to the *Augsburg Confession*. Here, it is rather harder to draw a clear distinction as the requirement for preachers and teachers to subscribe to a confessional standard has been felt as keenly within the reformed tradition as within the Lutheran. The sheer multiplicity of confessional documents, and their national and regional flavour mean that this has been felt more strongly in certain places and at certain times, whereas

---

[9] Ibid.
[10] Ibid., p. 16.
[11] Ibid., pp. 3–4.
[12] Ibid., p. 24.

the Lutheran position has always been clearer, the commitment being required to the *Augsburg Confession* alone.[13]

Given the situation outlined above, it is possible to see how the tradition practises its confessional nature. It is impossible to point to one confession and state that it is the definitive statement of the doctrine of the reformed tradition. Rather, the tradition has stated time and again, in radically different contexts, what it considers essential to faith. Given, as we noted above, the fact that such statements are rarely used in public worship, it would seem to be the case that it is the formulation of such statements that is of significance, rather than their use. Purely anecdotal evidence of this is provided by a debate within the United Reformed Church concerning an alternative version of the statement of faith in inclusive language, which the church debated in the General Assemblies of 1994 and 1995 (and was adopted in 1995). The debates on the floor of General Assembly were as heated and theologically charged as any that can be remembered, all for the sake of a statement of faith which would virtually never be used in a liturgical context.

Thus far, we have restricted our reflection on confessions to the place they hold within the tradition in terms of their history, conception and use. There is, however, a more fundamental question which concerns what the tradition is doing in developing confessional statements. Here, the content of – and formal position of – such statements can seem to be at odds with the general practice of the tradition in continually producing new confessional texts. A brief examination of the context of the *Westminster Confession* in the constitution of the Church of Scotland will highlight the issue. The *Articles Declaratory of the Constitution of the Church of Scotland in Matters Spiritual* appear as an appendix to the uniting Act of Parliament of 1929, which united the Church of Scotland in the form in which it is known today. The first article concludes with the statement that:

> The Church of Scotland adheres to the Scottish Reformation; receives the Word of God which is contained in the Scriptures of the Old and New Testaments as its supreme rule of faith and life; and avows the fundamental doctrines of the Catholic faith founded thereupon.[14]

---

[13] Ibid., p. 6.
[14] Weatherhead, *The Constitution and Laws of the Church of Scotland* (Edinburgh: Church of Scotland, 1997), p. 159.

J.L. Weatherhead in *The Constitution and Laws of the Church of Scotland* comments on the articles declaratory, noting that 'There is a clear distinction in the *Declaratory Articles* . . . between what is fundamental (*Article 1*) and what is expedient and may be altered by the Church (all the other *Articles*)'.[15]

Given this, it is interesting to note that in the *Second Article*, the following is stated:

> The principal subordinate standard of the Church of Scotland is the Westminster Confession of Faith approved by the General Assembly of 1647, containing the sum and substance of the Faith of the Reformed Church.[16]

From these three brief quotations, two significant issues emerge – first, the relationship between the authority of scripture and confessional statements, and secondly, the relationship between confessional statements and doctrine.

Given that Article 1 of the *Articles Declaratory* has a status that the others do not have, it is of note that the authority of scripture is placed here within the articles with a prominence not given to the *Westminster Confession*. Scripture is presented within the first Article as the *supreme* rule of faith, whereas the *Westminster Confession* takes its place as a subordinate standard. Scripture is that which is immovable, whereas the confession is, theoretically, changeable. This fits with a historic pattern within the history of reformed confessions of faith. Barth quotes a number of examples of this, one of which comes from the *Bern Consensus* of 1532, which states:

> If anything were presented to us by our pastors or others which might *lead us closer to Christ* and in the power of God's Word be more supportive of common friendship and Christian love than the views presented here, we *will gladly accept it and not block the course of the Holy Spirit*. For it is not directed backwards to the flesh but always forwards towards the image of Christ Jesus our Lord.[17] [Barth's emphases]

Barth quotes other examples of this kind of statement as emerging in confessions such as the *Second Zurich Confession*, the *First Basel Confession*, the *Second Helvetic Confession* and the *Scots Confession*.[18]

---

[15] Weatherhead, *The Constitution*, pp. 5–6.
[16] Ibid., p. 159.
[17] Quoted in Barth, *Reformed Confessions*, p. 24.
[18] Barth, *Reformed Confessions*, pp. 24–5.

Reformed confessions have a tendency to proclaim themselves to be secondary in nature to scripture. They point away from themselves towards scripture, and are subordinate in nature to the authority of scripture. Therefore, the Church of Scotland, in the position it grants the *Westminster Confession* in the second of the *Articles Declaratory*, is following a well-trodden reformed path.

The second issue regarding the position of the *Westminster Confession* within the Church of Scotland, however, is more intriguing. The notion that the confession contains the 'sum and substance' of the faith suggests that the Confession is, in essence, a summary of the doctrine contained within the scripture itself. This notion is one that makes the presupposition that scripture contains doctrine, and that this doctrine can be summarized in a fashion authoritative for church life within a confessional statement. We noted in Chapter 1 the huge number and diverse range of images that the New Testament alone uses for the church.[19] If this extends to the whole of scripture and across a range of doctrinal issues, a vast range of complex and often contradictory issues emerges. Scripture, by the nature of the literature involved (law, history, poetry, prophecy, gospel, epistle and apocalyptic) is simply not doctrinal in the sense in which a confession of faith is doctrinal. The sheer range and variety of confessions of faith, all of which are seeking to represent a scriptural position, bear witness to the nature of the difficulty.

The relationship between scripture and confessional texts returns us to some of the complexities of the nature of doctrine shown in Chapter 2. In emerging later than the New Testament texts and the formation of the church itself, we have termed doctrinal statements post-rationalizations of the church. Confessions of faith are, by their nature, doctrinal statements and therefore equally are a post-rationalization, not simply of the church, but of scripture. This is at times clearly understood and stated, as we have noted in Barth's work on the *Confessions*; therefore, confessions of faith are temporary, replaceable and arise from particular contexts and occasions as statements of biblical faith rationalized from within the context of their composition. This sits uneasily with the notion of a confessional text approved in 1647 being a subordinate standard for a twenty-first century church.

---

[19] See above, p. 2.

It must be realized that the constitutional position of any church may not accurately reflect either its practise or its ethos. The Church of Scotland is a good case in point. John McPake, in an unpublished paper presented to a consultation on reformed Identity in Great Britain and Ireland, comments on the fact that although all office bearers within the church are required to sign the *Formula* of the church, which affirms that the fundamental beliefs of the church are found within the *Westminster Confession,* the confession itself forms little or no part of the education of ministers within the church.[20] Indeed, it must be noted that in many parts of the Church of Scotland, the *Westminster Confession* might as well not exist for the attention it receives.

To conclude our thinking on the nature of confessing as a practice of the reformed churches, we can begin to see that it itself is, to some extent, one of the practices by which the church reforms and renews itself. In their fundamentally provisional nature, confessions invite continued attempts to express the faith in each new time and place. This is always done with reference to the scriptures, and therefore they point to the reality that one of the ways the church understands the practice of reform and renewal is by reading, and re-reading scripture. We have noted, however, a tendency alongside this for the confessions themselves to become historically fixed, as in the traditions that hold to sixteenth and seventeenth century confessional standards.

Attending to a confessional voice: *The Basis of Union of the United Reformed Church*

Having briefly attempted to outline some important contours concerning the place of confessional texts within the reformed tradition, we shall now turn to one specific text in an attempt to hear the voice of the concrete historical church itself as it expresses its understanding of the church. The *Basis of Union of the United Reformed Church* has been chosen for two primary reasons. First, it is the church of which I am a member and ordained minister of Word and Sacrament, which, given the importance of recognizing the denominational context of any theologian noted in Chapter 1, makes this statement an

---

[20] McPake, John L., *How do We Understand Our Present Reformed Identity?* Unpublished, 2002.

obvious choice. Secondly, it has been chosen as a relatively recent example of a confessional text, which will serve to illustrate how such texts are formulated with reference to past confessions of faith and contemporary situations.

We have noted that confessions of faith arise out of particular contexts. The *Basis of Union of the United Reformed Church* arose in its original form as a result of negotiations between the Congregational Union of Great Britain and the Presbyterian Church in England. These negotiations began in 1964 and resulted in the formation of the United Reformed Church in 1972 following the acceptance of the *Basis of Union* at the Congregationalist and Presbyterian Assemblies of 1971 and the passing of the *United Reformed Church Bill* in Parliament.[21] Thus, the confessional texts of the United Reformed Church were driven by a newly realized ecumenical context requiring a fresh statement of the faith of what would be a new united church.

Such negotiations for union frequently provide the impetus for new confessional texts. Vischer selects a number of examples of such texts from Africa, Asia, Australasia and Europe in his collection of contemporary reformed statements of faith.[22] They are by no means the only occasions. Vischer also notes particular political situations have led reformed churches to re-state their faith. Of note are texts from the United Church of Christ in Japan which arose after the World War II, and a renewed commitment to unity and to responsibility to the past after a politically forced union in 1941 was lifted following the end of the war.[23] Another example would be from Cuba, where following Castro's socialist revolution in 1959, the Presbyterian Church felt compelled to re-state its faith in a new situation.[24] From the myriad of occasions which have given birth to confessions of faith, it was ecumenical engagement which provided the immediate context for the writing of the *Basis of Union of the United Reformed Church*.

The two traditions that united in 1972 stood within the wider reformed tradition, but had distinct histories. The Congregational tradition stems from the Calvinist stream of the Reformation, and placed stress on the independence

[21] David Cornick, *Under God's Good Hand: A History of the Traditions which have Come Together in the United Reformed Church in the United Kingdom* (London: The United Reformed Church, 1998), pp. 175–9.

[22] Vischer, *Reformed Witness*, pp. 267–467.

[23] Ibid., pp. 60–1.

[24] Ibid., pp. 166–7.

of the local church. Stemming from what is broadly known as the 'Puritan' Movement, Congregationalism incorporated both the 'old' and the 'new' dissent movements. A heavy emphasis was placed also on 'non-conformity' (to the established Anglican Church, and to the 'establishment' more generally). The main confessional document of the Congregational movement (in so much as it has one) is *The Savoy Declaration* of 1658. This document is heavily dependent on the *Westminster Confession* of 1647, which is the main confession of the Presbyterian churches, but differs in areas of church government and church/state relations.

English Presbyterianism has a rather different history. It was also a movement of the Reformation period, and strongly Calvinist, but with a stress on the Presbyterian form of church government. English Presbyterianism, however, was largely wiped out in the seventeenth and eighteenth centuries, when the majority of congregations became Unitarian. English Presbyterianism, as it was at the time of unification in 1972, came more directly from Scotland. As Scots emigrated during the industrial revolution and throughout the nineteenth century, Presbyterian churches were founded throughout England. Initially a Presbytery of the Church of Scotland, later the Church became independent, although still fully in communion with the Church of Scotland and with a great deal of fluidity of ministry between the two right up to 1972. In 1981 the United Reformed Church (henceforth URC) joined with the Churches of Christ, who also come from Presbyterian origins. The Churches of Christ are marked particularly by their practice of believers' baptism, and on union in 1981, the URC formally accepted both forms of baptism as legitimate – infant and believers' – with the strong proviso that the sacrament of baptism may not be repeated. The most recent union took place in 2000 when the Scottish Congregational Church united with the URC. The text of the *Basis of Union* as it exists today retains the same essential shape and elements as in the original act of Union in 1972, but is a result, in its present form, of the unions of 1972, 1981 and 2000 coupled with amendments made by the General Assembly from time to time.

The title *The United Reformed Church* is revealing. In using the word 'Reformed', the Church is obviously placing itself within a theological tradition in contra-distinction to the traditions of the uniting bodies, Congregationalist and Presbyterian, who defined themselves by forms of church government.

The insertion of the word 'United', however, indicates something other than simply that this church is the result of a union. In choosing the word, it is a statement of something which is fundamental to the nature of the URC: this is an ecumenical church, not simply a reformed one. David Cornick reflects this when he notes that 'The URC is therefore struggling with its identity, with what it means to be both United *and* Reformed, to be true to the heritages which are ours, and yet open to the promptings of God's Spirit to become what God would have us be'.[25]

The tension between being united and reformed is one which is reflected in the heading of the very first section of the *Basis*, 'The Church and the United Reformed Church'.[26] In what way is 'church' being used here? Within the context of the church it refers to itself. Hence, it is understood that the URC is church, but it is not the church alone. One might wish to say that it is fully a church, but not in and of itself fully the church. Interestingly, this is at once a statement which is both intrinsically ecumenical and at the same time non-ecumenical. Here, we are using the word ecumenical in two slightly different but related ways. It is ecumenical in the sense that it does not deny being church to other church bodies, and it recognizes that it can only be fully the church because the church is wider than the URC. It is non-ecumenical in the sense that Barth speaks of reformed confessions not being ecumenical,[27] in that there is no attempt to state anything universal concerning the church. Implicit within the statement 'The Church and the United Reformed Church' is an acceptance that the church can at once be a body defined by national boundaries, without, at the same time, being structurally part of a visible universal church. The reformed tradition has held particularly closely to national expressions of the church. Barth comments on this when he states that:

> The Reformed approach was that their confessions would have only the particular public recognition of city or national church fellowships or eventually of a coalition of these . . . Such a *particular confessing church* sought to prove and defend the truth of its confession solely through its connection to Holy Scripture and not through its formal connection to a

---

[25] Cornick, *God's Good Hand*, p. 189.
[26] URC, *The Manual*, p. A1.
[27] Barth, *Reformed Confessions*, p. 1.

universal church or a normative exposition of Scripture . . . The legitimate
pathway to universality is here the pathway of particularity.[28]

The URC is following a traditional reformed approach at this point. The
church is the church in one particular place and time through its connection
to scripture, not through universal confessions of faith or visible structures.
Therefore, the URC is both fully the church in its own right, and equally
part of the church in the sense of a wider ecumenical body. The ecumenical
implications of this, we shall discuss later.

Under the heading 'The Church and the United Reformed Church' come
10 paragraphs which essentially concern the nature of the church. It is worth
quoting these in full:

1. There is but one Church of the one God. He called Israel to be his people,
   and in fulfilment of the purpose then begun he called the Church into
   being through Jesus Christ, by the power of the Holy Spirit.
2. The one Church of the one God is holy, because he has redeemed and
   consecrated it through the death and resurrection of Jesus Christ and
   because there Christ dwells with his people.
3. The Church is catholic or universal because Christ calls into it all peoples
   and because it proclaims the fullness of Christ's Gospel to the whole
   world.
4. The Church is apostolic because Christ continues to entrust it with the
   Gospel and the commission first given to the apostles to proclaim that
   Gospel to all peoples.
5. The unity, holiness, catholicity and apostolicity of the Church have been
   obscured by the failure and weakness which mar the life of the Church.
6. Christ's mercy in continuing his call to the Church in all its failure and
   weakness has taught the Church that its life must ever be renewed and
   reformed according to the Scriptures, under the guidance of the Holy Spirit.
7. The United Reformed Church humbly recognises that the failure and
   weakness of the Church have in particular been manifested in division
   which has made it impossible for Christians fully to know, experience
   and communicate the life of the one, holy, catholic, apostolic Church.

---

[28] Ibid., pp. 11–12.

8. The United Reformed Church has been formed in obedience to the call to repent of what has been amiss in the past and to be reconciled. It sees its formation and growth as a part of what God is doing to make his people one, and as a united church will take, wherever possible and with all speed, further steps toward the unity of all God's people.

9. The United Reformed Church testifies to its faith, and orders its life according to this Basis of Union, believing it to embody the essential notes of the Church catholic and reformed. The United Reformed Church nevertheless reserves its right and declares its readiness at any time to alter, add to, modify or supersede this Basis so that its life may accord more nearly with the mind of Christ.

10. The United Reformed Church, believing that it is through the freedom of the Spirit that Jesus Christ holds his people in the fellowship of the one Body, shall uphold the rights of personal conviction. It shall be for the Church, in safeguarding the substance of the faith and maintaining the unity of the fellowship, to determine when these rights are asserted to the injury of its unity and peace.[29]

The first significant thing to note in the opening paragraph is the essentially Trinitarian nature of the church. The church is construed as being formed by the God of Israel, Jesus Christ and the work of the Holy Spirit. Intrinsic to this statement is also the relationship between Israel, the people of God and the church. This is not clarified but it is clear that there is a relationship conceived, an issue which we will examine more extensively in the next chapter. The church is the church 'of God', that is, the church belongs to, or even is owned by God. It is Jesus Christ who calls the church into being, but this is done 'by the power of the Holy Spirit'. What is made completely clear by this statement is that the church is only what it is because of the action of the Triune God. Given these preliminary remarks, we shall proceed to examine this text from four different but related perspectives: first, the social nature of the church; secondly, the relationship between the church and the world; thirdly, the question of the provisionality of the church; and finally the question of the unity of the church.

---

[29] URC, *The Manual*, pp. A1–2. Henceforth, all references to the Basis of Union of the United Reformed Church will simply note the relevant paragraph number in the main body of the text.

Throughout these paragraphs the church is frequently referred to as a people. Israel is called by God to be a 'people' and the church fulfils this (paragraph 1); the church is holy because Christ is with his people (paragraph 2); it is God's people with reference to the call to unity (paragraph 8) and is a people in the fellowship of the Body (paragraph 10). The conception of the church at work here is very much a social one. The church is elect (paragraph one referring to the 'call' of the church) as a social entity, rather than as a collection of individuals who have been elected.

This understanding of the church as people places its self-identity firmly within a biblical understanding of the church, but it also rests within the historic confessional expressions of the tradition too. Interestingly, however, this understanding stands in contrast to the *Westminster Confession of Faith* and the *Savoy Declaration* (being the primary confessions of faith of the Presbyterians and Congregationalists, respectively). These state (and the text of the *Savoy Declaration* exactly follows the *Westminster Confession* at this point) that, 'The catholic or universal Church, which is invisible, consists of the whole number of the elect, that have been, are, or shall be gathered into one, under Christ the head thereof; and is the spouse, the body, the fullness of him that filleth all in all.'[30] It is not the church as a social body, a people that is elect; rather, the church is the gathered elect (i.e., individuals who are elect; gathered together). Here, we can see an outworking in a confessional statement of some of the doctrinal concerns that we engaged with in the previous chapter. The Westminster Confession and the Savoy Declaration follow Calvin's ecclesiological logic of the church being made up of the gathered elect, and therefore, implicit within this is his notion of the invisible church. Interestingly, the *Basis of Union* at this point stands far closer to the *Heidelberg Catechism*, which confesses that '. . . out of the whole human race, from the beginning to the end of the world, the Son of God, by his Spirit and word, gathers, defends, and preserves for himself unto everlasting life, a chosen communion in the unity of the true faith.'[31] Here, it is the collective nature of

---

[30] David Thompson, *Stating the Faith: Formulations and Declarations of Faith from the Heritage of the United Reformed Church* (Edinburgh: T&T Clark, 1990), pp. 37 and 106.

[31] Quoted in Rohls, *Reformed Confessions*, p. 166. An alternative translation is given in the Book of Confessions of the Presbyterian Church in the United States of America: 'I believe that, from the beginning to the end of the world, and from among the whole human race, the Son of God, by his Spirit and his Word, gathers, protects, and preserves for himself, in the unity of the true faith, a congregation chosen for eternal life.' (PCUSA, *Book of Confessions*, p. 37).

the church as an elect body which predominates – a logic that, as we have seen, Barth follows in his re-reception of the doctrine of election. It is quite possible that in the text of the *Basis*, we are seeing the influence of Barth's thought. Rohls notes that in terms of confessional development historically, it is in the Scots Confession that a shift takes place, from the election of the church to the election of individuals who form the church.[32]

It is interesting that the URC has followed an expression of the reformed tradition somewhat removed from its own heritage. We simply note this and add that it is, in some ways, an indication of the way the tradition does re-form itself, understanding its confessional texts in a provisional fashion, rather than in a continuous historical line of tradition, which in the case of the URC, would force it into an expression more clearly in continuity with the *Westminster Confession* and the *Savoy Declaration* than it has chosen.

The role of the individual in relationship to the whole church is one that receives particular attention within the *Basis*. Paragraph 10 attempts to hold in tension the rights of individual 'personal conviction', with 'safeguarding the substance of the faith and maintaining the unity of the fellowship'. This paragraph stands in tension with the social understanding of the election of the church which has preceded it. One has to question whether this is fundamentally a theologically driven issue or whether enlightenment concerns, with the autonomy of the individual and human rights discourse, are playing a more dominant role at this point in the statement. Ultimately, even here, the social entity maintains a priority over the individual. This understanding of the social nature of the church finds expression in the statements of the *Basis* concerning ministry too. Paragraph 19 stating that, 'The Lord Jesus Christ continues his ministry in and through the church, the whole people of God called and committed to his service and equipped by him for it'. Here, it is the whole church as a social entity which continues the ministry of Christ, rather than individuals who continue that ministry who come together in the church. There is a clear recognition of the ministry of individuals, but ministry itself is of the church as a social entity. This social entity does not simply exist; rather, it has a ministry – it has what one might term a 'vocation'.

---

[32] Rohls, *Reformed Confessions*, p. 167.

The vocation of the church is expressed in a section of the *Basis*, which immediately follows the 10 opening paragraphs concerned with the nature of the church quoted above. This section, entitled 'The United Reformed Church and the Purpose of the Church' states that:

> 11 Within the one, holy, catholic, apostolic Church the United Reformed Church acknowledges its responsibility under God:
> - to make its life a continual offering of itself and the world to God in adoration and to worship through Jesus Christ;
> - to receive and express the renewing life of the Holy Spirit in each place and in its total fellowship, and there to declare the reconciling and saving power of the life, death and resurrection of Jesus Christ;
> - to live out, in joyful and sacrificial service to all in their various physical and spiritual needs, that ministry of caring, forgiving and healing love which Jesus Christ brought to all whom he met;
> - and to bear witness to Christ's rule over the nations in all the variety of their organised life.

It is interesting that the statement separates, by a subheading, the nature of the church and its purpose. Paragraph 11 essentially concerns what the church does, not what the church is. Implicit within the *Basis* is an assumption that the vocation of the church arises from the being of the church. Being precedes doing. Yet, this distinction cannot clearly be maintained. Paragraph 6 speaks of the church being open to the reformation of the Spirit, but paragraph 11 speaks of one of the purposes of the church as being to receive the life of the Holy Spirit, which follows the worshipping purpose of the church. How else does the church receive the Spirit other than in the doing of its worship? It would be possible to reverse this logical order, and say that it is in the doing of the church (as implied in the above statement concerning the 'Purpose of the Church') that the being of the church happens. The question concerning the appropriate place for the consideration of the ontology of the church is emerging again here. Following similar moves that we noted in Chapter 2, the structure of the *Basis* is presuming that ontology must receive precedence, although this leads to inconsistencies and is a position that the *Basis* fails to maintain completely.

In the section subtitled 'The Faith of the United Reformed Church' (which directly follows that concerned with the 'Purpose' of the Church), we find the following in paragraph 12: 'It [the URC] acknowledges the faith of the

Church catholic in one God, Father, Son and Holy Spirit continually received in Word and Sacrament and in the common life of God's people'. Paragraph 13 continues, 'The United Reformed Church believes that, in the ministry of the Word, through preaching and the study of the Scriptures, God makes known in each age his saving love, his will for his people and his purpose for the world'. Paragraph 14 then continues with statements concerning the two sacraments of Baptism and the Lord's Supper. Baptism is '. . . a gift of God to his Church, and . . . an appointed means of grace' and the Lord's Supper is considered '. . . in obedience to the Lord's command his people show forth his sacrifice on the cross by the bread broken and the wine outpoured for them to eat and drink, he himself, risen and ascended, is present and gives himself to them for their spiritual nourishment and growth in grace'.

Within paragraphs 12–14, what emerges is that the up-building of the church happens in proclamation (preaching), the celebration of the sacraments and in 'common life' together. It is in these activities that the United Reformed Church understands that its identity is primarily formed. We find ourselves at this point with a set of questions similar to those we posed when considering the thinking of Gunton in Chapter 2. Gunton points to preaching and the sacraments as the things through which the church comes to be, and we find a similar position being maintained within the *Basis* of the URC. In following an approach to an understanding of the church found within a confessional text, we have found ourselves in the same place as we did when considering more 'academic' doctrinal elucidations in Chapter 2. For Calvin, Barth and Gunton, Word and Sacrament are the primary means of grace which uphold the church, and could be said to form its identity, and we have found exactly the same within a contemporary confessional text. In terms of a theological understanding of the reform and renewal of the church, we need to take with us the question of how this happens.

Before leaving the question of the sociality of the church as expressed in the *Basis*, one other factor is worth noting. Paragraph 12 refers to the gift of faith being received through the work of the Holy Spirit not only in Word and Sacraments, but also in 'the common life of God's people'. The sociality of the church is found not only in distinct forms of religious activity, but also simply in the being together of the church in the ordinary, everyday activities of a collective group.

We have already touched on the theme of the vocation of the church, and this becomes clearer when the question of the relationship between the 'people' of the church and the 'peoples' of the world is addressed in the *Basis*. At this point, we return to statements made in the section of the *Basis* entitled 'The Church and the United Reformed Church'. The third and fourth paragraphs begin to state the relationship between the church and the world. The 'people' of the church is in a relationship with the 'peoples' of the world. When the *Basis* states that, 'The Church is catholic or universal because Christ calls into it all peoples and because it proclaims the fullness of Christ's Gospel to the whole world', we see the fundamental relationship of the church to the world. According to this understanding, the whole world is actually called into the church, there is an ecclesial movement outwards, towards the world. This is not simply to state that the church is the world, or that the world is the church, but to state something about the vocation of both. The fact that all are called into the church is making an implicit statement about both the incompleteness of the church and the sovereignty of God over the world. God is in relationship with the whole of the world in that God has actively called the world. The church is that which, through the activity of the God who has brought it into being, proclaims this vocation or calling to the world and proclaims that the world is also called into the church. This is made even clearer in the article concerning the apostolicity of the church. Paragraph 5 states that, 'The Church is apostolic because Christ continues to entrust it with the Gospel and the commission first given to the apostles to proclaim that Gospel to all peoples'. The historic continuity implied in the notion of 'apostolicity' does not suggest that the church is in any way a static, or complete entity. If God's call is a call to the whole world, and the vocation of the church is to make that call known, surely the church will not be complete, and truly one, holy, catholic and apostolic until all creation is brought into response to the call of God? This introduces eschatology into the understanding of the church, something which is suggested, but not stated. We must note again here some of the similarities with the themes that emerged in the previous chapter. The question of the way the understanding of the election of the church helps shape the church's understanding of what it is to be in relationship with the world was one of the key issues that emerged in Barth's reframing of the doctrine of election. We see a very similar outworking here within this confessional text – the church, in effect, mediates the election of the world.

What is particularly of note is that the church does not simply offer itself to God in worship, it offers its own life and the life of the world. We see the inter-connectedness of the church and the world at this juncture. The church has a responsibility to the world as well as to God (to put it more accurately, because of its responsibility to God). This is also indicated in the section on service and ministry. The phrase 'forgiving and healing love which Jesus Christ brought to all whom he met' is used to show that the ministry of the church is not simply to her members, but, as in the life of Christ, to all with whom the church has contact. The ministry of the church is a ministry to the world that the church offers to God in worship.

This responsibility to the world is perhaps most boldly stated in the final clause of paragraph 11. One does have to seriously question the meaning of the statement 'and to bear witness to Christ's rule over the nations in all the variety of their organised life'. What does this mean, and how does it happen? As often in such documents (and perhaps here we see some of the limitedness of confessional texts), this is left as a bold statement which is not expounded. What it does show again is the relationship between God, the church and the world. Christ rules (however that may be) over the nations, and thus, the church must bear witness to this. This is indicative of the relationship between the church and the world in wider terms, as perceived by the URC. This informs the statements the church makes about church/state relations. The *Statement Concerning the Nature, Faith and Order of the United Reformed Church* states in paragraph 8 that:

> The United Reformed Church declares that the Lord Jesus Christ, the only ruler and Head of the Church, has therein appointed a government distinct from civil government and in things spiritual not subordinate thereto, and that civil authorities, being always subject to the rule of God, ought to respect the rights of conscience and of religious belief and to serve God's will of justice and peace for all humankind.

That the church is not subordinate to the state in matters 'spiritual' could be taken as a rather vague statement. It is, however, made clearer in the second version of the statement (designed for liturgical use), which clarifies the meaning of the word 'spiritual' somewhat. The alternative version (which is held by the General Assembly to share the same essential meaning as the version quoted above) states that:

> We believe that
> Christ gives his Church a government
> distinct from the government of the state.
> In things that affect obedience to God
> the Church is not subordinate to the state,
> but must serve the Lord Jesus Christ,
> its only Ruler and Head.
> Civil authorities are called
> to serve God's will of justice and peace for all humankind,
> and to respect the rights of conscience and belief.
> **While we ourselves**
> **are servants in the world**
> **as citizens of God's eternal kingdom.**[33]

This statement brings the matter into sharper focus. Here it is not 'spiritual matters', but 'all things which affect obedience to God' which are not subject to the civil authorities. What is also significant is that God's will is conceived of as for 'all humankind'. The church and the members of the church are servants of this will of God for the world (i.e., servants of the world, by the will of God) as 'citizens of God's eternal kingdom'. Here the sociality of the church is being construed in terms of the autonomy of the church over its affairs, and over its relationship to the affairs of the world. The social structure, it is implied, has its own authority and 'power structures', which are not subordinated to any other authority.

What emerges from the *Basis* is what might be termed a triadic relationship between God, the people of God and the world. The church exists for the sake of God and the sake of the world. God is in a particular relationship with both the world and the church, and the vocation of the church is to bear witness to God within the world. No one element of the triad can be broken. God's relationship with the world is, in part, dependent on the people of God, and the relationship of the people of God with God demands a relationship between the

---

[33] URC, *The Manual*, p. A20.

people of God and the world. The sociality of the church, as examined above, is one which does not exist simply for itself, or for God, but for the world too. In this sense, it is possible to speak of the church as having a vocation. This leaves us, once again, with the question of how the sociality of the church comes into being and how the vocation of the church is exercised.

To speak of a relational triad of *God–people of God–world* is to speak of dynamic, rather than static relations. This too is implied within the *Basis,* where the incompleteness of the church is considered. This theme requires consideration alongside the question of the unity of the church. The incompleteness of the church is a theme taken up in paragraphs 5 through to paragraph 9 of the *Basis,* which deal with the continually reforming nature of the church and the ecumenical vocation of the church. The church is described as existing in 'failure and weakness', and its vocation only continues through 'Christ's mercy'. This requires the church to be continually 'renewed and reformed according to the Scriptures, under the guidance of the Holy Spirit'. The church is not static because divine activity continually calls the church to reform. This is ultimately recognized in the fact that the URC 'reserves its right and declares its readiness at any time to alter, add to, modify or supersede this *Basis* so that its life may accord more nearly with the mind of Christ'. At this point, we see one of the classical marks of the reformed approach to confessions emerging within this contemporary text – that of the provisionality of the confession itself. We shall not dwell further on this matter, having explored it already.

This implied 'incompleteness' is also a central, underlying notion in paragraphs 7 and 8, which deal with the division of the church and the ecumenical vocation of the church. The *Basis* states that, '. . . the failure and weakness of the church have in particular been manifested in division which has made it impossible for Christians fully to know, experience and communicate the life of the one, holy, catholic, apostolic Church'. This is a large, sweeping claim and one that some world communions would not accept. It is interesting to note that this 'failure and weakness', and thus the incompleteness of the church, are construed here only in the terms of the relations between specifically Christian bodies, not world religions or the life of the world itself. This continues in the wording of paragraph 8, where the church sees its 'formation and growth as a part of what God is doing to make his people one, and as a united church will take, wherever possible and with all speed, further steps towards the unity of all God's people'. Because the church is divided, it is not fully 'one, holy, catholic and apostolic', and thus the church is in a very real sense incomplete.

If God's call is a call to the whole world, and the vocation of the church is to make that call known, surely the church will not be complete, and truly one, holy, catholic and apostolic until all creation is brought into response to the call of God? The question I would wish to pose at this juncture to the *Basis* of the URC is this: If the church were united and reconciled among its many, present, parts, would the church be then complete and in no further need of 'reformation and renewal'? To answer in the affirmative would be to forget what the *Basis* says about the catholicity of the church, that 'Christ calls into it all peoples'. Surely, it is only when this is so (which is to introduce the eschatological category again) the church will truly be one, holy, catholic and apostolic?

The incompleteness which the *Basis* speaks of in its ecumenical dimension returns us to a question left open earlier, which is the attitude of the URC towards ecumenism inherent within its understanding of the nature of the church. The URC is clearly ecumenical in its self-understanding as only being the church with other churches and in its commitment to seeking visible union with other churches. However, part of the underlying thinking here presents an ecumenical problem; one which returns us to the issue of the church that is visible and invisible. The *Basis* recognizes that disunity means that Christians have not fully experienced the one, holy, catholic and apostolic church. This does not stop the URC, however, from understanding itself as fully church while also being part of the wider, universal church. As an example of a church which constructs itself around national boundaries (although we should remember that the URC is a church in three 'nations' – Scotland, Wales and England), it follows the classical reformed process of having its own confessional documents which constitute it for a specific and limited geographical area. In this sense, and in the sense that Barth notes in his examination of reformed confessions, there is no attempt to be ecumenical in the sense of being truly universal. While this leaves space for the full acknowledgement of other denominations as 'church', it leaves a peculiarly invisible understanding of the church. The church is already the church universal even though it is not visibly so and has no structural unity within it. It is perhaps this issue which ultimately underlies a difficulty which emerged in an informal trilateral dialogue between the Church of England, the Methodist Church and the United Reformed Church. Paragraph 47 of the report of the trilateral states that:

> It became clear at the first meeting that the other two churches had some questions about the willingness of the United Reformed Church to express its commitment to the full visible unity of the Church in the terms agreed between the Methodists and Anglicans in *Commitment to Mission and Unity*... The United Reformed Church representatives had taken for granted that their church's commitment to the goal of an organically united Church, as restated most recently at the 1996 General Assembly when it resolved to express that commitment through
>
> > 'active participation in initiatives leading towards
> > organic union'
>
> was recognised as equivalent.[34]

There are four characteristics of visible unity that the document *Commitment to Mission and Unity* describes – a common profession of faith, the sharing of one Baptism and Eucharist, a common ministry and a common ministry of oversight. In its eagerness to be ecumenical in the most exemplary fashion, the URC has perhaps failed to grasp the very visible nature of the church. In happily stating itself as 'a Church of the Church', it runs the risk of failing to take visible structures seriously as an instrument of unity, relying on a notional pre-existing invisible unity. It is perhaps not so surprising, then, that ecumenical partners of the URC detect a lack of commitment to visible unity, as inherent in the URC's statements concerning the church is a doctrine of the invisible church which is open to the interpretation that visible structural unity is only of secondary importance. Matters of visible unity in terms of the interchangeability of ministry and common structures of oversight become less pressing, given the URC's perception of the wider church as already fully the church. This perhaps leads to a situation where there is, in fact, less impetus to seek realized visible union than within traditions which have a more overtly structural and visible understanding of the church. This allows for a peculiar situation where the URC is at once deeply ecumenically committed, and yet

---

[34] United Reformed Church, *Conversations on the Way to Unity 1999–2001: The Report of the Informal Conversations Between the Church of England, the Methodist Church and the United Reformed Church* (London: United Reformed Church), p. 16.

sits loosely to matters of concern for visible, structural union. This in turn, explains why ecumenical partners distrust the URC's commitment to such a structural visible union.

Within the *Basis*, there is no explicit mention of the invisible church; however, as a concept, it emerges most clearly in paragraph 16:

> (16) The United Reformed Church gives thanks for the common life of the Church, wherein the people of God, being made members one of another, are called to love and serve one another and all men and to grow together in grace and in the knowledge of the Lord Jesus Christ. Participating in the common life of the Church within the local church, they enter into the life of the Church throughout the world. With that whole Church, they also share in the life of the Church in all ages and in the Communion of Saints have fellowship with the Church Triumphant.

In many ways, this paragraph unites well the key themes we have identified within the *Basis*; the sociality of the church as a people, the incompleteness of a church called to continually grow, and the relationship between God, church and world. It is the final section of the paragraph which reveals something of how this is construed. References to the 'Communion of Saints' and the 'Church Triumphant' are serving here, within the context of the *Basis*, as an alternative way of construing the church as essentially invisible. It may be this commitment which, in turn, leads to the URC lacking commitment to structural visible unity, with its attendant questions of the interchangeability of ministry and a common ministry of oversight.

Inherent within the understanding of the provisionality of the church and its incompleteness lies an important place for eschatology within the *Basis*. But here, there is a slightly confusing mixture of realized and future eschatology at work. References to 'fellowship with the Church Triumphant' suggest a realized eschatology based upon a dualistic understanding of the church. This leaves a conception of a church in eschatological completeness eternally other than the visible church within time. However, alongside this, the incompleteness of the church implied in terms of the call for the church to be perpetually reforming and open to new and better statements of the faith and church structures implies a strong future reference. The church is being called on within history to become what it is not already. The *Basis* never attempts to reconcile these two implicit understandings at work within the text.

Re-formation and confessional identities

Our examination of the nature of confessional identities within the reformed tradition, coupled with a listening to the ecclesiological reflection of a particular reformed confessional text, has lead us to a number of observations.

First, there is within the nature of confessional texts within the reformed tradition a number of tensions. Such texts at once illustrate the reality of change and continuity within the tradition. In seeking to be open to the perpetual reformation of the Spirit through Scripture, a necessity arises to continually re-frame confessional statements, and hence we see the development of myriad confessional texts within the tradition world-wide. The essentially doctrinal nature of such texts, however, is an attempt to state, in a complete form, the 'sum and substance' of the faith, and is therefore an attempt to state the 'truth' in a timeless fashion. The provisionality of confessional texts, particularly as implied by their status subordinate to scripture, is undermined by claims inherent in such texts to correct doctrinal formulation. It is perhaps these inherent claims that lead to historic confessions remaining for centuries a subordinate standard, as in the case of the Church of Scotland.

The tension between continuity and change is illustrated in the text of the *Basis of Union of the United Reformed Church*. This text makes explicit its temporary and incomplete nature, by maintaining as an article of faith, the need for perpetual reformation and in stating the right of the church to change and alter the text itself as circumstances require. However, we noted (particularly with reference to the social nature of the church, but the point could equally well be illustrated through the sections of the text that deal with church/state relations) that the text is influenced by previous texts and statements that arose within the early history of the reformed tradition. We also noted places where the text differs considerably from some previous statements. The main point of continuity rests in the place given to scripture within the text itself, which remains constant within reformed confessions. As we noted, however, this position rests uneasily with the very notion of a confessional text when the doctrinal nature of such texts contrasts with the un-doctrinal nature of the texts of scripture.

In conclusion, we need to ask to what extent an examination of the nature of confessional texts, and an examination of one particular text, has helped us begin to see the constructive space in which a theology of the reform and renewal of the church can emerge? Some of the key themes that have emerged within our thinking about confessional texts overlap with those identified in the last chapter. There are key areas of doctrine which emerge strongly in both – particularly the doctrine of election and how that shapes our ecclesiology. Alongside this, our engagement with both has pushed us back to the question of how it is that Word, sacrament and common life together form, re-form and renew the life of the church. It is understood both in the engagement with particular theologians and with this one very particular confessional text that this is the case. How, though, are we to develop this line of thought?

In this chapter and the last, we have seen, while engaging with different kinds of theological material, some examples of where we see both change and continuity within the theological project, as engaged both by individual theologians and by the church itself in the adoption of its confessional statements. For example, we noted Barth's re-conception of the doctrine of election, and noted a very similar shift taking place in the way in which the *Basis* understands the election of the church as primarily social, rather than the result of individual election. We have also noted the way in which confessional texts leave themselves fundamentally open so that scripture can be continually engaged, and the faith continually newly expressed.

We move now to a close examination of one very particular example of the way in which confessional texts adopted by the churches have changed quite dramatically since the time of the reformation. In the next chapter, we will take the example of the relationship of the church to Israel – a theme we have touched upon already – and examine how confessional statements have fundamentally shifted in what they say about this. This will hopefully move forward our project in two ways. First, it serves as a worked example of confessional re-formation, and secondly, it will begin to explore further, and in a new way, the issues that surround the doctrine of election as it pertains to the way this enables us to understand the relationship of two different social realities that are dynamic within history – Israel and the church.

4

Confessional Re-formation: The Example of the Church and the Jewish People

Whereas Chapter 3 concentrated on the nature of confessions generally, coupled with a very specific reading of one particular confessional text, this chapter seeks to examine one particular theme across a range of confessional texts, both historic and contemporary. This will assist us in locating key factors that cause the church to actively re-form the confessional texts which are the self-expression of its identity. The issue of Israel and Judaism has been chosen for three primary reasons. First, it is a theme which we noted emerged right at the start of the *Basis of Union of the United Reformed Church*. Secondly, it is one particular and clearly defined area in which substantial change within confessional texts can be observed, and therefore it serves as a clear case study with which the factors that have caused this particular re-formation are identified. Thirdly, it has been chosen because Israel and Judaism lay claim to the title the 'People of God' – a title which emerged as clearly significant within the last chapter. As such, Israel – and Judaism – understands itself as a divinely formed sociality; therefore, the choice of Israel and Judaism can serve as far more than a simple case study, as a theological reality in its own right that may assist us in our attempt to offer a theological understanding of the dynamic process of social identity formation.

This topic also serves as an illustration of the relatedness of the work of individual theologians and the way in which that thought both runs in parallel to, forms and is formed by confessional texts of the churches. To illustrate this point, we will also briefly examine the shift in thinking within the reformed tradition that can be observed between John Calvin and Karl Barth. Both engage with the question of Israel and the Jewish people, and both do so particularly as they offer an exegesis of Romans 9–11, which, as we will see, is a seminal text in theological discussions around Jewish–Christian relations. It will be enlightening to note the similarities and divergences between their engagement with the issue alongside the development that can be seen in confessional texts that are themselves the church itself articulating its faith. While it is impossible to demonstrate a direct link between the work of these individual theologians and churchmen and the confessional development of the church as a whole, it does illustrate indirectly the way in which theology is a practice of the life of the church, undertaken by individuals as well as collectively, which itself forms one of the practices which underlies processes of reform and renewal.

Much consideration has been given by the church to its relationship with the Jewish people since the *Shoah*. This can be understood in both a positive and a negative light. Negatively, Christian responses to Judaism since the *Shoah* have been based on guilt, the sense of responsibility that Christianity bears for the deep anti-Semitism that lies behind the events in Europe in the 1930s and the 1940s.[1] This has led to significant efforts to engage in constructive dialogue with Jews, which has borne fruit in greater understanding and tolerance. As such, to label this a negative response seems churlish, as great good has come from it. There is, however, an emerging positive response too. This lies not in attempting to deal solely with the past on its own terms, but in engaging constructively and theologically with Judaism and Israel itself. There is an emerging idea that the Jews, as the people of God, are not simply a separate religion or ethnic group with which the church must engage in dialogue, but rather that they are foundational for the church and Christianity as such. Without theology listening to Judaism, and seeking to understand not only the past history of Israel, but the present Jewish people of God, the church is impoverished. This move seeks not only to build a situation whereby the sins of the past may not be repeated, but also fundamentally to challenge Christian theology to a more complete and full picture of God and God's relationship to creation. This shift signifies something fundamental to the question of ecclesial identity – Israel would appear to have become a means of understanding the identity of the church itself.

---

[1] For discussion of this point, see Richard Harries, *After the Evil: Christianity and Judaism in the Shadow of the Holocaust* (Oxford: Oxford University Press, 2003), p. 8ff.

Calvin and the classic reformed confessional texts

David Steinmetz notes that because of the expulsion of Jews from France in 1394, it is unlikely that Calvin ever met a Jew until his period in Strasbourg.[2] While this is presumably a situation that did not continue at the time he moved into the area of the Holy Roman Empire in which Jews were allowed to reside, it is possible that this lack of personal engagement with Jews underlies Calvin's lack of concern with the Judaism of his own period. For Calvin, overwhelmingly (although perhaps not exclusively), concern with Israel and Jews resides primarily at the exegetical level and concerns Israel until the time of Christ. In some senses, this is also related to Calvin's concern for the fact that there is one covenant that includes Israel and the church, not two. Calvin introduces this theme in the *Institutes,* stating that 'The covenant made with all the Patriarchs is so much like ours in substance and reality that the two are actually one and the same. Yet they differ in the mode of dispensation.'[3] This notion of the dispensations is, for our purposes, quite significant. The covenant with Israel has effectively become the covenant of the church, one dispensation giving way for another. Thus, for Calvin, the question is largely irrelevant concerning the Jewish people of his own time; that dispensation is past, we live in the midst of a new dispensation, even though it is of the same covenant.

Calvin is frequently quite scathing about the Jewish people. In his commentary on Romans, he states that 'none of us can excuse the Jew for having crucified Christ, treated the apostles with barbarous cruelty, and for having attempted to destroy and extinguish the Gospel . . .'[4] There is a strong sense in which the Jews have forfeited the covenant, they have 'stripped themselves of all these privileges, so that it was of no advantage to them to be called the children of Abraham'.[5] However, as one might expect from a careful commentator on Paul's letter to the Romans, there is a more complex understanding at work, even though Calvin essentially upholds this basically

---

[2]   David Steinmetz, *Calvin in Context* (New York/Oxford: Oxford University Press, 2010), p. 217.
[3]   Calvin, *1559*, p. 429.
[4]   *Calvin's Commentaries: The Epistles of Paul the Apostle to the Romans and to the Thessalonians* (David W. Torrance and Thomas F. Torrance (eds), Ross Mackenzie (trans.), Grand Rapids, MI: Eerdmans, 1960), p. 220.
[5]   Calvin, *Romans*, p. 194.

supersessionist position. When commenting on Paul, as he writes in ch. 11:1, 'I ask, then, has God rejected his people? By no means!' (Rom. 11.1), Calvin states that:

> Paul's answer is negative and qualified. If the apostle had absolutely denied that the people were rejected, he would have contradicted himself. By inserting a correction, however, he shows that the rejection of the Jews is not of such a character as to render void the promise of God.[6]

The move that Calvin makes is to speak of the way in which the election of Israel is continued within the life of the church, which contains Jews as well as Gentiles. Thus, he introduces a distinction within Israel between those who have been rejected, and those with whom the covenant promise has been maintained. 'Thus the general rejection was not able to prevent some seed from being saved, for the visible body of the people was rejected in such a way that no member of the spiritual body of Christ was lost'.[7] There is a sense that within the rejection of the Jewish people as a whole, there is still the secret election of some individuals who, therefore, bear witness to the fact that God's promise is not revoked. Randall Zachman sums up Calvin's position by stating that:

> Calvin viewed the Church as still being within the Synagogue, for there is present within it an elect remnant, even as the Church is still in the Roman Church, even though deeply hidden from view. There is hope for the hidden elect even in a place where to all appearances there is no hope. Sometimes that election is manifest by individual Jews coming to faith in Christ, but usually not, as otherwise the elect would not be hidden.[8]

In essence, Calvin's understanding of the Jewish people contemporaneous to himself is of a rejected people – rejected because they were responsible for the death of Christ. Within that people, however, were a hidden remnant that maintained the promise of God. What is very clear is the sense that the church is the inheritor of the covenant with Israel, which is continued within the body of Christ.

---

[6] Ibid., p. 239.
[7] Ibid.
[8] Randall C. Zachman. *Reconsidering John Calvin* (Cambridge: Cambridge University Press, 2012), p. 73.

Where references to Israel appear in classical reformed confessions, they generally speaking follow something of the logic of Calvin's thinking on the topic. By and large, they are unconcerned with the Jewish people of the time, and by and large they think in terms of one covenant that the church has inherited.

The *Scots Confession* of 1560 presents what could be conceived of as a short history of Israel in the section that concerns 'The Continuance, Increase, and Preservation of the Kirk':

> We must surely believe that God preserved, instructed, multiplied, honoured, adorned, and called from death to life his Kirk in all ages since Adam until the coming of Christ Jesus in the flesh. For he called Abraham from his father's country, instructed him, and multiplied his seed; he marvellously preserved him, and more marvellously delivered his seed from the bondage and tyranny of Pharaoh; to them he gave his laws, constitutions and ceremonies; to them he gave the land of Canaan; after he had given them judges, and afterwards Saul, he gave David to be king, to whom he had promised that of the fruit of his loins would one sit forever upon his royal throne. To this same people from time to time he sent prophets, to recall them to the right way of their God, from which sometimes they strayed by idolatry. And although, because of their stubborn contempt for righteousness he was compelled to give them into the hands of their enemies, as had previously been threatened by the mouth of Moses, so that the holy city was destroyed, the temple burned with fire, and the whole land desolate for seventy years, yet in mercy he restored them again to Jerusalem, where the city and temple were rebuilt, and they endured against all temptations and assaults of Satan till the Messiah came according to the promise.[9]

This is the entire paragraph concerning the continuance of the church, and it concerns almost exclusively the continuance of Israel until the time of Christ. Israel – or the Jews – is not once mentioned as an ethnic and religious body contemporary to the time. This statement should also be read in the context of the later statement concerning 'The Kirk':

> This Kirk is catholic, that is, universal, because it contains the chosen of all ages, of all realms, nations, and tongues, be they of the Jews or of the

---

[9] Presbyterian Church in the United States, *Our Confessional Heritage: Confessions of the Reformed Tradition with a Contemporary Declaration of Faith. Recommended for Study in the Churches by the 117th General Assembly* (Louisville: Presbyterian Church in the United States, 1978), pp. 54–5.

Gentiles, who have communion and society with God the Father, and with his Son, Christ Jesus, through the sanctification of his Holy Spirit.[10]

Israel is clearly understood in the first section quoted as being the church, founded by God from the beginning of time. However, the second section indicates that the Jewish people are, after the incarnation of Christ (the subject considered in the intervening sections), only of the church if they have communion with Jesus Christ and the Holy Spirit, not simply with God, the Father. There is a clear and distinctive break in the understanding of Israel before and after Christ, following that which we have identified within Calvin and his understanding of the differing dispensations.

Another elucidation of the question of Israel and the Jews is offered in the *Second Helvetic Confession* of 1561, where, concerning 'The Two Peoples', it states:

> Generally two peoples are usually counted, namely, the Israelites and Gentiles, or those who have been gathered from among Jews and Gentiles into the Church. There are also two Testaments, the Old and the New. The same church for the old and the new people. Yet from all these people there was and is one fellowship, one salvation in the one Messiah; in whom, as members of one body under one Head, all united together in the same faith, partaking also of the same spiritual food and drink. Yet here we acknowledge a diversity of times, and a diversity in the signs of the promised and delivered Christ; and that now the ceremonies being abolished, the light shines unto us more clearly, and blessings are given to us more abundantly, and a fuller liberty.[11]

Here again, what is stressed is the continuity of covenant, rather than a before- and an after-Christ. While there are two peoples in the two periods of history, there is but one covenant that incorporates the Jews and the Christian church. It is not made clear exactly what the meaning of this was for the Jewish people of the period; what is made clear is that there is one Messiah within this covenant, and that the covenant people are united under one head – the head of Christ. Both Jews and the Gentiles are seen as 'the church'. What is clear is that Israel – or the Jewish people – in no way constitutes the people of God

---

[10] PCUSA, *Confessional Heritage*, p. 59.
[11] PCUSA, *Book of Confessions* (Louisville: PCUSA, 1999), p. 85.

as the church; rather, the point is that God's covenant is one covenant, and as such has a unity that cannot be seen to have been severed at the time of Christ; the church continues the covenant God made with Israel. Where this leaves contemporary Jews is not expressly made clear, but supersessionism seems to be intrinsic.

The *Westminster Confession* has an equally covenantal understanding of the Jewish people. Again, there is only one covenant spoken of, but two different administrations – that of the time of the law and that of the time of the gospel.[12] The *Westminster Confession,* however, sees the administration of the old covenant as preparing for the new in a direct way:

> . . . under the law it was administered by promises, prophecies, sacrifices, circumcision, the paschal lamb, and other types and ordinances delivered to the people of the Jews, all foresignifying Christ to come, which were for that time sufficient and efficacious, through the operation of the Spirit, to instruct and build up the elect in faith in the promised Messiah, by whom they had full remission of sins and eternal salvation; and is called the Old Testament.[13]

Again, the Jews are seen only in the terms of Christ, as *foresignifying,* as old covenant. There is again no sense of the illegitimacy of the claim of the Jewish people to be the people of God, but this is only comprehended in terms of the period of history before Christ.

This very brief and by no means conclusive view of classical reformed confessions gives us an idea of the way in which the topics of Israel and the Jews are treated in such texts. It is possible to draw some limited conclusions from this evidence. First, the Jews are a topic addressed in relationship to the themes of the church, the covenant and election. Secondly, Israel and the Jews are not addressed as a present reality, but only in the terms of the people before Christ. This is significant, as when we examine more recent confessional statements, we see that the major themes that frame the discussion of Israel and the Jews are the same; what is different is that Israel and the Jews are addressed in contemporary confessional documents as a living, present reality.

---

[12] Thompson, *Stating the Gospel,* p. 20.
[13] Ibid.

Karl Barth and contemporary reformed confessions of faith

Just as it is impossible to determine a clear link between the thought of Calvin and the classical reformed confessions, so it is equally impossible to determine a clear link between Karl Barth and later twentieth century reformed confessions of faith. However, as one can discern a clear line of thinking from Calvin through the classical confessions, one can equally discern a similar pattern between Barth's thinking about Israel and the church, and contemporary confessional statements of the reformed tradition. Equally, it is possible to see how just as biography potentially impacted upon Calvin's attitudes towards the Jews in his time, so were Barth's views undoubtedly coloured by his engagement with the Jewish people of his time, and particularly, his period of time in Germany in the 1930s during the rise to power of Hitler, the persecution of the Jews leading to the *Shoah* and the German Church Struggle in which he initially played a key role within the Confessing Church.

There is some considerable scholarly dispute about Barth's attitude and actions towards the Jewish people within Germany in the 1930s, but undoubtedly, this context framed the period in which much of his formative thinking on the question of the doctrine of election and the relationship of the church and Israel was developed, Volume II.2 of the *Church Dogmatics* being published in 1942. Eberhard Busch has mounted a strong defence of Barth's position in response to some of these critiques.[14] Among other evidence adduced, is a letter from Barth written in 1934 in which he states that: 'The solution to the Jewish question that is currently being sought in Germany is an impossibility – humanly, politically, Christianly . . . It is necessary that the Evangelical Church makes itself heard with a resounding 'no' 'and, 'enter the fray in diligent support of the members of the synagogue'.[15] This line of thought from the political situation facing Germany in the 1930s, finds its full theological expression in his Doctrine of God, where he treats the question of the election of the community.

---

[14] Eberhard Busch, 'Indissoluble Unity: Barth's Position on the Jews during the Hitler Era', in George Hunsinger (ed.), *For the Sake of the World: Karl Barth and the Future of Ecclesial Theology* (Grand Rapids/Cambridge: Eerdmans, 2004), pp. 53–9.

[15] Quoted in Busch, 'Indissoluble Unity', p. 55.

The elect community is, for Barth, very clearly both Israel and the church, 'What is elected in Jesus Christ (His "body") is the community which has the twofold form of Israel and the Church'[16]. In this logic, 'We cannot, therefore, call the Jews the "rejected" and the Church the "elected" community'. This does not stop Barth from using some very strong, and initially anti-Semitic sounding language concerning Israel. 'Israel is the people of the Jews which resists its divine election . . . By delivering up its Messiah, Jesus, to the Gentiles for crucifixion, Israel attests the justice of the divine judgment on man borne by God Himself'.[17] While statements such as these superficially seem to be following a line very similar to that noted by us in Calvin, the difference is actually very significant. In seeing Israel and the church as the elect community, Barth is very clearly not speaking simply of Israel before Christ, he is speaking of the Jewish people of his time. Equally, while his harsh words about the Jewish people and their blame are stark, there is a sense in which the Jewish people are here representing human sinfulness more universally, and what is of absolute significance is that this sin is borne not by the continued suffering of this people, but by Christ upon the cross. This logic, however, Barth spells out in language that strikes us as utterly extraordinary, particularly in the context of the 1940s. When he speaks of 'The Jews of the ghetto give this demonstration involuntarily, joylessly, and ingloriously, but they do give it. They have nothing to attest to the world but the shadow of the cross of Jesus Christ that falls upon them',[18] we are perhaps rightly shocked. He is, however, as his dense reading of Romans 9–11 that accompanies his doctrine of election at this point, following to a significant degree the tensions in the language that St. Paul uses. Equally, as Busch points out, in distinction to the German Christians who sought to expunge parts of scripture that they found to be too Jewish, Barth wishes to remain firmly committed to God's revelation in scripture and to grapple with the complexities and difficulties of the text. That, perhaps, makes Barth's text very difficult too.[19]

Ultimately, the significant move that Barth makes is to understand the one covenant as having a twofold nature, and one that continues into the present

---

[16] CD II.2, p. 199.
[17] Ibid., p. 198.
[18] Ibid., p. 209.
[19] Busch, 'Indissoluble Unity', pp. 59–61.

in the form of the Jewish people and the Christian church. The church is very much secondary in certain senses. So, the miracle is that God has called an abundance of people 'from the nations who as such are not elected, who as such have no part in its promise, distinction and endowment . . .'[20] God is the God of Israel, and Jesus is the Messiah of Israel, through which the covenant is broken open to engraft within it the peoples of the world. Barth continues his exegesis of Romans 9–11, placing the section concerning the engrafting of branches in the context of the resurrection. In his extended exegesis of this section, the logic of his thinking becomes (following St. Paul) clearer, 'In the resurrection of Jesus Christ God himself has cancelled both the *finis* of the Jewish rejection of Christ and also that of the rejection of the Jews, acknowledging, against the will of Israel, His own will with Israel, the Messiah of Israel as the Saviour of the world, and therefore also and all the more fully of Israel itself'.[21] The judgement of Israel, as with the world as a whole, is taken up in the cross and the resurrection of Christ (later, Barth will speak of Christ as the 'Judge Judged'[22]); thus, the judgement of Israel itself is ended. This all leads very strongly in the direction of a theology of one covenant in two dispensations. In rooting this understanding (following Paul) so closely in the work of Christ, the ongoing nature of the covenant with Israel can only be understood in Christological terms in so far as Jesus is the Messiah of Israel. There is no sense in which Israel has a theological reality outside of this, and Israel can have no understanding herself of her theological reality.

While Barth uses language and forms of expression that we may not presently be comfortable with, the theological leap from Calvin is clear. Whereas for Calvin, and the classical reformed confessions, supersessionism was the clear reality, and Israel was of significance before Christ, and in as much as the church has inherited the covenant from Israel, in Barth, this situation has radically shifted. Barth is offering a very close reading of Romans 9–11, just as Calvin was, but in his reading, he finds a very different reality to that which Calvin discovered. The experience of the German Church Conflict and of the Jewish policies of the German state under Hitler and of the German Christians clearly force Barth to engage anew with scripture, and in doing so, reforms theology

---

[20] CD II.2, p. 229.
[21] Ibid., p. 291.
[22] See CD IV.1, p. 211.

significantly in terms of its understanding of the relationship of Israel and the church. While, as with Calvin, we cannot demonstrate a clear link between Barth and more contemporary reformed confessions of faith, the indirect link is clear. Much of the logic of Barth's presentation we will see re-emerge within these confessions of faith, which develop yet further this highly significant re-framing of the doctrines of election, the church and Israel.

We have already referred to the opening statement of the *Basis of Union of the United Reformed Church*. It states:

> There is but one Church of the one God. He called Israel to be his people, and in fulfilment of the purpose then begun he called the Church into being through Jesus Christ, by the power of the Holy Spirit.[23]

This statement in many senses continues the earlier confessional tradition examined above. Israel is addressed in relation to the church, and is seen as being called by God to be a people, as the church is called by God to be a people. No clear distinction is made between notions of the old and the new covenant although the wording is such that this could either be read into the text, or not. What is of interest is the fact that Israel is mentioned right at the start of the statement as a whole, and located firmly within the context of ecclesiological discussion. It is also obviously related to the idea of election, even though this term is not used. The church is termed the 'fulfilment' of the purposes begun in Israel; this could easily be read in line with the *Second Helvetic* or *Scots Confession* discussed above. However, there is a sense in which in relating Israel and the church so clearly at the beginning of this statement, we are also invited to call to mind the significant shifts in reformed thought in the twentieth century, particularly that of Barth.

A recent statement from a gathering of European reformed theologians and church people, *The Church in Reformed Perspective*, marks far more clearly a significant shift in the direction of Barth, and his reading of Romans 9–11, 'The Church is the gift and event of the Holy Spirit. As such she has been incorporated into God's covenant with Israel and joins together men and women from all peoples into a universal fellowship.'[24] Here, in a confessional-style statement concerning the church, Israel is once again centrally placed at the beginning of

---

[23] URC, *Manual*, p. A1.
[24] *The Church in Reformed Perspective: A European Reflection* (Geneva: John Knox Series, 2002), p. 15.

reflections. In comparison with the URC statement quoted above, in this case, the covenant is explicitly mentioned, but now it is the church that is stated as having been 'incorporated' into God's covenant with Israel. The church is not the fulfilment of something begun in Israel, but is actually taking its life and origin from God's covenant with Israel itself. Here, we see Israel being treated together with the themes of ecclesiology and covenant. Israel, however, is more clearly identified as a present and living reality.

The 1976 *Confession of Faith of the Presbyterian Church in the United States* goes much further in addressing the question of the relationship of the church to Israel. It states that:

> The followers of Jesus
> remained at first within the people of Israel.
> As persons from all nations joined them,
> they were separated from the Jewish community.
> Yet they continued to accept Israel's story as their own
> and to consider themselves part of the people of God.
> We can never lay exclusive claim to being God's people,
> as though we had replaced those
> to whom the covenant, the law, and the promises belong.
> We affirm that God has not rejected his people the Jews.
> The Lord does not take back his promises.
> We Christians have often rejected Jews throughout our history
> with shameful prejudice and cruelty.
> God calls us to dialogue and cooperation
> that do not ignore our real disagreements,
> yet proceed in mutual respect and love.
> We are bound together with them in the single story
> of those chosen to serve and proclaim the living God.[25]

In this statement, we see the continuation of the covenantal thought pattern evidenced in the *Second Helvetic Confession* – that there is only one covenant, not an old and a new covenant. What this particular statement does, however, is to take the radical next step of saying that the covenant continues with Israel and the Jews *to this day*. The church alone is not the people of God, but rather,

---

[25] Vischer, *Reformed Witness Today*, pp. 253–4.

Israel and the church. The reasoning is spelt out clearly; God does not break his promises.

Another recent statement makes the same point, but this time, in relationship to the theological category of election. The Leuenberg Church Fellowship, a fellowship of Lutheran, Reformed and Methodist churches within Europe, makes this statement in their agreed text, *The Church of Jesus Christ*:

> This election of the Church is inseparably connected with the election of Israel as the people of God (Ex. 19:5f.; 1 Kings 8:53; Ps. 77:16.21; Is. 62:12). As his people God has called Israel to faith (Is. 7:9) and has shown it through his guidance the way to life (Ex. 20:1–17; Deut.30:15–20) and has in this way made it the light of the nations (Is. 42:6). This promise to Israel has not been rendered invalid by the Christ event because God's faithfulness upholds it (Rom. 11:2.29).[26]

Again, the emphasis is on the faithfulness of God to his promises, which means that the election of Israel cannot be revoked. As in the text from the Presbyterian Church in the United States, this is then worked out in a practical call for dialogue between Christianity and Judaism. Once again, it must be noted that Israel is seen as central to understanding the church, that is, to the ecclesial enterprise, and also central to the theme of election. Here, again, there is a consistency with earlier reformed confessions, but once again, Israel is no longer seen as 'ancient Israel', but as the Israel and Judaism of today, the living people of God.

What then is the significance of Israel and Judaism for the Christian church, more specifically for ecclesiology? Equally, how do we begin to understand the development in thought between the classical confessional statements and the more recent confessional material? We have already indicated the role that Karl Barth's thinking has played, and the work of individual theologians engaging in the practice of Christian theology is certainly one of the driving factors in the renewal of the doctrine of the church regarding Israel and the church. However, in discussing both Calvin and Barth, we have already seen how biographical factors influence theological thought, and it is clear that there are a range of factors that are at work compelling theological reformation.

---

[26] Leuenberg Church Fellowship, *The Church of Jesus Christ: The Contribution of the Reformation towards Ecumenical Dialogue on Church Unity* (Frankfurt am Main: Lembeck, 1995), p. 102.

The events of the twentieth century obviously provide the context for more recent statements. The unspeakable horrors of the *Shoah* have undoubtedly caused the churches to contemplate deeply their relationship with Judaism and Israel. Another recent document from the Leuenberg fellowship, *Church and Israel: A Contribution from the Reformed Churches in Europe to the Relationship between Christians and Jews*, indicates well the impact that the events of the 1930s and 1940s have had on Christian responses to Judaism. 'The churches look back on times of persecution of the Jews and especially on the Shoah, which exceeded all previous persecution in its programmatic brutality and intensity. The churches know that they failed in that situation; a number of churches in the Leuenberg Fellowship have therefore confessed their guilt towards Israel and their share of guilt in the Shoah in different ways and given voice to their failure.'[27] This act of confession – and the related feelings of guilt – have prompted the churches to re-consider their relationship with Israel and Judaism. What becomes apparent is that the context of the late twentieth century calls for a new understanding and perspective – one not available or called for in the sixteenth century. The statement continues:

> The churches have failed because of indifference and fear, pride and weakness; but they also failed, above all, as a consequence of wrong interpretations of texts from the Bible and the terrible theological errors to which they led. Sometimes in Christianity there has been an idea that the rejection and devaluation of Judaism, even to the extent of overt anti-Semitism, could be considered an important aspect of how Christians understand themselves.
>
> If, in view of this past, we are able to come to a new, theologically responsible clarification of the relation between the Church and Israel, this will give the Church greater freedom and also constitute a theological enrichment and a deeper insight into its own nature.[28]

Here, the churches are actually condemning their theological heritage, and accepting failure and theological error. The accepted reality is that bad theology had led the church to think and act in ways that made the *Shoah* possible.

It is not the purpose of this book to assess the extent to which classical reformed confessions share a part in the direct blame for an anti-Semitism

---

[27] Leuenberg Church Fellowship, *Church and Israel: A Contribution from the Reformation Churches in Europe to the Relationship between Christians and Jews* (Frankfurt am Main: Lembeck, 1992), p. 96.
[28] Leuenberg, *Church and Israel*, p. 96.

that had such devastating consequences in the twentieth century. The need felt for contemporary confessions to redefine classical understandings of Israel and Judaism makes clear a dissatisfaction with the classical statements themselves. The process that lies behind this can perhaps be best understood as part of the process of re-remembering. What was considered as justifiable theology and action on the part of the church, based upon the interpretation of biblical texts and theological thinking, has been re-thought, re-remembered and re-formed. Reformed churches, at least many of them, still accept classical reformed confessions as a 'subordinate standard', or at least 'bear witness' to such statements alongside other, more recent, confessional statements. The old formulations have not been discarded, but rather, their consequences have been understood in new ways. In the relationship of the church to Israel and Judaism, a re-reading of biblical texts has taken place – alternative theological understandings that have not traditionally been part of mainstream thinking have moved to central places within confessional documents. What we can see is a living tradition which in the light of contemporary actions and events is caused to re-think its past understanding in a process that requires the development of new – or at least alternative – collective memories.

Part One of *Church and Israel* begins, 'There are several reasons for defining the relationship between the church and Israel. The church is rooted in Israel. Israel's Holy Scriptures constitute one part of the Christian Bible, the Old Testament.'[29] Here, a very old tradition is being called upon. The statement that the church is rooted in Israel is one which the *Scots Confession* upholds and affirms to the point of offering a concise history of Israel within the confession itself. Equally, as we saw, a number of the classical confessions concern themselves with the importance of the Old Testament. An old confessional memory is at once being invoked, and at the same time, being re-remembered in the light of later history and events.

It is notable that the major themes under which Israel and Judaism are discussed have not changed between the time of the classical confessions and the more contemporary statements quoted. The major themes are church, covenant and election. As such a theological memory is being invoked. At the same time, what has changed is the understanding of what these themes are addressing.

---

[29] Ibid.

Israel cannot, after the *Shoah,* be understood only as 'ancient' Israel. The horrors of the gas chambers did not happen to an 'ancient' people, but to people known by many within the churches in Europe. Equally, the existence of the state of Israel, something also undoubtedly greatly influenced by the *Shoah,* presents the church with a concrete reality of a geographical entity and a nation with defined borders that cannot be ignored. It is in this context that the memory of classical formulations are re-read, re-thought, re-formed and re-remembered.

This process is not one that is in any sense limited to the reformed tradition. It takes on a particular nature in the reformed tradition because of the perpetual tendency to re-state the faith, but it has also been a very significant aspect of life within the wider church too. The Vatican II *Declaration of the Relation of the Church to non-Christian Religions* clearly lays out a similar stream of thought to that reflected in the later reformed confessions. It states:

> Sounding the depths of the mystery which is the church, this sacred council remembers the spiritual ties which link the people of the new covenant to the stock of Abraham.
>
> The church of Christ acknowledges that in God's plan of salvation the beginnings of its faith and election are to be found in the patriarchs, Moses and the prophets. It professes that all Christ's faithful, who are people of faith are daughters and sons of Abraham (see Gal 3:7), are included in the same patriarch's call and that the salvation of the church is mystically pre-figured in the exodus of God's chosen people from the land of bondage . . .
>
> Likewise, the church keeps ever before its mind the words of the apostle Paul about his kin: "they are Israelites, and it is for them to be sons and daughters, to them belong the glory, the covenants, the giving of the law, the worship, and the promises; to them belong the patriarchs, and of their race according to the flesh, is the Christ" (Rom 9:4–5), the Son of the Virgin Mary . . . the apostle Paul maintains that the Jews remain very dear to God, for the sake of the patriarchs, since God does not take back the gifts he bestowed or the choice he made.[30]

Here again, we see the acknowledgement that God does not go back on his word, and therefore the covenant with the Jews continues. This is simply stated as a mystery, rather than receiving a detailed outworking, but it constitutes

---

[30]   Austin Flannery, O. P. (General ed.), *The Basic Sixteen Documents: Vatican Council II: Constitutions, Decrees, Declarations* (New York: Costello Publishing Company, 1996), p. 572.

a radical statement. Michel Remaud notes that this statement, of all the statements of Vatican II, stands somewhat alone in that it refers not at all to the traditional teachings of the church – be they pontifical, conciliar or patristic.[31] In the light of our reflections above concerning the relationship between the major themes that occur surrounding the topic of Israel in the classical and contemporary reformed confessions, this seems somewhat surprising. It also seems surprising simply because of the weight normally given to traditional teachings within the Roman Catholic Church. No firm conclusions can be drawn from this, but it is interesting to note that, surrounding the topic of the Jews and Israel in the post-*Shoah* context, the churches' response, across the denominational board, has been radical and has caused a re-ordering of thought in the authoritative statements the churches have made. The church has fundamentally had to question its identity in the light of the relationship between itself and the Jews in a process of remembering and re-remembering the past in the light of a new situation.

The process of re-formation

How exactly are we to understand this process of re-formation which appears to be happening to the confessional positions of the churches regarding Israel? One answer is suggested within a confessional text itself – that of the Evangelical Church of the Rhineland in a statement adopted in 1980, *Towards Renovation of the Relationship of Christians and Jews*. After an initial statement that 'accepts the historical necessity of attaining a new relationship of the church to the Jewish people', the text then goes on to state that:

The church is brought to this by four factors:
1. The recognition of Christian co-responsibility and guilt for the Holocaust – the defamation, persecution and murder of the Jews in the Third Reich.
2. The new biblical insights concerning the continuing significance of the Jewish people within the history of God (e.g. Rom. 9–11), which have been attained in connection with the struggle of the Confessing Church.

---

[31]   Michel Remaud, *Israel, Servant of God* (London and New York: T&T Clark, A Continuum imprint, 2003), pp. 9–20.

3. The insight that the continuing existence of the Jewish people, its return to the Land of Promise, and also the foundation of the state of Israel, are signs of the faithfulness of God toward his people . . .
4. The readiness of Jews, in spite of the Holocaust, to (engage in) encounter, common study and cooperation.[32]

This suggests a number of issues that lie at the heart of the renewing of the relationship between Christians and Jews and demonstrate key processes at work in the re-formation of confessional positions that have recently arisen.

The fact of the *Shoah* undeniably takes a central place in the process of re-formation. The point is made in the following way by Remaud:

> Explicitly or implicitly and whether we like it or not, the Nazi genocide is present in our discourse on Judaism and in our encounters with the Jews. Anyone who might claim to disregard this reality is obliged to accept as obvious the following fact: it is during the past few decades that the Christian Churches have really started to undertake research in Judaism and in the significance of Jewish existence. Virtually all the great documents striving to break with a past of anti-Judaism or theological anti-Semitism and using fresh terms to reflect on Judaism after Jesus Christ have appeared since the Second World War . . . Before Auschwitz, could Christian thinking have taken a fresh look at the significance of the permanence of Israel?[33]

The historical fact of the *Shoah* is inescapable and unavoidable, and it is perhaps still too early to fully comprehend its significance. Richard Harries states that, 'For twenty years or so after the Holocaust there was a stunned, appalled theological silence. The enormity of what had happened could not be registered in ordinary theological terms and indeed the very attempt to do this seemed an act of gross insensitivity.'[34]

The impact of the *Shoah* on Jewish–Christian relations has been well documented,[35] but what concerns us is that it is a historical fact. It is not a

---

[32] World Council of Churches, *The Theology of the Churches and the Jewish People: Statements by the World Council of Churches and its member churches* (Geneva: WCC, 1988).

[33] Remaud, *Israel*, p. 40.

[34] Harries, *After the Evil*, p. 25.

[35] See Paul M. van Buren, *A Christian Theology of the People Israel* (3 volumes, New York: Seabury Press, 1980 & 1983 and San Francisco: Harper and Row, 1988); Peter von der Osten-Sacken, *Christian-Jewish Dialogue: Theological Foundations* (Philadelphia: Fortress Press, 1986); Richard Harries, *After the Evil: Christianity and Judaism in the Shadow of the Holocaust* (Oxford: Oxford University Press, 2003); Frymer-Kensky, Tikva, et al., *Christianity in Jewish Terms* (Colorado: Westview Press, 2000).

theological or philosophical enquiry that has spear-headed this process of re-formation of the confessional positions of the churches, but rather an event. This returns us to a theme that emerged from our discussion of the *Basis of Union of the United Reformed Church* – that of the relationship between God, the church and the world. Such a massive and unspeakable event within the life of the world led to a process of reflection that is resulting in theological and ecclesial re-formation. Christopher M Leighton, in an essay entitled *Christian Theology After the Shoah* reflects on the church's process of reformation. He states that:

> When Christians embark upon a process of reformation, they reach into their earliest memories to recover the generative ground from which the tradition derives its sense of direction. Although Christians once regarded the times of the fledgling Christian movement as a golden age, recent scholarship portrays this age as a time when fragile and defensive communities were caught in the midst of intense struggles. These scholarly reappraisals have also stressed the Jewishness of Jesus as well as the Jewish roots of Christianity, thus these reappraisals are loaded with significance for the contemporary church and its understanding of the Jewish people.[36]

The impact of the *Shoah* is seen as forcing the church to return to the root sources of its identity, and Leighton is suggesting that this has emerged at a time when scholarly opinion was already forcing a change of perspective when considering Christian origins. This return to the original sources of the memory of the tradition has led in a number of different directions. First, perhaps, to the immediate questions that surround the history of the church and the attendant impact this had on the evolution of National Socialist Germany and the policy of genocide. Osten-Sacken relates the history in the following terms:

> . . . it cannot be disputed that, throughout the centuries, churches and theologies have again and again, to a depressing degree, aroused and encouraged attitudes that were hostile to and contemptuous of the Jews, appealing to the bible to support them; and the consequences have often been deadly. Even when the churches did not directly violate Jewish life in the physical sense, they contributed, to a degree that can hardly be overestimated, to the fact that when attacks were made on Jewish existence, the power of resistance and readiness for protest was either not allowed to spring up at all

---

[36] Frymer-Kensky et al., *Christianity in Jewish Terms*, p. 44

or was undermined. The readiness for partly active, partly passive betrayal of the Jews before and after 1933 grew up on fertile ground – ground prepared theologically and by the church over a period of centuries.[37]

It is this history, of theoretical and actual anti-Semitism, that the church found when engaging in an examination of its history in a bid to comprehend what had actually happened in the *Shoah*. Of particular note is Osten-Sacken's reference to the use of scripture to support such anti-Semitism. Leighton argues that this biblical approach rests in a typological reading of scripture as followed by the church Fathers, and offers an example in an interpretation of the 'Parable of the Wicked Tenants' (Matthew 21:33–46). Here, the parable is read in such a way that the tenants represent Israel and Judaism, and culminates in them murdering the landowner's son, so that the indictment at the end of the parable: 'Therefore I tell you, the Kingdom of God will be taken away from you and given to a people that produces the fruits of the Kingdom', comes to be read as the removal of the covenantal status of Israel and the Jews.[38]

The return to Christian origins, which Leighton identifies as being part of the process of reformation of the church, recalls us to the reasons given by the Evangelical Church in the Rhineland for a re-construction of Jewish–Christian relations. To return to Christian origins is to return to scripture itself. Together with the historical fact of the *Shoah*, perhaps the other most influential aspect of the process of the re-formation of confessional texts regarding Jewish–Christian relations has been a re-engagement with scripture. A process of reading and re-reading scripture has taken place that has fundamentally re-shaped the church's position regarding Israel and the Jews. This process has centred particularly on a re-reading of Paul's letter to the Romans, Chapters 9–11. Osten-Sacken takes these chapters as what he terms 'an initial approach to the rest of our discussion'[39] – something indicative of the place these chapters have in the whole dialogue. Remaud observes that:

What is, according to Romans 9–11, the situation of Jews who have not accepted Christ? The answer is not simple. To designate Jews who have not accepted the gospel, Paul expresses himself in at least four different ways which, at first sight, appear hard to reconcile among themselves. These

[37] Osten-Sacken, *Foundations,* p. 12.
[38] Ibid., p. 38.
[39] Osten-Sacken, *Foundations,* p. 19.

apparent contradictions point to the complexity of the subject and must act as checks against any tendency to draw hasty or unqualified conclusions from isolated passages.[40]

Van Buren states the matter this way:

> Paul was sure that God had not rejected his beloved people Israel (11:1, 2, 11, 28, 29...). How could he? They were, after all, Abraham's heirs and so heirs of the promises (11:1, 28b).
>
> So may Paul be read, if, contrary to the whole history of Christian exegesis, we take him at his word that he was a Jew, and Israelite, a Pharisee, and blameless in his keeping of Torah – at least until his calling seemed to demand an identification with his new Gentile converts.[41]

What van Buren is pointing to is that in failing to read Romans 9–11 in a way that takes seriously 11.1–2 as meaning that God's covenant continues with the Jewish people, the church has failed to take scripture seriously. It is in returning to scripture and engaging again with it that the matter can be seen now in a new light. Remaud makes a very similar point:

> We cannot but suspect that where Paul wrote, 'There can be neither Jew nor Greek' (Gal. 3.28), the Gentile-Christian would interpret 'There is no more Jew, there is only the Greek', and consider a culturally Graeco-Latin Christianity as the necessary fulfilment of the hope of Israel. History has shown that, when Paul put the Gentile Christian on guard against any temptation of arrogance toward Israel, there were good grounds for his warning, a warning that has largely gone unheard.[42]

Again, the point being made is that Christian history has misread scripture, and returning to it serves us in reframing more responsibly the relationship between Judaism and Christianity.

The third cause identified in the statement of the Evangelical Church of the Rhineland for a restatement of the relationship between Christians and Jews is the fact of the 'return to the Land of Promise'.[43] This point takes us into the realm of politics and international state relations as well as theologies of the land and covenant. It is impossible to deal adequately with this subject here, so

---

[40] Remaud, *Israel*, p. 123.
[41] Van Buren, *People Israel*, Vol. 2., p. 148.
[42] Remaud, *Israel*, pp. 130–1.
[43] WCC, *The Theology of the Churches and the Jewish People*, p. 92.

we limit ourselves to a few pertinent remarks. First, the existence of the nation state of Israel created after the end of the World War II is another example of the life of the world causing the churches to re-form their perspectives regarding Jewish–Christian relations. Van Buren, in a commentary to WCC texts regarding Jewish–Christian relations, puts the matter this way:

> Nothing in the church's tradition has prepared it for dealing with the State of Israel. Indeed, tradition has assumed as a matter of theological principle that a Jewish state was an impossibility: the Jews, we have taught, having rejected their Messiah and so their own inheritance, are condemned to wander the face of the earth in exile, until they turn to Christ or are confronted by him upon his return in glory. It is therefore not surprising that the churches have had difficulty in accounting for this new phenomenon, and that no consensus has yet arisen concerning the State of Israel. Furthermore, the absence of any analysis of the relationship between the Jewish people and the Land in all major documents of the WCC may be due to understandable apprehensions: fear of awakening eschatological fervour; aversion to the sacralization of any territory or institution; concern for the predicament of the Palestinians or of Christians in Arab or Islamic lands.[44]

What seems to have emerged is a situation whereby the formation of the state of Israel, by its very concrete historical reality, forces the churches to reawaken the question of Jewish–Christian relations. In the process, the churches have found it very much easier to deal with the Jewish people as a whole, both in Israel and as scattered throughout the world, than they have to deal with the existence of a state. A number of issues may account for this, as van Buren points out, but perhaps a central one is whether this state is to be understood theologically or politically. Israel is a secular state: it is founded by resolution of the United Nations. Given the theological understandings of the significance of the land, however, this state is one that carries great theological resonance for the churches. The existence of Israel has also brought about a situation whereby the dividing line between criticism of the policies of a nation state (and indeed, the foreign policy of other nation states) and anti-Semitism becomes very unclear. Is it anti-Semitic to criticize Israel? For some, it would appear that this is the case; however, this is perhaps to misunderstand the situation. The damaging supersessionist position held by the churches over

[44] Ibid., p. 170.

the centuries arose within a situation where there was no state of Israel. It was a supersessionism regarding the Jewish people, not a particular state. The reversal of this situation in recent confessional texts pertains equally to the Jewish people as a whole, rather than being in any way related to the state of Israel.

We cannot, in this work, examine the vexed question of how the present state of Israel is to be considered theologically. But, it is necessary to say how this work is using the terms Israel and the Jewish people. Where the state of Israel is concerned, it is referred to as such; where the terms 'Israel' or 'Jewish people' are used, it refers to the Jewish people as a whole, as a theological entity found scattered around the world. I would also take the position that theological or political criticism from either the churches or political bodies is as legitimate regarding the policies of the state of Israel as it is regarding the policies of any other nation state.

The final point made by the Evangelical Church of the Rhineland concerns common study and cooperation between Christians and Jews as having drawn the church into a process of re-formation regarding the relationship between Jews and Christians. This point cannot be elaborated at length, but it is significant. The churches have transformed their position regarding the Jews and Israel as a result, in part, of an active process. It is through meetings, dialogues, common work and the resulting personal relationships that have developed. We noted earlier the place that common life together receives in the URC *Basis of Union* as being seminal for the up-building of the church, and here, we see this process at work, albeit on a different scale to that referred to by the *Basis* (which, at that point, is speaking of the life of local congregations). It is through active participation, in the forming of living relationships between individuals and groups, that the churches' process of re-formation regarding the position of Israel within confessional texts has partly arisen. Here, it is within the practice of this dialogue that ecclesial re-formation has emerged.

The implications of re-formation

We noted at the beginning of this chapter that not only did the re-formation of the churches' position regarding Israel in confessional texts offer us an insight into how, at the denominational and ecumenical level, re-formation might occur, but that this process offers challenges to, and insights into, the very nature of the church itself. We need now to examine the questions that this process of re-formation pose to any attempt to understand what might be significant within our understanding of the church itself.

We have shown, through our examination of confessional texts, the general contours of the place of Israel in contemporary church texts. This can essentially be summarized in the statement that God has not revoked the covenant with Israel, and therefore Israel is the elect people of God continuing in a covenant relationship. This is fundamental to questions concerning the theology of the church, as to confess Israel as being the covenant people of God is to confess that there is such a concrete historical reality of the people of God other than the church. What then is the relationship between the church and this other people, and what does the existence of this people of God, Israel, tell us of the *God-People of God-World* triadic relationship that we identified in Chapter 3?

The Leuenberg text concerning the church and Israel outlines four broad approaches that have been taken to this question. The first is the conception of *'two ways',*[45] a notion which suggests there are two ways of salvation that run in parallel and find their origin and goal in one God. The second identified construction is the idea of the '"uncancelled covenant" and the idea of inclusion in the One Covenant'.[46] This is the notion that there is one covenant, begun with Israel, into which the Gentiles have been called in Christ. Thirdly, Leuenberg identifies the 'pilgrimage of the nations to Zion',[47] which rests on the eschatological notion of the incorporations of the nations into Zion at the end of time, the church and Israel sharing in this one eschatological hope. The last model identified is the idea of 'One People of God comprising Israel and the Church'.[48] This rests on the idea that there is only one true people of God, which has an inner distinction between Israel and the church. While problems and issues are identified within the Leuenberg text regarding all of these models,[49] they share in common the fact that both Israel and the church, however they are related, are the people of God.

---

[45] Leuenberg, *Church and Israel*, p. 124.
[46] Ibid., p. 125.
[47] Ibid., pp. 126–7.
[48] Ibid., pp. 127–8.
[49] Ibid., pp. 124–8.

Perhaps the most radical suggestion concerning the relationship between Israel and the church has come from George Lindbeck in his concluding response to the collection of essays, *Christianity in Jewish Terms*.[50] Lindbeck's proposal is twofold – first that supersessionism be eliminated from the understanding of the church – something which, as we have seen and Lindbeck points out, has largely happened in the official teaching of many of the mainstream denominations. Secondly, he suggests that the church regain an understanding of itself as Israel. Lindbeck introduces this proposal by suggesting that 'the understanding of the church as Israel can and should be recovered, together with the reading of what Christians call the Old Testament as genuinely and centrally the church's book (which does not deny that the same text, read as Tanach, is also Judaism's property)'.[51] Lindbeck suggests that there would be various results from making such a move. It would change our attitude to scripture, meaning that 'the whole Old Testament is as essential as the New for Christian communal self-understanding'. It would also, he argues, shift the church away from an individualistically construed understanding of itself as 'a limited liability corporation formed by individuals freely contracting together for the furtherance of their personal projects' because 'the church is a people that God has gathered out of many nations to bear corporate witness along with Israel to the promise made to Abraham and Sarah that their seed would bless all humankind'.[52]

Whichever 'model' of the relationship between Israel and the church identified within the Leuenberg text one adopts, Lindbeck's point here stands. To accept the continuing election of Israel and to accept the intrinsic relationship between the church and Israel in which this results, is to force the church to take the Old Testament far more seriously in its ecclesial reflection on its self-identity. The Old Testament, speaking of God's covenant with the people of God, becomes as powerful in the search for a theological articulation of the identity of the church as the New Testament is. Lindbeck identifies other implications for his proposal to understand the church as Israel, which must also be taken seriously by any church that confesses the ongoing nature of God's covenant with the Jewish people. Lindbeck suggests that a re-appropriation of

---

[50] Ibid.
[51] Ibid., p. 358.
[52] Ibid., pp. 362–3.

the Old Testament will bring about the recovery of critical voices within the tradition, that is, the notion of the loyal prophet – of the people, and committed to the people, but critical of the people. He argues that this provides a way through the bitter arguments within and between the churches.[53] Lindbeck, in working through the implications of the newly conceived relationship between Israel and the church, is arriving at a position that responds remarkably well to what we outlined in the introduction as the need to engage theologically with the concrete reality of the church, not simply an idealized form of the church.

There is one last significant issue to which Lindbeck points, which is the significance of the contemporary Jewish community for the self-understanding of the church. He states that:

> One final example of what Christians can gain from understanding the church as Israel in nonsupersessionist terms is that it frees them to hear God speak not only through Old Testament Israelites, but also through postbiblical Jews; this freedom follows from the belief that the covenant with Israel has not been revoked. The Jews remain God's chosen people and are thus a primary source for Christian understandings of God's intentions.[54]

This point returns us to the central issue that the Jewish–Christian dialogue raises for ecclesiological reflection – what does it mean for the church that the Jewish people are also the covenant people of God? Alan Brockway, in his concluding reflection on the documents of the WCC and its member churches begs a similar question: 'If the church did not replace Israel in the covenant with God – the Jewish people remaining God's people – how, then, are the churches to understand their own status vis-à-vis the God of Israel? The apparently simple affirmation of the covenant . . . cannot for ever be left hanging without development of its ecclesiological implications.'[55]

It is possible to understand Lindbeck's call to engage post-biblical Jewish voices as one means of continuing to develop the ecclesiological and theological reflection on the nature of the church in a situation where the churches confess the ongoing nature of God's covenant with the Jewish people. The historical relationship between Israel and the church has been confessed by the churches from the earliest period, but what has not happened to any significant extent

---

[53] Ibid., p. 364.
[54] Ibid., pp. 364–5.
[55] WCC, *The Theology of the Churches and the Jewish People*, p. 184.

is an examination of the way Jewish self-identity is perceived, articulated and practised, and how this might inform the identity of the church in its own perception, articulation and practise of its self-identity. One example of a systematic theological engagement that has attempted this is the work of Paul van Buren, who in the third part of his trilogy concerning the Jewish–Christian 'way' seeks to develop a Christian theology in the light of his engagement with Jewish self-understanding.

A full account of van Buren's work is unnecessary to this particular enquiry, but it is worth quoting the first two paragraphs of his work on Christian theology within his trilogy, *A Theology of the Jewish Christian Reality*, the subheading of which is 'The Church as Starting Point':

> As there is a Jewish reality in this world, so there is a Christian reality. The name of the former is the Jewish people, or the people Israel. The name of the latter is the Church. The Church is as visible, as much a historical entity, as is the Jewish people. Jews sometimes worry about who is a Jew. Christians sometimes worry about who is a Christian. In both cases, the worry is about the inclusion of actual people in an entity that is itself part of our actual world. The Church with which we shall be dealing, then, is a historical entity, in the same sense in which the Jewish people is a historical entity.
>
> As a historical entity, the Church is visible. One need not be a believer to see that there is and has been the Church as an identifiable historical factor in the history of the world, and especially of the West, since the first century of the Common Era.[56]

These two paragraphs bring together a number of our concerns. Van Buren begins his enquiry into Christian theology with the existence of the concrete historical reality of the church, rather than choosing a starting point in the realm of the doctrinal matrix. This points to one of the key demands the re-formed confessional status of the ongoing covenant with the Jewish people makes of the church. The concrete historical reality of a social entity which is the Jewish people has demanded the re-formation of the life of the churches regarding Jewish–Christian relations. This, in turn, demands that the church, as a concrete historical social entity, which is also the people of God, becomes central to both the actual dialogue itself and the theological work that dialogue requires. Van Buren has moved the emphasis from a post-rationalization of the

---

[56] van Buren, *A Theology of the Jewish-Christian Reality, Part 3*, pp. 1–2.

church (as evidenced in a more purely doctrinal approach) to the reality of the church as it actually is. As such, the very first doctrinal move van Buren makes is to state the visibility of the church. Beginning with the concrete historical church itself means that the doctrinal position of the invisible church simply cannot be maintained. The Jewish–Christian encounter has not taken place between the concrete historical social entity of the Jewish people and an invisible idealized church. Rather, it has taken place with the concrete historical social entity of the church as the people of God itself as it exists in time and space. This fact alone offers us the hope that engaging with Jewish voices concerning how the people of God are formed and how their self-identity is formed will assist in understanding the formation of the self-identity of the church.

This chapter has moved our discussion forward considerably. A comparison of historic and contemporary confessional texts as they address one ecclesiological issue (in this case, the place of Israel) illustrates the re-formation of the church and its confessional documents, which was highlighted in Chapter 3. This has allowed us to begin to identify the factors at work within the process of reformation. What has emerged is a process that involves the immediate context of the life of the church (illustrated by the fact of the *Shoah*), a continual returning to both scripture and the remembrance of the past (evidenced in the re-reading of the history of the Christian church and the re-reading of Romans 9–11) and the practices of church life (illustrated by the practice of dialogue central to developments in Jewish–Christian relations, and also by the particular practice of Christian doctrine itself, as practiced by individual theologians such as Calvin and Barth, but also in the councils of the church as they seek to express the content and implications of our faith in confessional statements). This correlates with the *God–People of God–world* triadic structure, and the central place of scripture within both the life of the church and the confessional texts that emerged in Chapter 3. In attempting to understand what is happening in the process of re-formation in the life of the church, all this serves to emphasize the incompleteness of the church and the eschatological dimension. The church is not simply the sum of its historical parts, it is also formed by a future open to God. It is for this reason that all confessional texts are only provisional in nature. It is this provisionality in general which allows for re-formation in the specific case of Jewish–Christian relations.

We noted in Chapter 3 that confessional texts, taken alone, present problematic issues for ecclesiology. While they provide a great benefit in that they are the voice of the church itself reflecting upon its own self-identity, they are limited in the sense that, as doctrinal in nature, they are also a form of post-rationalization, and also that they do not necessarily reflect the ethos or practice of church life accurately. Given this, our attempt to isolate the factors involved in the process of re-formation in this chapter shares some of those weaknesses. What we have identified are the processes at work in the re-formation of the church at denominational, national and international levels. What we have achieved is the identification of the broad contours and themes that must concern us. Our question must concern the process by which the identity of the church is formed and this must be examined in the context of the issue of the triad of *God-People of God* (both Israel and church)-*world*. Within this, we have found that this must hold a continuing fresh engagement with scripture, the remembrances of the past, and the concrete events of life in the world, together with the practices of the life of the church itself.

5

Biblical Re-formations

Covenantal re-formations

We turn now to the more constructive work of this book. Thus far, we have argued that a realistic theology of the church must address the question of how the identity of the church as a sociality, as the people of God, is formed, maintained and re-formed. In contrast to straight-forward systematic and doctrinal attempts to do this, which rest on idealized ontologies, the questions of processes, orientations and practices must be central to our enquiry. From our reading of one particular confessional text, it became clear that the existence of this sociality within a triadic structure of *God–People of God–world* is a central issue needing further exploration, alongside the future orientation implied in the understanding of the incompleteness of the church. From our examination of the process of confessional re-formation, it became clear that a return to origins, particularly a return to scripture; the immediate context of the world; and the place of practices are all central to understanding how it is that ecclesial identity is formed and re-formed. Equally, we have noted the demand made upon the churches and theology to hear the voices of the Jewish people regarding the process of the formation and re-formation of the self-identity of the people of God brought by the recent re-formation of the confessional position of Israel. This is obviously closely allied to the call to return to scripture, particularly the Hebrew scriptures.

This chapter seeks to deepen our examination of all of these themes, returning to the Hebrew scriptures and offering a reflection on the way in which the Hebrew scriptures understand renewal. We will pay particular attention to the idea of the covenant, and the renewal of the covenant, but we will also offer some reflections on the way in which scripture itself reads and re-reads itself. Along with this, we will also endeavour to hear the voices of Jewish commentators and theologians as they reflect upon the significance of covenant. This is, in part, an attempt to respond to the need to explore the ecclesiological implications of the confession of the church of the ongoing nature of God's covenant with Israel. Responding to the challenge that Linkbeck sets out, we will endeavour to receive something of ecclesiological significance from our attempt to understand the reformation and renewal of the church through engaging very specifically with the texts of the Hebrew scriptures, and Jewish (and Christian) commentators.

In terms of our engagement with the Hebrew scriptures, we will draw on slightly different approaches. In our examination of the covenant, we will take a broadly canonical approach. Rolf Rendtorff is one particular scholar who represents this kind of approach. The approach attempts to take seriously the final shape of the canon as the theological text which 'became the foundation of the faith, doctrine and life of the two biblical faith communities, the Jewish and the Christian.'[1] This allows us to see the significance of the order of the presentation of the covenant(s) within the scriptures, and to elucidate the understanding within that canonical presentation of covenantal renewal and the formation of the social identity of Israel. We will also, however, take note of certain ways in which the canon contains within itself readings, and re-readings of itself. This becomes apparent when one brings not only canonical but historical–critical tools to bear. Both, as we shall see, offer rich understandings of the way in which renewal is understood within the Hebrew scriptures.

There are two particular Jewish thinkers that we will engage with, particularly with reference to the issue of the covenant and election. Michael Wyschogrod is a Jewish author who has grappled with the question of Jewish theology and philosophy, primarily in his work, *The Body of Faith: God in the People Israel*. He perceives his work to be in a small field which contains the work of those such as the medieval Jewish philosopher, Maimonides, and the later work of people like Hermann Cohen and Franz Rosenzweig.[2] Another Jewish theologian, David Novak, addresses similar questions to Wyschogrod in his work, *The Election of Israel: The Idea of the Chosen People*.[3] Novak too

---

[1] Rolf Rendtorff, *The Canonical Hebrew Bible: A Theology of the Old Testament* (David E. Orton (trans.), Leiderdorp: Deo Publishing, 2005), p. 2.

[2] Michael Wyschogrod, *The Body of Faith: God in the People Israel* (San Francisco: Harper and Row, 1983), p. xiv.

[3] David Novak, *The Election of Israel: The Idea of the Chosen People* (Cambridge: Cambridge University Press, 1995).

stands in the theological and philosophical academic tradition, though more markedly within a tradition of a rabbinic dialogical approach. The concerns of Wyschogrod and Novak with questions of identity, covenant and election make them obvious choices for dialogue, so too does the fact that both have been deeply engaged with the Jewish–Christian dialogue. They particularly (though not exclusively) will be our chosen dialogue partners throughout this section of the work.

The suggestion that philosophy and systematic theological thought are alien to Judaism opens up a theme that will emerge throughout this chapter. Wyschogrod states that had there been no Jewish philosophy at all, this would be easily explicable on the basis that 'philosophy is a legacy of the Greek spirit, and biblical and rabbinic Judaism are not a philosophy but a way of life and a mode of national-religious existence'.[4] In comparing Judaism with Christianity, Wyschogrod suggests various reasons as to why theology as a discipline does not have the same centrality within Judaism as it does within Christianity. Perhaps surprisingly, the first thing he notes is the element of 'Jewish incarnation'.[5] He suggests that:

> 'The election of Israel is an election that does not exclude the flesh of this people. No theory can therefore encompass such an election, since theory can deal with a faith that consists of teachings but not one that reaches into the existence of a people. Existence can be expressed in narrative form and it can also be thought about, but such thought is always tentative, partial, incomplete, subject to correction by life processes that no theory can forecast but only follow'.[6]

This idea interestingly mirrors almost exactly the criticisms we noted in Chapter 2 of this book concerning doctrinal approaches to ecclesiology. Theoretical approaches can deal with systematic bodies of teaching and idealized accounts of theoretical ontology, but they cannot deal easily with the realities of the existence of a people. Wyschogrod's perspective is that Jewish modes of thought can act as a corrective to this kind of problem. Equally worth noting is that his attention to the incomplete and tentative nature necessarily implicit in any thought regarding the physical existence of the Jewish people

---

[4] Wyschogrod, *The Body of Faith*, p. 40.
[5] Ibid., p. 33.
[6] Ibid.

mirrors well the way we have argued that confessions of faith function within the reformed tradition, as temporary and revisable.

A covenant with all: Noah and the first covenant

Within the canon of scripture, the first covenant is that which God makes with Noah. While this text might well be one of the latest in compositional terms, its position within the opening chapters of Genesis gives it a function within canonical thinking which provides what might be termed a 'covenantal backdrop' to later expressions of the covenant between God and Israel. The covenant with Noah is not a particular covenant, as with the idea of a covenant with Israel, that is, it is not a covenant which brings into existence a particular people. Rather, it is a covenant with all living beings:

> Then God said to Noah and to his sons with him, "As for me, I am establishing my covenant with you and your descendants after you, and with every living creature that is with you, the birds, the domestic animals, and every animal of the earth with you, as many as came out of the ark. I establish my covenant with you, that never again shall all flesh be cut off by the waters of a flood, and never again shall there be a flood to destroy the earth". (Gen. 9. 8–11)

This covenant is one that encompasses all 'living flesh', and also one that is not restricted to either time or place; it is for Noah and all his descendents; Noah, at this point, is the ancestor of the whole human race. This covenant is one which arises within the context of what might, loosely, be termed 'law'. The 'Noahide law' is primarily a Jewish concept, emerging from the written and the oral *Torah*, the written component being found in Genesis 9.1–8, which immediately precedes the passage quoted above. It entails the command to multiply, the command not to shed the blood of human life and the command 'you shall not eat flesh with its life, that is, its blood' (Gen. 9.4). Although the covenant is not explicitly dependent upon the keeping of this law, this law is inherent to the expression of this first covenant. Also inherent in this covenant are a sign and the notion of remembrance in the giving of the sign of the 'bow', which is for the purposes of reminding God not to forget this covenant (Gen. 9.12–15). The nature of this covenant as one which is not simply with Noah, but for all his descendants (i.e., all humanity) is not simply stated; rather, the means of its mediation are given. The bow is to function as a sign by which God will remember the covenant, and the fact of God's remembrance will ensure the continuation of the covenant. This extraordinary way of speaking of divine activity offers us a glimpse of one of the central themes with which we will now need to concern ourselves – memory as the mediator of covenantal reality. Memory relates us to our past; without memory, there can be no sense of our present. In portraying God as remembering, the author of this story is offering us a radical insight into the nature of God. God is one who relates within history through the process of 'calling to mind' – remembrance.

The story of the covenant with Noah also returns us to the issue of the *God–People of God–World* triadic structure. The nation of Israel came to understand itself as in a particular covenantal relationship with God, but the wider context of this more specific covenant made with Noah is the covenant of God with all flesh. This serves as an important corrective in any discussion of covenant which concerns either Israel or the Christian Church; when speaking of a specific covenant with Israel or of the Church, one cannot speak solely of an exclusive one. The Hebrew scriptures present an actively remembering God in a covenantal relationship with the whole of creation before there is any specific mention of a covenant with Israel or any thought of a 'new' covenant in Christ. Israel and the Christian Church can only ever claim to be a covenantal people within (or drawn out of) the covenantal people of the whole earth, the descendants of Noah. In this sense, the Noahide covenant is not simply historical in the linear terms of past, present and future; it also confronts what we might call the 'spread-outness' of historical life in the world. It is a concept which deals with the complex realities of historical life in the world, which consists not simply of 'humanity', but distinct social groupings, of nations and peoples.

David Novak introduces the Noahide covenant and law as being a 'border concept' (*Grenzbegriff*). He defines this in the following way:

> It mediates between Judaism and the non-Jewish world in both time and space. For the Noahide (*ben Noah*) designated both that which preceded the emergence of Judaism, that is, "pre-Judaic" man, and that which *confronts* Judaism in the present, that is, "co-Judaic" man. Because of this dual status, the concept of Noahide law has been one which has been used both in understanding the condition which enabled Judaism to emerge,

and Judaism's view of what lies directly beyond the point where it ends. The former type of understanding may be termed *vertical*; the latter *horizontal*.

Some treatments of Noahide law have emphasized the vertical aspect more than the horizontal; others have reversed the emphasis. However, since the conceptual term "Noahide" designates both dimensions, no matter how much one's emphasis tended towards one direction, he always had to take into consideration the other dimension.[7]

Within a Jewish perspective, what Novak is identifying here is very similar in structure to the *God–People of God–World* structure we noted emerging with the *Basis of Union of the United Reformed Church*. To understand the social nature of covenant, and therefore, to understand either Israel or the Church, is to understand the intrinsic relationship that each has both with God and with the world (and between Israel and the Church; their relationship with one another).

The covenant with Noah draws out three particular issues which will concern us as we examine the notion of covenant, and the renewal of covenant, as it emerges within the Hebrew scriptures. First, covenant is essentially a social phenomenon, as it is not simply with Noah, but with all humanity (his descendents). Secondly, the covenant is mediated within history through remembrance, and thirdly, the covenant is mediated through signs and practices (i.e., the bow and the Noahide 'law'). Unlike the Abrahamic covenant, this does not form a particular people, but rather assumes a general sociality; it is made with 'all flesh', not with a distinct group. The major themes that are of particular interest in our enquiry concerning the re-formation of the people of God, however, are already present.

The covenant with Abraham: The election of a sociality

The covenant with Abraham is the foundational covenant which is then referred to and recalled throughout the texts of the Hebrew scriptures and the Christian New Testament. Apart from genealogical information, Abraham[8]

---

[7] David Novak, *The Image of the Non-Jew in Judaism* (New York and Toronto: The Edwin Mellen Press, 1983), p. xiii.

[8] Until Gen. 17.5, the name is 'Abram', for the sake of consistency, I shall refer to Abraham throughout the text.

apparently comes from nowhere. Nothing is recounted as being special about Abraham; we are not told that he is particularly good, or great. He is simply called. Genesis recounts that

> Now the Lord said to Abram, "Go from your country and your kindred and your father's house to the land that I will show you. I will make of you a great nation, and I will bless you, and make your name great, so that you will be a blessing. I will bless those who bless you, and the one who curses you I will curse; and in you all the families of the earth shall be blessed."
>
> So Abram went, as the Lord had told him. (Gen. 12.1–4)

Implicit in the first Genesis account of the covenant made with Abraham that follows in Chapter 15 is the content of the call of Abraham. The whole of Chapter 15 deals with two component promises – the promise of offspring for Abraham and the promise of the land. Accompanying this is what might be termed a covenantal sacrifice. Moshe Weinfeld in *The Promise of the Land* undertakes to determine the nature of this covenant with Abraham by means of a comparison with the grant formula in the ancient Near East.[9] Weinfeld concludes that the main point concerning the nature of this covenant is that it is unconditional. Thus, Abraham is promised an heir and also the land, but with no apparent demand made in return: 'God as the suzerain commits himself and swears, as it were, to keep the promise'.[10] He remarks that the type of grant with which he compares the covenant with Abraham normally contains a historical introduction, and indeed Chapter 15 contains such an introduction. We are told that the Lord said to Abraham 'I am the Lord who brought you from Ur of the Chaldeans, to give you this land to possess'. (Gen. 15.7) This historical note is complemented later in the chapter in the Lord's address to Abraham in his dream. Here, we find not a past reference but a future reference:

> Then the Lord said to Abram, "Know this for certain, that your offspring shall be aliens in a land that is not theirs, and shall be slaves there, and they shall be oppressed for four hundred years; but I will bring judgement on the nation that they serve, and afterward they shall come out with great possessions." (Gen. 15. 13–14)

[9] Moshe Weinfeld, *The Promise of the Land: The Inheritance of the Land of Canaan by the Israelites* (Berkeley and Oxford: University of California Press, 1993), p. 222 ff.

[10] Weinfeld, *The Promise*. p. 251.

Thus, at this decisive moment in the history of Israel, the conclusion of the covenant with Abraham, divine reference is made to both the past and the future. The call of Abraham is remembered and his journey from *Ur*, and the future of his descendents is accounted. It is in the context of both the past and the future that 'On that day the LORD made a covenant with Abram, saying, "To your descendents I give this land, from the river of Egypt to the great river, the river Euphrates . . ."' (Gen. 15.18).

Simon DeVries has noted the position of the statement 'on that day' at the very opening of the sentence.[11] His exhaustive analysis of the Hebrew terms for the day past, the day present and the day future defies easy summarization. However, it is useful to note one of his conclusions that the term *bayyomhahu* (the day past) when used as an epitome can be defined as 'a summarizing characterization concerning a particular day in which Israel's God was in some way seen to be active in crucial confrontation with his people'.[12] Thus, he states concerning Genesis 15:18 that 'the forward position of *bayyomhahu* calls attention to this "day" as a moment of unique self-revelation on the part of Yahweh, intervening in Abram's life to shape it toward the fulfilment of his promises in the history of the people who should come forth from his loins'.[13] This emphasis on this 'day' makes clear the significance of a particular moment in the past, a particular event on a particular day. It serves to demonstrate the importance attached by the author to this particular moment in such a way that the reader too becomes aware of its historical significance.

In the account of the covenant with Abraham, the action of God in the world is presented historically. The people of Israel find their origin in a text that views history both in terms of the past, present and future *and* in the spread-out terms of land, geographical boundaries and political entities.

Genesis 17 offers another account of the covenant between Abraham and God. In this account, we find the first use of what has come to be known as the 'covenant formula' – the phrase 'I will be your God and you will be my people'. Rendtorff has offered an exhaustive examination of this formula and

---

[11] Simon J. DeVries, *Yesterday, Today, and Tomorrow: Time and History in the Old Testament* (London: S.P.C.K, 1975), p. 73.

[12] DeVries, *Yesterday, Today*, p. 136.

[13] Ibid., p. 74.

designates it as having three primary versions, which he defines as: A = I will be God for you; B = You shall be a people for me; and C = where the two are combined.[14] Genesis 17 presents us with an example of the first form (A):

> I will establish my covenant between me and you, and your offspring after you throughout their generations, for an everlasting covenant, to be God to you and to your offspring after you. And I will give to you, the land where you are now an alien, all the land of Canaan, for a perpetual holding; and I will be their God. (Gen. 17.7–8)

Again, we see that the covenant makes the promise of the land to Abraham as well as the promise of offspring for Abraham. This time, there is a content to the covenant other than simply an unconditional gift. The offspring of Abraham are to be known by a sign – circumcision. It is possible to draw some parallels here with the covenant with Noah. First, as with the Noahide law, there comes a requirement for the recipient of the covenant (circumcision) and secondly, there is a sign, this time not a bow in the clouds, but the physical mark of circumcision. It must be noted (as it is by W. J. Dumbrell[15]) that this is not a sign specifically of remembrance, but of separation. It is, nonetheless, a physical reminder of the reality of covenant, which plays its part in reminding the possessor of the sign of his part in the covenantal community and acts theologically as a marker of separation from the surrounding communities.[16]

We must now turn to some of the issues that these texts raise in an attempt to hear the particular Jewish contributions that Wyschogrod and Novak make concerning their significance for the identity of Judaism. Novak addresses the election of Israel in the context of creation. He notes the correlation between the election of Abraham and the creation of the world. Both events hold within themselves the same inherent logic in that there is no indication given within scripture of any particular reason for each act. Genesis begins with the account of creation itself, and does not offer reasons or an account of the inner life of God prior to creation; creation simply happens as God has decreed. So too,

---

[14] Rolf Rendtorff, *The Covenant Formula: an Exegetical and Theological Investigation* (Edinburgh: T&T Clark, 1998), p. 13.

[15] W. J. Dumbrell, *Covenant & Creation: An Old Testament Covenantal Theology* (New South Wales: Paternoster Press, 1984), p. 75.

[16] One must note that the practice of circumcision is one which, historically, is prevalent throughout the Semitic world, and therefore the reality that it is a sign of separation is questionable. It is clearly functioning in this way in the text, however.

the election of Abraham functions in the same way. Commenting on Genesis 12:1–4, Novak notes that:

> In this elementary text there seems to be no clue as to why God elects Abraham and his progeny or why Abraham obeys the call to respond to being elected by God. Unlike in the case of Noah, who is elected to save human kind and the animal world from the Flood "because (*ki*) I have seen that you are righteous (*tsadiq*) before Me in this generation" (Genesis 7:1), and who obviously responds to God's call because of the biological drive for self-preservation, there is no reason given here for either God's choice or Abraham's positive response to it.[17]

Novak goes on to suggest that any righteousness involved on Abraham's part is a response to election, not the reason for it.[18] This election is, however, not simply the election of the man Abraham; rather, it is a generic election, 'Abraham is elected as the progenitor of a people. Every member of this people is elected by God and every member of this people is called upon to respond to his or her generic election'.[19] This generic election requires a communal, and therefore, also a *public* response. Implicit within this is the understanding that the election of Israel and Judaism is intrinsically public. That is, it is to be visible, rather than hidden. Novak understands the promise of election as one that sets up what is the essential relationship between God, creation and the elect people: a correlative relationship. Israel's relationship with the world is correlative of God's relationship to Israel.[20] Novak locates this notion in a quotation from Genesis 18.17–19 and his comment on this passage:

> "How can I conceal what I am doing from Abraham? And Abraham shall surely become a great and important (*atsum*) nation, in whom all the nations of the earth shall be blessed. For I know him, so that (*le-ma'an*) he will command his children and his household after him to keep the way of the Lord to do what is right (*tesdaquah*) and just (*mishpat*)." (Genesis 18:17–19)
>
> The question now is to determine the connection of the blessing of the nations of the earth to Abraham and his people keeping the way of the Lord to do what is right and just.[21]

---

[17] Novak, *Election of Israel*, p. 115.
[18] Ibid.
[19] Ibid., p.117.
[20] Ibid., p.120.
[21] Ibid., p.121.

The question has moved from the fact of election, to the practice of election. The question is not what the ontological relationship between God, Israel and the world is, but rather the 'keeping the way of the Lord', that is, an active *doing*, a practice (or practices), which is the means by which Israel – and Judaism – is understood as being a blessing by the God of all creation to that creation. At this point, we see in Novak's approach something of the nature of Jewish theology and philosophy as explicated by Wyschogrod – namely, that theological reflection begins with the existence of the Jewish people, the embodied people of God within the world. An embodied people relates to the world, and other 'peoples' bodily, that is, in actions and practices, rather than in any theoretical or conceptual way. Such practices are consequent to the fact that God *knows* Abraham. This is the basis of the particular relationship between God and Israel and is also the basis upon which it becomes possible that Abraham will keep the way of the Lord: 'Without God's knowing him and his being aware of it, Abraham would not be able to recognize the way of the Lord and keep it'. This knowledge is presented by Novak as being a 'relationship of direct and intimate personal contact',[22] and intimacy Novak relates to sexual contact; 'knowledge' is used to designate sexual intimacy as well as the knowledge God has of Abraham.

This theme of intimacy is one that is also followed by Wyschogrod, who addresses the notion of divine *eros* in the context of the election of Israel and the Jewish people. Wyschogrod notes that it is not Abraham who chooses God and therefore moves towards God, but God who chooses Abraham and moves towards him. He uses the language of love, speaking almost literally of God having fallen in love with Abraham. This love, then, cascades throughout the Jewish people: 'If God continues to love the people of Israel – and it is the faith of Israel that he does – it is because he sees the face of his beloved Abraham in each and every one of his children as a man sees the face of his beloved in the children of his union with his beloved'.[23] He then goes on to unpack the consequences of this in terms of helping us understand the nature of God's jealous anger: jealous, because God's beloved has betrayed God.

---

[22] Ibid.
[23] Wyschogrod, *The Body of Faith*, p. 64.

It is by means of an extensive working through of this theme of love for Abraham and Israel that Wyschogrod attempts to answer the question that inevitably arises whenever one stops to consider the logic of election – why is it that God elects some, and not others? Why does God elect Abraham and his offspring in particular?[24] He breaks down the oft-made distinction between *eros* and *agape*. The love of God for Israel is understood both as the desiring love between two people, as expressed in sexual intimacy, and the love of a parent for a child. He addresses the way in which this finds expression with regard to all the peoples of the world. He explores the reality of fatherhood, and what it means that God is father, rather than an 'impartial judge'. He suggests something that he recognizes we are usually very unwilling to recognize: that parents do not love all their children impartially, as children are all different, and they are all loved in their particularity. He goes so far as to suggest that some are inevitably loved more than others. It is the fact that love is particular and not general, that makes this love truly fatherly love, rather than that of the impartial judge. Without favouritism, God would not be father at all, because God would not love the particular. Therefore, he can ultimately state that: 'When we grasp that the election of Israel flows from the fatherhood that extends to all created in God's image, we find ourselves tied to all men in brotherhood, as Joseph, favoured by his human father, ultimately found himself tied to his brothers'.[25] Election, therefore, reveals the fatherly, and therefore particular, love of God, and is actually the guarantor of the fact that God is father of all the nations. For Wyschogrod, the election of Israel is actually the means by which the personal relationship between God and all peoples is realized. Similarly, to Novak, this is an intimate personal relationship that brings God, Israel and the world into a relationship.

Within this line of Jewish thinking, therefore, the Abrahamic covenant is foundational to the creation of the sociality of the people Israel. The act of election is essentially a gracious act, not determined by the prior action or merits of Abraham. It is also an act that construes the relationship between God, the people of God and the world. Equally, the covenant becomes a way of life, a practice that itself forms the identity of the people. Covenant does not function as a theory, or even offer a particular ontology of the people of God;

---

[24] Ibid., p. 58.
[25] Ibid., pp. 64–5.

rather, it brings into being a set of concrete relationships between God, the people of God and the world, which are upheld in practices.

The Sinai covenant: The centrality of the practice of law

The Abrahamic covenant serves as the fundamental basis upon which the idea of covenant recurs. Thus, towards the beginning of the Exodus narrative, we hear that:

> God also spoke to Moses and said to him: "I am the LORD. I appeared to Abraham, Isaac and Jacob as God Almighty, but my name 'The LORD' I did not make myself known to them. I also established my covenant with them, to give them the land of Canaan, the land in which they resided as aliens. I have also heard the groaning of the Israelites whom the Egyptians are holding as slaves, and I have remembered my covenant. Say therefore to the Israelites, 'I am the LORD, and I will free you from the burdens of the Egyptians and deliver you from slavery to them. I will redeem you with an outstretched arm and with mighty acts of judgement. I will take you as my people, and I will be your God. You shall know that I am the LORD your God, who has freed you from the burdens of the Egyptians. I will bring you into the land that I swore to give to Abraham, Isaac and Jacob; I will give it to you for a possession. (Exod. 6.2–8)

This passage precedes the account of the Exodus and establishes the relationship between the Abrahamic covenant and the Exodus. The account is clearly historical in nature; it recalls the call of Abraham and the covenant with him. We also find a parallel with the Noahide covenant in that God is referred to as remembering. This account is not suggestive of a new covenant being formed with the Israelites, but rather, is presenting the divine action of the Exodus as being as a result of the covenant with Abraham being remembered.

This passage is also of significance because it is the first time within the canon that Israel is addressed by God as a people. Using Rendtorff's typology of the covenant formula, we see that it appears here in its two-part form, 'I will take you for my people and will be God for you'. He comments that:

> What is unusual here is the verb . . . 'take', which occurs in no other formulation of the covenant formula. But it is certainly not by chance that

this word appears at this precise point, where God addresses Israel as people for the first time; for it is only in the immediately preceding narratives that Israel has in fact become a people (cf. Ex. 1.7, 9). Consequently it is also with good reason that in God's address to Abraham in Genesis 17 only Formula A about Yhwh's being God should be used; whereas now the two-part formula follows, with which Yhwh 'takes' the 'people' of Israel to be his people. We can also see why the second part of the formula, which talks about Israel's being a people, comes first; for it is this which embodies the new thing that is now announced.[26]

The notion of the covenant emerges here in its canonical position as having a new substance – that of God taking the whole people to Godself. The historical preface clearly states that this is the covenant with Abraham, but it has found a new manifestation at this point in the clear taking of Israel to be a people. It would be possible to express this as a re-formation of the covenant. It is clearly not new, and represents no break with the past, but finds a new expression. This happens because God remembers. God's memory is not simply a static occurrence; rather, the remembrance brings the covenant to a new expression within the context of the Exodus. This memory also serves as a future-orientated hope – because of the remembrance of the covenant by God, there is hope for the possession of the land in future. The covenant, then, is functioning as a calling to mind of the past, and the calling to mind of a future, which results in a renewed expression of the covenant within the context of slavery in Egypt.

The covenant at Sinai has a bilateral nature far more overt than either the Noahide or Abrahamic covenants. The liberation from Egypt, the promise of the land and the keeping of the law, all form an integrated whole in the Sinai covenant. The divine address to Moses at Sinai in Exodus 19 relates these themes clearly:

> Thus you shall say to the house of Jacob, and tell the Israelites: You have seen what I did to the Egyptians, and how I bore you on eagles' wings and brought you to myself. Now, therefore, if you obey my voice and keep my covenant, you shall be my treasured possession out of all the peoples. Indeed, the whole earth is mine, but you shall be for me a priestly kingdom and a holy nation. (Exod. 19.3–6)

---

[26] Rendtorff, *The Covenant Formula*, p. 16.

The action of God in bringing the people out of Egypt, as foretold to Abraham, becomes the central event by which the people will know the validity of the covenant and the law. It is in the covenant and the law that the identity of the people as a nation will be formed. The past history, the knowledge of the covenant and the reality of the law are the realities which form a particular social entity. We find also a parallel with the Noahide covenant in that 'the whole earth is mine'; the covenantal reality of God with the whole of creation is not forgotten; rather, within that creation, this particular people will be 'a priestly kingdom and a holy nation'.

The covenant is to be 'kept', and immediately after the command to keep the covenant follows what is known as the 'book of the covenant', the legal code. The question arises as to whether this is a different covenant from the covenant with Abraham, which we noted was essentially gracious in nature. The formulation of the covenant as it is presented later in Exodus, in Chapter 34, does not make this absolutely clear. Exodus 34.10 introduces what might be termed a re-affirmation of the covenant following Israel's failure to follow the law in building the golden calf. The text states that: 'He said: I hereby make a covenant', which suggests that this is something new. After a further explication of law, the chapter ends, 'The LORD said to Moses: Write these words; in accordance with these words I have made a covenant with you and with Israel' (Exod. 34:27), which equally sounds like a new covenant. The intervening part of the chapter, however, makes it abundantly clear that the covenant is rooted in the promise of the land which Israel will inherit (Exod. 34.11–12), which clearly recalls the covenant with Abraham. It is also of note that the whole of Chapter 34 is presented as God's re-making of a covenant in the light of the failure of the Israelites to keep the covenant. It would appear, then, that this is not a new covenant as such, but rather is a renewal of the covenant made first with Abraham now finding renewed expression as a bilateral, rather than a purely gracious, covenant. This view is supported when one examines Exodus 32, which relates specifically to the building of the golden calf. Here, Moses is recounted as appealing to God specifically to remember the covenant with Abraham:

> Remember Abraham, Isaac and Israel, your servants, how you swore to them by your own self, saying to them, 'I will multiply your descendents like the stars of heaven, and all this land that I have promised I will give to

your descendents, and they shall inherit it forever'. And the LORD changed his mind about the disaster that he planned to bring on his people. (Exod. 32.13–14)

In the light of this, the expression of the covenant with the Israelites in Chapter 34 is more clearly seen as a renewal rather than a specifically new covenant. The gracious nature of the covenant with Abraham is recalled, and is presented here as stronger than the peoples' breaking of the law in building the golden calf. The content of the law itself will concern us more fully in Chapter 7, which will demonstrate how that law serves as a set of covenantal practices for the remembrance of the covenant – practices which form and re-form the social identity of the people.

For Wyschogrod the law, *Torah*, is something given only to Israel and is that which upholds the covenant, and is by definition not a universal law, 'The Torah grows out of Israel's election and Hashem's saving acts performed for his people. The Torah is Israel's obligation under the covenant, in the absence of which there would be no obligation toward the Torah. In fact, only the history of Israel is part of the Torah'.[27] The observance of the law is a practice, not the acceptance of certain principles or theories. The law is both a result of, and an upholding of the covenant by which God relates in an intimate, personal, way to Israel, through which the fatherhood of God is made known and realized to all the peoples of the world.

At this point, it is worth noting a criticism that Novak makes on this very point, regarding this precise text from Wyschogrod. Novak suggests that Wyschogrod (and we should make clear here the very high regard in which Novak holds Wyschogrod[28]) fails adequately to maintain the dialectic between grace and merit.[29] Novak suggests that Wyschogrod has emphasized the gracious nature of election at the expense of the law, 'The Jewish people is at least as much for the sake of the Torah as the Torah is for the sake of the Jewish people. Here there must be something about the Torah, for which they live as much as it lives for them, that is part of the prehistorical created order'.[30] The prime problem that Novak sees in Wyschogrod's presentation is precisely

---

[27] Wyschogrod, *The Body of Faith*, p. 211.
[28] Novak, *Election of Israel*, p. 241ff.
[29] Ibid., p. 246.
[30] Ibid.

concerning the question of the 'nations' and their relationship to God and to Israel. He argues that the Torah not only upholds Israel itself, but does function as the revelation of a higher standard which, particularly in the prophetic literature, one sees functioning as the higher standard by which both Israel and the nations will be judged. He states that: 'The practical implication of assuming that the Torah is solely for the sake of affirming the election of Israel is to see no transcendent standard governing Israel's relationships with the nations of the world'.[31]

Novak elaborates at some length what exactly are the *tesdaquah* (right) and the *mishpat* (just) and how they function within Judaism in relationship to the rest of creation. It is in the midst of this discussion that we begin to see something of Novak's understanding of the vocation of Israel and Judaism. Locating it in the judgement of the cities of Sodom and Gomorrah, Novak suggests that the knowing of Abraham by God, the personal intimate relationship we have explored above, constitutes the way of the Lord in righteousness and justice (*tesdaquah* and *mishpat*). These Novak sees as separate, but related,[32] and they are the means by which one can see the connection between the blessing of all the nations of the earth in Abraham and the people keeping the way of the Lord in what is right and just. *Tesdaquah* (right) is, according to Novak, the 'transcendent aspect of God's relationship to creation because it is something totally gracious'.[33] This grace is the grace of creation and election as seen in the covenant with Abraham. It is a grace which pertains to creation and the covenant with Noah with all the peoples of the earth (indeed, all living flesh) and as such is transcendent. Novak uses this notion to offer an explanation for the contingency of existence – the idea that there is something rather than nothing because of the gracious creating will of God.

Alongside, as well as in contrast, Novak locates *mishpat*. This is what effects creation as an ordered and structured existence and underlies the continuity of its existence. Novak elucidates *mishpat* as the order, structure and continuity of existence, 'Minimally, that coherence is seen in the principle of contradiction, by which things maintain their distinct identities in relation to each other'.[34]

---

[31] Ibid., pp. 246–7.
[32] Ibid., p. 121.
[33] Ibid., p. 125.
[34] Ibid., p. 126.

He unpacks this notion at length, and it will not serve our purposes to follow his argument. However, it is in the fundamental relationship between Israel and the way of the Lord that Novak sees the relationship between Israel and the nations. Novak argues that although the *mishpat* was known before the call of Abraham (particularly in the commandments which follow the covenant with Noah), it is in God's knowing of Abraham, and Abraham's response to God's knowing of him, that the source of this ordering and structuring of creation is in turn known. Hence, it is in the election of Abraham and Israel that the *mishpat* of God is made present within creation. In a fascinating reading of Genesis 13.13, he suggests that we see the reason for the acceptance by Abraham of God's election. This is connected to the *tesdaquah* and *mishpat*. Abraham concerns himself that justice be done to the people of Sodom, despite their status as evil sinners. Abraham pleads on their behalf for justice; that the due law be followed. In doing so, he is imitating the right and justice of God, and concerning himself with the wellbeing of the peoples of the world, just as God does. 'Knowing that he is known by God, Abraham is now in a position to act truly as *imitator Dei*. His being known by God is not only something he enjoys and can celebrate; it is something he can act on.'[35] He acts on this, by involving himself in the case of Sodom when, by rights, he need not concern himself with it.

For Novak, election is an act of free grace which has a content. In being known by God, Abraham equally knows God, and is therefore with God within and for the world. Through the content of the law (the enactment of justice), Israel is the presence of God within the world. It is in this sense that Novak understands the correlation between election and God's relationship with the world. It is interesting to note the similarities between Wyschogrod's account of election and Novak's. For both, the election of Israel is not something which is for the sake of Israel alone, it is rather for the sake of the whole of creation. For Wyschogrod this takes the expression of making known God's fatherhood to the whole of creation, and for Novak it takes form in the expression of Israel as the presence of God's grace, right and justice within the created order. Equally, for both, the fact of this election, which is for the sake of the whole world, is upheld by a set of practices; the observance of the law. It is in the

---

[35] Ibid., pp. 135–6.

practice of ethics (rather than in a set of ethical *beliefs per se*) that the covenant is upheld.

For both Novak and Wyschogrod, there is no clear division between law as it is revealed in *Torah*, and the intrinsic law which Novak characterizes as *mishpat*, which provides the inner logic of the election of Abraham. This perspective allows us again to address the relationship between the covenant with Abraham, which is essentially gracious, and the covenant as enacted at Mount Sinai, which is legal and bilateral. Particularly in the context of the covenant with Noah, and revealed too in the logic of the election of Abraham, there is a divine order and *mishpat* that governs creation as a whole. The *Torah* exists as the particular calling of Israel to manifest the *mishpat* of God within the whole of creation, the whole of creation ultimately being called to embody that *mishpat*. There is then a dialectic between a gracious election and covenant and a bilateral and dependent covenant that rests upon the keeping of the law. There is, however, clearly only one covenant and one election, the covenant with Abraham finding a particular re-formation, renewal and embodiment in the giving and keeping of the law by the people for the sake of the nations. For Wyschogrod, the nature of the gracious covenant with Abraham takes the lead, the *Torah* being specifically for the maintenance of the sociality of the people; for Novak, the *Torah* has a more general relevance to the whole of creation through the category of *mishpat*. What is significant is the fact that for both, the law as a category both upholds Israel as an elect people and also determines the way in which Israel is a blessing for the whole of creation, rather than existing simply for its own sake.

New covenants?

In contrast to the accounts of the Sinai covenant in Exodus, we find that in Deuteronomy, the covenant is presented somewhat differently. Moses is recorded as saying:

> The LORD our God made a covenant with us at Horeb. Not with our ancestors did the LORD make this covenant, but with us, who are all of us here alive today. The LORD spoke with you face to face at the mountain, out of the fire. (At that time I was standing between the LORD and you to declare to you the

words of the LORD; for you were afraid because of the fire and did not go up the mountain.) And he said:

I am the LORD your God, who brought you out of the land of Egypt, out of the house of slavery; you shall have no other gods before me. (Deut. 5.2–6)

This covenant is presented as being a present one, here and now. It is for the living, who are present at that moment. As a re-reading of the Exodus account, the significance has shifted, from continuity with the covenant with Abraham, to discontinuity. The emphasis here is on *these* people, not *those* of the past. Is this, then, a new covenant, different from the covenant that has gone before?

It is of interest here to note DeVries' analysis of the significance of 'today', the 'day present'. He notes that where 'today' is used within the Hebrew Scriptures:

> Here the immediately past, the present, and the immediate future merge into one another. Certain memorable events have happened, are happening, and are about to happen to give "this day" its central significance. Always it is something that has decisive effect for the time to come: after "today" things will never be the same . . . every aspect of public life is touched upon. The epitome with *hayyom* has its *SitzimLeben* in Hebrew life and society as a whole.[36]

This suggests that in this context, 'today' is acting in a far wider sense than simply a means of designating time. DeVries categorizes 'today' in this passage as being an 'identifying characterization',[37] suggesting that it acts in such a way as to characterize something of the event itself. This suggests that all is held within this characterization – the significance of the covenant; the reality of the covenant with the gathered people there and then; all the attendant implications of the past covenant with Abraham; and the future orientation of the covenant in terms of the promise of the land. All are being stressed by the use of the term 'today'. Rendtorff concludes, as we have here, that this is not a new covenant, but rather that '. . . this emphatic concentration on the present situation cannot be viewed as a departure from the tradition according to which

---

[36] DeVries, *Yesterday, Today*, p. 275.
[37] Ibid., p. 174.
[38] Rendtorff, *The Covenant Formula*, p. 83.

God had already entered into a covenant relationship with the patriarchs, and then with the Exodus generation.'[38]

A wider examination of this text from Deuteronomy and its use within the canon equally suggests that it is the present reality of the covenant which is being stressed upon, not the creation of a new covenant. Deuteronomy is presented as that which has been forgotten; it is that which has become unknown and is once again to be remembered. It is the book 'found' in the temple during renovations, which has been forgotten. When it is read to Josiah, he responds saying:

> Go, inquire of the LORD for me, for the people, and for all Judah, concerning the words of this book that has been found; for great is the wrath of the LORD that is kindled against us, because our ancestors did not obey the words of this book, to do according to all that is written concerning us. (2 Kgs. 22. 13)

Leaving aside questions of historicity and the dating of texts, and concentrating on the canonical presentation of the finding of this book, we find it possible to understand why the covenant is presented in the way it is within Deuteronomy by understanding the impact on those hearing it once it has been discovered. 2 Kings relates that:

> Then the king directed that all the elders of Judah and Jerusalem should be gathered to him. The king went up to the house of the LORD, and with him went all the people of Judah, all the inhabitants of Jerusalem, the priests, the prophets, and all the people both small and great; he read in their hearing all the words of the book of the covenant that had been found in the house of the LORD. The king stood by the pillar and made a covenant before the LORD, to follow the LORD, keeping his commandments, his decrees, and his statutes, with all his heart and all his soul, to perform the words of this covenant that were written in this book. All the people joined in the covenant. (2 Kgs. 23.1–3)

The author could not go to greater length to stress the social nature of this event. It is all the people, great and small. In this context, the fact that the covenant is not simply an old covenant, but is a new covenant becomes extremely significant. The emphasis being taken by those hearing the Deuteronomic account is the fact that this covenant is a covenant for the here and now, a covenant with immediate relevance to the people hearing the text publicly read. However, a clear relationship between this covenant and the covenant with Abraham is implicit in the narrative. In the context of forgetting, the reminder of the ancient covenant could not be clearer. What is happening in this text is not overruling of an old covenant, but rather stressing of the present reality of that covenant. This clear stress on the present arises from the law having been forgotten, the religious life of Israel having fallen into disrepair, coupled with the finding of the book of the law. The renewal of the covenant in this context represents a response to the concrete situation of the life of the nation coupled with a return to scripture in the remembering of the book of the law.

A similar account of the reading of the law before the people occurs in Nehemiah, in the context of the post-exilic return to Jerusalem. Once again, all the people are gathered for a reading of the law (Nehemiah 8) which precedes the celebration of the festival of booths, a national confession and a covenant ceremony. In this context, however, explicit mention is again made of the covenant with Abraham. At the start of a lengthy reiteration of the history of the people, Ezra is recalled as saying:

> You are the LORD, the God who chose Abram and brought him out of Ur of the Chaldeans and gave him the name Abraham; and you found his heart faithful before you, and made with him a covenant to give to his descendents the land of the Canaanite, the Hittite, the Amorite, the Perizzite, the Jebusite, and the Girgashite; and you have fulfilled your promise, for you are righteous. (Neh. 9. 7–8)

Once again, the covenant accounts are being read in public, in a situation of recovery from national disaster in the return from exile, and in this context, the words of Deuteronomy again become a powerful reminder of the present reality of the covenant for those gathered at that time. Any 'new covenant' in the account from Deuteronomy, placed in the context of Ezra's account of the history of Israel, clearly becomes not a new covenant as such, but rather, once again, a renewal of the covenant. Hence, there is a signing of a 'firm agreement in writing' (Neh. 9.38) as a physical expression of a renewed commitment on the part of the people to the covenant.

In contrast to the accounts of the covenant we have examined to this point, the references to the covenant in the later prophetic books of the Hebrew scriptures, for the first time, introduce the distinct notion of a new covenant. The book of Jeremiah states:

> The days are surely coming, say the LORD, when I will make a new covenant with the house of Israel and the house of Judah. It will not be like the covenant that I made with their ancestors when I took them by the hand to bring them out of the land of Egypt – a covenant that they broke, though I was their husband, says the LORD. But this is the covenant that I will make with the house of Israel after those days, says the LORD: I will put my law within them, and I will write it on their hearts; and I will be their God, and they shall be my people. No longer shall they teach one another "Know the LORD," for they shall all know me, from the least of them to the greatest, says the LORD; for I will forgive their iniquity, and remember their sins no more". (Jer. 31. 31–34)

This is the only appearance of the distinct phrase 'new covenant' within the Hebrew Scriptures, but the idea is present elsewhere, notably in Ezekiel, which states:

> Yes, thus says the Lord GOD: I will deal with you as you have done, you who have despised the oath, breaking the covenant; yet I will remember my covenant with you in the days of your youth, and I will establish with you an everlasting covenant. (Ezek. 16. 59–60)

This notion of a new covenant seems to suggest a loss of continuity, as distinct from one continuing covenant. This, however, is not quite the case. Rendtorff points out that the fundamental issue at stake is not a change in God. God is constant and has not broken the covenant. This new covenant focuses not on a fundamental change in God, but on a fundamental change that God will bring about in the people such that the law will be so ingrained within them and fundamental to them that it will be kept anew. He suggests that 'The covenant, which always existed, is put into force afresh; and the same is true of Israel's relationship to God'.[39] So, once again, it would appear to be the notion of a renewal, or re-formation of the reality of the covenant, which is emerging within the text. The writings place themselves in the context of exile, a time of national crisis, where both the identity of the people and the hope of the

---

[39] Ibid., p. 73.

people are under threat. In this context, the idea of renewal of the covenant points interestingly both to the past, in terms of calling to mind the covenant which has been broken, and also to a future hope in which the covenant will be restored.

Equally interesting is the distinction used concerning 'those days' within Jeremiah 31. DeVries notes that the 'day future' is a day of action, divine or human. He states, 'What then is "that day" future? It is God's or man's new opportunity for decisive action . . . Like "that day" past, it marks a new turning point in man's journey through history in conversation with God'.[40] The future is not something passive, but is a time of action – it is a concrete, historical time. Lying at the heart of this vision of a new covenant lies the covenant formula: 'I will be their God, and they shall be my people'. The historical and social aspects of the life of the people of God are maintained in this vision of future hope.

Intrinsic to the notion of a new covenant is the eschatological category – reality will be transformed at some future point. This is an issue to which we will return in the next chapter, as the re-formation of the people of God takes place not only in the context of remembering of the past, but in the anticipation of the future. This is evidenced throughout the biblical history of the covenant. The covenant looks forward to the future creation of a people and the inheritance of the land in the covenant with Abraham. The re-affirmation and re-formation of the covenant at Sinai looks both backwards to the Abrahamic covenant and forward to the realization of the promise of the inheritance of the land. In the context of national religious decline, or national disaster as in the Exile, the covenant re-forms the people through the memory of what is past and the promise of future restoration. It is always a re-reception of the one covenant, but it is always historically situated in the present moment. The renewal of the covenant is not simply a reception of the tradition; a repetition of the covenant. Rather, it is always a repetition with variation. It is the one covenant, experienced anew and formed anew. In that formation, various signs and practices accompany the covenant, be it circumcision, the keeping of the law, the restoration of cultic practices of the temple, the reading and signing of the covenant or the vision of a renewed covenant that requires no

---

[40] DeVries, *Yesterday, Today*, p. 331.

outward activity because it is written 'within'. It is one covenant, reformed and renewed in the instigation of new practices which mediate that covenant anew into the present historical moment.

Renewing the canon: Scripture re-reading scripture

Thus far, we have kept to a reasonably canonical reading of scripture as we've addressed the way in which the renewal of the covenant is practised. However, a different approach regarding a somewhat different topic yields some similar conclusions such that it is worth taking note of them, albeit at not such length. The Jewish biblical scholar Bernard M. Levinson has undertaken some detailed and helpful exegetical work on the reception and renewal of legal traditions within the canon itself. A brief examination of his argument and conclusions in *Legal Revisions and Religious Renewal in Ancient Israel* will aid us considerably.

Levinson is setting out to address one of the issues that faces any community that is living with a canon which is essentially fixed. He is examining this problem from the interesting perspective of inside the canon of the Hebrew scriptures. Taking a more historical critical starting point, he recognizes that some texts within the canon emerge from much later periods than others, and that this can give us an insight from within scripture itself as to how a community lives with a fixed canon 'while adapting that unchangeable canon to realities of social, economic, political, and intellectual life never contemplated at the time of its composition'.[41] He examines various texts that demonstrate a divergent reading of the law. For example, he sees in the book of Ruth a late text, emerging within the post-exilic Persian period, but that is written as if in the period of the Judges prior to the monarchy very much earlier.[42] He suggests that Ruth offers, '. . . something of a counter-narrative that seeks to revise and liberalize the requirements of Deuteronomy regarding gleaning rules (Deut 24:19), the exclusion of Moabites from the community (Deut 23:4–5[English, 23:3–4]); and the laws of levirate marriage (Deut 25:5–10).[43] The unfolding

---

[41] Bernard M. Levinson, *Legal Revision and Religious Renewal in Ancient Israel* (New York: Cambridge University Press, 2008), p. 14.
[42] Levinson, *Legal Revision*, p. 32.
[43] Ibid.

of the story of Ruth is understood as an 'authorial strategy' that actually 'constructs new law and recasts old law'.[44]

Levinson offers a more detailed set of readings of the reception of the Decalogue, and the punishment of future generations for the sins of their forbears. Exodus 20. 5 states that 'You shall not bow down to them or worship them; for I the LORD your God am a jealous God, punishing children for the iniquity of parents, to the third and the fourth generation of those who reject me'. Levinson notes that this doctrine creates theological problems regarding the justice of God and provides practical problems for a community as it 'creates an overwhelming sense of the futility of historical action'. Therefore, 'For both theological and existential-historical reasons . . . we can expect biblical authors to struggle relentlessly against the injustice of the Decalogue's doctrine'.[45] He offers readings of texts from Ezekiel and Deuteronomy that offer some radical re-readings of the Decalogue. In Ezekiel, Levinson cites 18.1–4:

> The word of the LORD came to me: What do you mean by repeating this proverb concerning the land of Israel, 'The parents have eaten sour grapes, and the children's teeth are set on edge'? As I live, says the LORD God this proverb shall no more be used you in Israel. Know that all lives are mine; the life of the parent as well as the life of the child is mine: it is only the person who sins that shall die. (Ezek. 18. 1–4)

Levinson notes that the 'correspondence between the rejected proverb and the doctrine of transgenerational punishment can hardly be accidental'.[46] The proverb that is being rejected is serving as a 'strategic foil for the far more theologically problematic act of effectively annulling a divine law'.[47] He argues that what Ezekiel is in part doing, is taking over an earlier civil law formulation, and using this to govern offenses against the deity.[48]

In a similar way to in Ezekiel, Levinson sees a re-working of the law happening in Deuteronomy. He notes that Deuteronomy was probably added to in the exilic and post-exilic period, although it is pertaining to be an ancient text.[49] It too, is therefore reflecting the concerns of a later community in

---

[44] Ibid., p. 45.
[45] Ibid., p. 60.
[46] Ibid., p. 62.
[47] Ibid., p. 63.
[48] Ibid., p. 64.
[49] Ibid., p. 83.

receiving the earlier canon. He sees Deuteronomy 7 as being a re-reception of the transgenerational doctrine. Deuteronomy 7. 10 stresses that God 'repays in their own person those who reject him'. Levinson argues that this is functioning slightly differently to the Ezekiel case. He states that 'the new teaching is presented as consistent with the very doctrine that it rejects: as an authoritatively taught re-citation of the original theologoumenon'.[50]

Levinson's exegesis leads him to four key conclusions:

(1) exegesis provides a strategy for religious renewal; (2) renewal and innovation are almost always covert rather than explicit in ancient Israel; (3) in many cases exegesis involves not the passive explication but the radical subversion of prior authoritative texts; and (4) these phenomena are found in the literature of ancient Israel before the closure of the canon.[51]

These are challenging conclusions, but of great interest, particularly when placed against the concerns that we have noted throughout this work for the role that the re-reading of scripture has in reform and renewal. Here, we are seeing not an example of the later re-reading of canonized texts, but the canon itself engaging with the exegesis of itself. This re-engagement and re-appropriation of texts, even to the point of radical departures from earlier parts of the canon, are presented by Levinson as part of the essential process of religious renewal within Israel.

What has emerged in this chapter is a complex web of issues that emerge from our engagement with the Hebrew scriptures, and particularly, Jewish understandings of covenant and election. We have seen how covenant is renewed through repetition with variation, and that this always happens in a concrete historical moment that draws into itself the past and the future. This repetition with variation is mediated through different covenantal practices and signs. We have also seen how the exegesis of scripture functions within the canon itself as an engine of religious reform and renewal. This complements our reading of the covenant material where the historical narrative is always re-appropriated in the present. A complex structural pattern is beginning to emerge, which assists us in understanding how divinely initiated sociality is formed and reformed within historically contingent life in the world. Having

---

[50] Ibid., p. 75.
[51] Ibid., p. 21.

attended to such voices, we now need to examine how such understandings inform our reading of the New Testament and our understanding of the processes of identity formation within the Christian Church. In doing so, we will continue to examine the covenant and election, specifically the Christian understanding of the 'new' covenant in Christ.

6

The Covenantal Identity of the Church

The 'New' covenant in Christ

Supersessionist readings of the New Testament have served to underline the passing away of the 'old' covenant, and particularly the notion of the covenant under the law. Thus, passages such as 2 Corinthians chapter 3, which refers to the 'old' covenant as 'set aside' and Hebrews 8.13, which speaks of it as 'obsolete and growing old' have often taken central place, which in turn leads to the inherent supersessionism within the historic Reformed confessions. The New Testament scholar James Dunn has argued convincingly that the relationship between 'old' and 'new' is rather more complex – the 'new' being understood more in the terms of 'renewed' or 're-formed' in the way we understood the notion of 'new' in the 'new covenant' in Jeremiah.[1] Following this line of thinking will assist us in seeing how it is that the New Testament follows the trajectory of that we explored in the previous chapter in terms of the processes of reformation and renewal. It will assist us to follow Dunn's argument, augmenting it from other contributions to the discussion.

Dunn argues that for St. Paul, the law has come to function in the way it was understood in Jeremiah. Thus, he quotes 2 Cor. 3.3:

> . . . you are a letter of Christ, prepared by us, written not with ink but with the Spirit of the living God, not on tablets of stone but on human hearts. (Dunn's translation).[2]

---

[1] James Dunn, 'Judaism and Christianity: One Covenant or Two?', in Mark J. Cartledge and David Mills (eds), *Covenant Theology: Contemporary Approaches* (Carlisle: Paternoster Press, 2001), pp. 33–55.

[2] Cartledge, *Covenant Theology*, p. 41.

The idea is clear – that the law is still central to the covenant, but now is appropriated differently, extending the reading of Jeremiah we offered above[3]. Dunn also cites Phil. 3.3 and Rom. 2.28–9 in support of this view. He sees in these passages a clear resonance with the idea of the New Covenant as found in Jeremiah, and that this, '. . . confirms that he did not think of the new covenant as wholly new in its terms, only in its effectiveness.'[4] He follows this by a reading of Paul concerning the law, where, after discussion of texts such as Rom. 3.27, 13.8–10, Gal. 5.16–25 and Phil. 3.3, he concludes that traditional reformation period readings of Paul which attempt to set the new against the old in a law/gospel antithesis are mistaken, 'For *both* covenants the objective is the same: how may the law best be fulfilled, how best may the will of God be done? The issue is the law's implementation, not its abrogation.'[5] He is recognizing both a continuity and a discontinuity with regard to the law. The law is essential to both, but the means of fulfilling the law are understood quite differently, one rooted in observance of written law, the other in the terms of incorporation into Christ who is the fulfilment of the law. A not dissimilar position is taken by N. T. Wright, who sees Jesus as the 'climax of the covenant'. He suggests that, 'For Jews of his day (and many other days), Torah was at one and the same time the charter of the people of God and the full and final revelation of God himself. If, then, Jesus has taken on this double role, it is no surprise to find him taking on precisely the role of Torah in Paul's understanding of the plan of the one God.'[6] Christ, then, becomes the fulfilment of the law, and incorporation into the body of Christ becomes the way the law is then fulfilled within the community of the church. This raises once again questions of how Jews and Christians understand the law and the differences between themselves.

David Novak discusses the difference between Jewish and Christian understandings of the law, and notes that both relate to the law, but to differing extents, and the Christians have taken to themselves part of the content of the Torah, but not other parts:

> The part of the Torah not appropriated by Christianity has consisted of those commandments that are addressed to the people of Israel in their very

---

[3]   See above, p. 146.
[4]   Cartledge, *Covenant Theology*, p. 41.
[5]   Ibid., pp. 43–4.
[6]   N. T. Wright, *The Climax of the Covenant: Christ and the Law in Pauline Theology* (Edinburgh: T&T Clark, 1991), p. 266.

separateness, such as the purity laws pertaining to diet, dress, and marital relations. It also includes those practices like Passover that celebrate pre-messianic events in the life of the people of Israel. The church has replaced these commandments with the sacraments that celebrate the life, death and resurrection of Jesus.[7]

This is an interesting perspective to place alongside that of Dunn and Wright. Their argument concerns specifically the question of whether the 'new' covenant in Christ is indeed 'new' in a literal sense, or rather is better understood in the way 'new' functions throughout the history of the covenant. We saw in the last chapter that for Novak, and Jewish thinking more generally, one of the key elements of the covenant and its law concerns the defining and practising of the relationship between Israel and the nations.[8] It follows that the church, in being called to a different relationship with the nations, will hold to different cultic practices than Judaism.[9]

Following an examination of the Sinai covenant, Dunn turns to what is essentially a prior question, which is the relationship of the church to the foundational covenant with Abraham. Dunn notes, as we have in the preceding chapter, the three distinct parts of the covenant promises with Abraham: the promise of seed, the promise of land, and the promise of blessing to the nations.[10] He notes that the first two have been more prominent than the third within Judaism. He then proceeds to explicate the Pauline understanding of the Abrahamic covenant, which he portrays as being more closely related to the third aspect, that of the covenant being a blessing to the nations. This is clearly bound up with Paul's understanding of himself as the apostle to the Gentiles (Acts 26.17–18; 9.15; 22.21), something Paul highlights as being specifically related to the Abrahamic promise of blessing to the nations in Gal. 3.8, where he draws to mind the promise of Gen. 12.3 and 18.18, 'Scripture, foreseeing that God would justify the Gentiles from faith, preached the gospel beforehand to Abraham, "In you shall all the nations be blessed."' (Dunn's translation)[11] Thus, he concludes his essay with the reflection that it is not so much that there are two covenants, but rather that the 'new' covenant is 'the means by

---

[7] Frymer-Kensky et al., *Christianity in Jewish Terms*, p. 120.
[8] See above, p. 147.
[9] This will be discussed further in Chapter 7.
[10] Cartledge, *Covenant Theology*, pp. 44–5.
[11] Ibid., p. 52.

which Gentiles were drawn into Israel (together with Jews) in fulfilment of Israel's historic mission to the nations'.[12] This argument is essentially that the foundational covenant with Abraham is one covenant upon which both Judaism and Christianity rest. The church, therefore, is not a covenant community which is of a different covenant from Israel; rather, in sharing the commonality of the Abrahamic covenant, its dispensation is different precisely in the way the *God-People of God–World* triangle is constructed. The church is the fulfilment of the promised blessing to the nations through Abraham, and therefore its identity in relationship to the world is different to the identity of Judaism, which perceives its blessing to the world to remain, at least at the present, manifest through a call to separateness.

If we accept Dunn's reading of the question of the new covenant, then given the prior understanding of covenant we have outlined in the preceding chapter with which it correlates, the church can, at its very inception, be understood as a re-formation. As the renewal of the covenant at Sinai was a re-formation of covenant in a newly expressed bilateral form of the Abrahamic covenant with active responsibility from both parties, equally, the founding of the apostolic church can be understood as a similar re-formation of covenantal social identity. The two are not exact parallels, for the obvious reason that the founding of what became a new social entity is a disruption and transformation far beyond the Sinai covenant.

Irving Greenberg helpfully denotes some of the key differences between what we might term the vocations of Israel and the church regarding the world. He suggests that Israel's being a blessing to the world finds expression in three key ideas – that Israel must be a teacher, a model and a co-worker. Israel must be a teacher because each generation must, 'pass on its values to others, starting with its own children'.[13] The idea here is that Israel must maintain its own self-identity if it is to fulfil any kind of vocation at all. Through passing on its values to future generations, it becomes possible for Judaism to continue to exist within the world. Its existence in the world is then that which serves as a model: 'Israel must be a community within which covenantal values are maximally lived, at least to the extent realizable now in an imperfect world. By so doing, Israel can create a liberated zone – a land within which equality

---

[12] Ibid., p. 54.
[13] Frymer-Kensky et al., *Christianity in Jewish Terms*, p. 148.

is respected. In serving as a model, Israel becomes "a light to the nations".[14] Through the maintenance of its separateness held within its role as teacher, Israel then embodies that which is a model to the whole of creation as the way of God for the world. The last element of Greenberg's notion is that Israel must be a, *'co-worker* for redemption. One people cannot lift up the whole globe by itself; Israel must work with others'.[15] In introducing the idea of redemption, and Israel working for redemption, Greenberg is drawing on a notion he develops of 'God's Universal and Particular Covenants'.[16] This notion is that God stands in covenant relationship with the whole world (the idea of the Noahide covenant) but works within creation in a series of particular covenants, of which Judaism and Christianity are two.

David Novak suggests a similar understanding to Greenberg, but in somewhat different terms, he speaks of a parallelism between Christianity and Judaism, both of which have emerged from the same sources. Therefore, he sees that, 'our theological logic in talking with one another should be that of analogy rather than that of either causal inference or teleology'.[17] This parallelism finds its expression ultimately in the eschatological perspective 'That opens the ground for God to make the truly final demonstration of an end that will include us all, making our presently parallel lines converge in eternity'.[18]

For both Greenberg and Novak, the relationship between Israel and the church is one which finds expression in the eschatological perspective, in God's future. For Greenberg, this offers an understanding (from within a Jewish perspective) concerning the relative vocation of the church. The vocation of the church is essentially to bring the Gentiles into relationship with God: 'Bringing considerably more people into covenantal relationships with God would be an important fulfilment (albeit not a complete one) of the promise that Abraham's people would be a blessing for the families of the earth'.[19] He is clear, though, that this is not a replacement for Israel, but an 'offshoot' from it. What he has noted (although it is not central to his own argument, but is significant for ours) is that the social model of the church has to be essentially different from

[14] Ibid.
[15] Ibid.
[16] Ibid., pp. 141–4.
[17] Braaten, *Jews and Christians*, p. 112.
[18] Ibid., p. 113.
[19] Frymer-Kensky et al., *Christianity in Jewish Terms*, p. 150.

that of Israel. Israel must maintain its self-identity of separateness by virtue of its call to be a model. In contrast, the church is not counter-cultural in the sense of being separate; rather, it is a covenantal expression of the will of God for the world while being part of what, for Israel, would be an alien society.

This fundamental difference in the vocation of the church and Israel begins to explain the differing ways in which law and ethics exist within both communities. Hauerwas notes that there is a fundamental difference in the way in which Judaism and Christianity relate to the question of family life and the importance of having children. It is a commandment within Judaism to reproduce, which is, of course, necessary for the continuation of an ethnic group. This is not the case in Christianity (Jesus was single and childless), 'What Jesus started did not continue because he had children but because his witness attracted strangers. Christians are not obligated to have children so that the tradition might continue; rather we believe that God through the cross and resurrection of Jesus and the sending of the Holy Spirit has made us a people who live through witness'.[20]

This is significant for two reasons. First, it suggests that it is the covenantal vocation of the church to participate in God's mission to the whole of creation, which re-casts the role the law plays within the life of the church. Law is not serving the function of creating a sociality which exists to serve as a 'model', as Greenberg defines Israel, but rather as a 'way' that calls all to follow it. This is perhaps illustrated well by the difference between the practices of circumcision and baptism. We have noted that circumcision functions precisely as a sign of separateness, it marks a boundary of exclusion.[21] Baptism, however, is primarily not a mark of separateness from the world, but one of inclusion in the church. Circumcision, therefore, remains a practice within Judaism and is performed automatically. If one is born Jewish, one will be circumcised. Baptism, in comparison, is a gracious practice concerning inclusion, functioning as a sign of the missionary vocation of the church within the world.

The second important insight Hauerwas points towards is the centrality of Jesus to the church's understanding of the law. Fundamentally, the way of Jesus is at the heart of Christian ethics. Hauerwas states the matter this way:

[20] Ibid., p. 138.
[21] See above, p. 150.

> The difference between Christians and Jews is not located in the law but in our different understandings of sanctification. Jesus has become for us the new law, making it possible for us to be his disciples. Discipleship is not a denial of the role of the law but rather, for Christians, names the way the law serves to make us manifestations of God's gracious election.[22]

There is a link here, being suggested (if not clearly stated) between Jesus, the law and the vocation of the church as a missionary community rather than a community of separateness (which follows the logic of Dunn and Wright's arguments noted above). The law functions within Judaism to mark out (sanctify) a community to be a vicarious exemplifer. Within the life of the church, the law cannot function in this way, as the vocation of the church is a missionary one. Therefore, ethics becomes the 'way of Christ', discipleship which furthers the existence of the church through conversion, not the continuity of the family.

Another way of putting this is to suggest that the focus of the collective memory which upholds the covenant has shifted. The focus within the church is not the Abrahamic covenant, or the law given at Sinai (although these continue to be an important part of that which is to be continually called to mind). Rather it is Jesus Christ. For the church, it is the remembrance of Christ which stands at the heart of the orientation to the past, and as Jesus is a Jew, and is the fulfilment of the Abrahamic covenant, the content of the Jewish scriptures become a central part of our collective memory too. Through this orientation, the church is also forced to keep its orientation to the world, as the universal call of Christ is addressed to the whole of creation and it is in the midst of the world, and history, that Christ becomes incarnate. Equally, the perspective of the future is one which finds its focus on Christ in the relationship of Christ and the kingdom of God.

Throughout this work, as a result of its concern to reclaim the Old Testament for the purposes of ecclesiology and our selection of the notion of the covenant from which to explore the process, orientations and practises of the reform and renewal of the church's identity, we have deliberately concentrated on understandings of the people of God. However, in the context of the new covenant and its orientation towards Christ, it is

---

[22] Frymer-Kensky et al., *Christianity in Jewish Terms*, p. 137.

necessary to call to mind one of the other major New Testament images of the church, that of the church as the body of Christ. Equally, our choice of material and dialogue partners has resulted in little discussion of the Trinitarian dimension of the formation and re-formation of the identity of the church. We must now examine the centrality of Christ for the identity of the church in an attempt to understand the issues around the image of the body of Christ and what that reveals about the nature of the reform and renewal of the church.

Jesus and the extensive ecclesial movement

Rowan Williams offers a series of important insights into the relationship between Jesus and the formation of the identity of the church as a covenant community:

> For both Jew and Gentile, the setting of the boundaries of a community was divine work: for the Jew because Israel was a people gathered and defined by the summons of God in the covenant tradition; for the Gentile because gods provided the sanctions of law and custom in the Greek city, and a divine monarch sanctioned the unity and cohesion of the *imperium Romanum*. Jesus stands as a potential rival to both; though his own unswerving relatedness, obedience, answerability, to the God of Israel held back most Christians from wholly disowning the Jewish past. But there should be no doubt that, as the defining focus of a new people, a new citizenship, a new kingdom, Jesus functions as a divine figure. And perhaps at a more lastingly significant level – he functions not simply as a god but as *the God of Jewish scripture* in two respects: he creates a people by *covenant* (as in the ancient and widespread tradition of the Last Supper), and by a summons that makes something radically *new*.[23]

The divine activity in initiating and renewing covenant community, which begins with Noah, continues within the life of Jesus Christ. Following Williams' understanding of the role of Christ as the divine activity within creation, we see both the continuity with the activity of the God of covenant,

---

[23] Rowan Williams, *On Christian Theology* (Oxford: Blackwell, 2000), p. 231.

as we have elucidated it within the Hebrew scriptures, and the radical discontinuity of creating something new. The specific function of the Lord's Supper merits more discussion, but its centrality as a covenant forming and renewing practice is central to understanding the place of Jesus Christ within the covenantal orientations of the church to the past, to the future and to the world.

That it is the historical Jesus Christ who initiates the calling of this covenant community into existence forces the church to orientate itself to the past, not simply to the foundational covenant in the call of Abraham, but to Jesus himself as initiator of this new covenantal community. In creating a community that stands as a 'potential rival' to existing understandings of the authority structures which create communities, the church is also forced to orientate itself to the world in a different fashion.

It is possible to understand the life, ministry, death and resurrection of Jesus as a specifically ecclesial movement. The centrality of the call of the first disciples as the opening up of the public ministry of Jesus in the Gospel accounts (Matt. 4.18–22, Mark 1.16–20, Luke 5.1–11, John 1.35–51) clearly delineates the centrality of the calling into existence of a sociality, a new community. These passages recall the account of the call of Abraham. For no apparent reason, Jesus calls these people to leave what they are doing, follow him and become something new. The logic of divine initiation, as revealed in the Abraham stories, is followed once again here. Within history, God calls individuals as a new sociality. This time, however, that sociality is not bound to the offspring of those called; rather, these people are called to '. . . fish for people'. The promise to Abraham that he would be a blessing to the nations finds its parallel in the same command. The appointment of the apostles can be understood as a continuation of the divine desire for a people who will participate in the divine mission to the world. In Mark's gospel, the specific account of the appointment of the twelve apostles (paralleled in Matt. 10.1–4 and Lk. 6.12–16) reads as follows:

> He went up the mountain and called to him those whom he wanted, and they came to him. And he appointed twelve, whom he also named apostles, to be with him, and to be sent out to proclaim the message, and to have authority to cast out demons. (Mk. 5.13–15)

Morna Hooker comments that in this, the disciples are 'to share his ministry'.[24] Jesus' ministry is one which, from the outset, is exercised in the gathering of people to share in that ministry. In contrast to John the Baptist, who is a prophetic figure, this is not purely a gathering around Jesus, but the disciples are empowered by him and sent out by him. This initial gathering must be understood as the beginning of an outward ecclesial movement. The initial concern is that the disciples be with Jesus; secondarily, that they are to be sent out. The notion of 'being with' takes on a far greater significance than simply being disciples as a prophet or teacher might form a group around them. They are to be with Jesus for the very purpose of being sent out: they are to participate in God's very ministry to historical life in the world.

Hooker notes that within Mark's gospel, the essentially social nature of Christianity is manifest: the disciples are called in pairs (Mk. 1.16–20), appointed as a group of 12 (Mk. 3.13–19) and sent out again in pairs (Mk. 6.7–13).[25] Equally, she notes the essential continuity of the nature of Israel as community. She states:

> The Exodus imagery reminds us that a new Exodus is taking place: God's people are being fed in the wilderness (6.32–44; 8.1–10); the waters of the sea are in his control (4.35–41; 6.45–52); a new covenant is being made (14.34). Jesus is the shepherd of a flock, and like a shepherd he will lead his flock into Galilee after the resurrection (14.27f; 16.7). The flock is scattered and reformed, but something even more drastic happens to the temple, and the vineyard and the fig tree. Yet these images imply the continuity between the old community and the new: Israel is recreated, not destroyed. And Mark's community would see itself as part of that new community, as the legitimate tenants of the vineyard. They, and not his natural kin, were the members of Jesus' new family (3.31–35).[26]

The invoking of the corporate memory of Israel within Mark roots this new ecclesial movement within the life of Israel, and serves to show the way the contours of its sociality parallel those of Israel itself. Mark is far from presenting us with a picture of an idealized community of disciples. The disciples are

---

[24] Morna D. Hooker, 'Mark's Vision for the Church', in Markus Bockmuehl and Michael B. Thompson (eds), *A Vision for the Church: Studies in Early Christian Ecclesiology* (Edinburgh: T&T Clark, 1997), p. 38.

[25] Bockmuehl and Thompson, *A Vision*, p. 38.

[26] Ibid., p. 39.

portrayed as frail, faltering historical beings. They argue among themselves about who is the greatest (Mk. 9.33–37), they attempt to stop children reaching Jesus (Mk. 10.13–16), James and John seek places of precedence within the group (Mk. 10.35–45) and they lack faith in a storm (Mk. 4.35–41). The divine initiative in drawing together a sociality to be with Jesus and share his ministry must never be understood to result in a perfected or idealized sociality. Despite this, it is the disciples who share with Jesus in his ministry. The disciples play an integral role in the feeding of the multitude (Mk. 14.13–21, Mk. 6.31–42, 8:1–10, Lk. 9.10–17, Jn. 6.1–13) and they are empowered and sent out to proclaim in the region (Mt. 10.5–15, Mk. 6.8–11, Lk. 9.2–5). Both of these episodes are symbols of Jesus extending his ministry out into the world through the disciples and demonstrate an outward dynamic at work in the ministry of Jesus. What begins with a call to be with Jesus develops into a sending out in the name of and with the power of Jesus.

The frailty of the disciples leads to a disintegration of what we have identified as the ecclesial movement within Jesus' ministry in the events of the passion. The denial of Peter, who at this juncture is functioning as a representative disciple (Mt. 26.69–75, Mk. 14.66–72, Lk. 22.55–62, Jn. 18.25–27), is the fracturing of the ecclesial community. This fracturing, however, becomes a renewal, or re-formation, of the ecclesial movement in the resurrection. Leaving aside the issue of the shorter end of Mark's gospel, the resurrection accounts stress the importance of the disciples being told of the event and of the disciples themselves being gathered as they witness resurrection (Mt. 28.1–10; Mk. 16.1–8, 14; Lk. 24.36–43; Jn. 20.19–23). Further to this, the account of the appearance on the road to Emmaus (Lk. 24.13–35 with a similar brief account in the longer ending of Mk. at 16.12–13) as two (not of the 12 disciples in this case) were leaving Jerusalem and returning home, forces them to return back to Jerusalem to the assembled company there. There is a quite literal re-grouping of the disciples as a result of this resurrection appearance. The account in John's gospel of the appearance in Galilee (Jn. 21.1–19) can be read in a similar fashion. Peter is recounted as saying 'I am going fishing' (Jn. 21.3), a return to a way of life representative of the time before the call to become a disciple and 'leave your nets'. Coupled with the denial of Christ, this is the unmaking of the new sociality initiated in the call of the disciples. The 're-making' of Peter in Jesus asking him three times 'Do you love me?' and the commandments to 'Feed my lambs', 'Tend my sheep', 'Feed my sheep' and 'Follow me' represent Jesus once again empowering Peter (and the disciples as a whole) in the task of upholding a new community, which continues Jesus' concern for the relationship between himself, the disciples as a whole and the world expressed in his prayer for the disciples in Jn. 17.1–26. Equally, the repetition of the question is indicative of an ongoing process, the confession of Jesus being not simply one which is made once, but remade again and again. The resurrection accounts concern not only the resurrection of Jesus himself, but the resurrection of the ecclesial movement begun in call, fractured in the passion and renewed in resurrection.

The resurrection of the ecclesial movement is not simply the re-gathering and internal strengthening of a particular sociality, it also contains the commissioning of that sociality in an outward movement. The accounts of the instructions to the disciples to 'Go, therefore and make disciples of all nations . . .' (Mt. 28.19, paralleled in Mk. 16.15 and Acts 1:8) is a 'Great Commission' that continues the ecclesial movement, but with its radical re-formation and extension in an outwards, worldly movement. It is what one might term an 'extensive ecclesial movement'. It begins with a call to be with Jesus, contains an outwards movement to the surrounding area within the confines of Israel itself, and at the end of the ministry of Jesus, the instruction to extend the movement throughout the whole world.

The orientation to the world is also a key dimension of the work of the Spirit. The baptismal formula of Mt. 28.19 links the universal mission of the church to the work of the Spirit and the relationship is even clearer in Acts 1:8. The ecclesial movement continues the activity of divine initiation through the gift of the Spirit in the events of Pentecost accounted in Acts 2. Commenting on this, Michael Welker states:

> The Pentecost event is a "miracle of Languages *and* of hearing". It is the event of the essentially worldwide proclamation of "God's deeds of power," which is made possible by an unforeseeable universal understanding. The disintegration and dispersion of human beings, the Babylonian confusion of languages (Genesis 11), and the connected rupture of the world are removed. But in this removal cultural, national, and linguistic differences are not set aside, but retained. The entire, differentiated representative world of a given time in its differentiation not only is addressed, but also understands the

proclamation of God's action of deliverance carried out on human beings. At great length and with the help of a quotation from the Joel promise of the universal pouring out of the Spirit, the account of the Pentecost event emphasizes that the representative world in its differentiation into many people, into Jews and Gentiles, into men and women, young and old, female and male slaves, is an active witness of this event.[27]

The activity of the Spirit in the proclamation and the hearing confirms that the sociality of the new (or renewed) covenant which centres on Christ is of a radically different orientation to the world than the Sinai covenant. The Christian church, orientated to Christ and empowered by the Spirit, is a divine sociality that is flung open to the whole of creation. Within Christ's church, the promise to be a blessing to the nations does not happen through an orientation to the world of separation, acting vicariously as we have understood the vocation of Israel, but an orientation of inclusion of the world in all its differentiation of peoples, nations and groups. The orientation to the world, and the re-formation that is intrinsically necessary when such an orientation is maintained, remains constant with the covenantal worldly orientation of Israel and Judaism. The content of that orientation, however, is radically inverted.

Throughout the book of Acts, we see the continued extension of the ecclesial movement and its re-formed orientation to the world. Peter goes to Simon the tanner, an unclean man and then moves out to Cornelius, a Gentile (although God-fearing), and through this event, the Holy Spirit is poured out on the Gentiles, Peter understanding his vision (Acts 10.9–16) to concern the 'cleanliness' of the Gentiles. The events of the Jerusalem Council (Acts 15) reflect the internal struggle within the community to recognize the radical re-orientation of the new ecclesial movement to the world, as opposed to a separation from the world. Acts 15, however, must also serve to remind us of the continued fragility of the community. There is no immediate certainty here, as one might expect in a community grounded in an idealized and eternalized infallible church. Rather, the struggle for discernment, particularly when coupled with the Pauline epistles and their explicit accounts of the sinful nature of early Christian communities, remind us that it is a historically

---

[27] Welker, *Spirit of God*, p. 230.

contingent and fragile community, capable of sin, that is divinely initiated and empowered to go out into the world.

This necessarily brief overview of one particular way of understanding the ministry of Christ reveals a number of significant things. As with the covenant with Abraham, the calling of the disciples can be understood as the divine initiative that calls into existence a covenant community. Jesus, understood as the incarnation of the God of Israel and Jewish scripture, calls into being a covenant community that follows similar dynamics to the forming of the covenant with Israel. This new covenant, as with the covenant with Israel, is fragile precisely because it is a concrete historical covenant, with its foundations in divine activity within history. As Israel is unfaithful and the covenant is, after times of national disaster, renewed, so too the disciples are unfaithful and called into a renewed sociality through the resurrection and empowered to new action in the work of the Spirit at Pentecost. This new covenant continues to be formed through an orientation to the past, that is, to the divine initiative revealed in the history and scriptures of Israel, and also to the past in the life and ministry of Christ, in which the church is called to share. The new covenant, through centring itself on the divine historical activity of Christ, finds its orientation to the world in an ecclesial movement with a perpetually outward direction. All the peoples of the world are called into a covenant relationship with Christ as the church moves out to the world. The new covenant finds itself orientated towards the future activity of the same living God that initiated its call into existence, as the church actively seeks and awaits the future redemptive action of the God who acts within history.

Such a reading of the New Testament as we are offering here stands in contrast to the idealized ontologies of the church examined in Chapter Two. There, we noted that it is the fact that the church is a mixed community which logically requires the interpolation of ecclesial dualisms of the visible and invisible. To understand the church solely as historical and rooted within historical contingency allows for change, development and re-formation, but also for sin. This is perhaps the reason why dualistic understandings of the church have often been considered so necessary. However, if we are to take the account of scripture seriously as it speaks of the sociality Jesus calls into existence, we are required to take seriously the reality that it was a divine initiative to call the church into existence within a historically contingent order, and as a church that itself is subject to that historical contingency. To state otherwise is actually to fundamentally question both the reality of the living God, the incarnation and the work of the Spirit. Jesus called into existence and empowered a group of human beings, subject to human frailty, to participate in his ministry to the world. To state that this visible historical reality is not the true church, is to suggest that the historically contingent reality Jesus initiated is neither the true thing in itself nor the true will of God. The true church, properly understood, is the reality called into being by Christ. It is a reality rooted in historical divine activity, empowered by the Spirit in its orientation and outwards ecclesial movement to the world and orientated to the future of the same divine activity as called it into being. By being historical, it is also subject to sin and error; hence, the church finds itself called to corporate confession. This happens in both an ongoing sense and at times very specifically, as in the case of confessing its error regarding the supersessionist understandings of Israel examined in Chapter Four. The disciples are both those who lacked faith during a storm, and are also those who did proclaim the gospel far away and beyond the confines of the nation Israel. To state that this church is not the real church is an affront to the divine initiation in Christ which called this church into being. To put it plainly, to say that the concrete historic church is not the real church is to deny that God has done as God has done. It is to deny that Jesus did initiate the church. It is to deny that the Spirit upholds and empowers the church in its historical human differentiation. It is to say that God was mistaken. It is to place human logical preferences in place of living divine historical activity. It also, ultimately, cannot allow for a proper understanding of the reform and renewal of the church which, as we have seen, is fundamental to the biblical revelation of what it is to be the covenant people of God.

Orientations to the future

The incompleteness of the church we noted as implicit within the self-understanding of the identity of the United Reformed church in its *Basis of Union*; the perpetual call to reformation and the processes involved in this – not least the confession of sin – as illustrated through the re-formation of confessional positions regarding Israel, reveals the fundamental centrality of the orientation to the future. Eschatology frames, as it were, the historical contingency of which we have been speaking, and the eschatological orientation of the church is intrinsic to the process of identity formation of the church. History is not contingent with reference to eternity *per se*; rather, it is contingent with reference to the future in-breaking of God, both within history and at the point where history as presently experienced is ended by the activity of God in its fulfilment.

It is interesting to note, as Craig C. Hill does in conclusion to his survey of the various eschatological strands of thinking within the Bible, that the particular vision of eschatology that a church has, has a bearing on the concrete shape and life of that church. He notes:

> Churches with a future eschatological orientation tend to be more stable and institutionalised. They often have considerable structure and locate authority in recognized offices and traditions. Such things are more fluid in a church with a strongly realized eschatology. Authority is more charismatic, and structure tends to be flatter, with fewer levels and intermediaries.[28]

He goes on to note that churches with a future eschatological orientation tend to centre their thinking more on the cross, rather than the resurrection (and vice versa). He notes that churches emphasizing the future orientation have various strengths in enabling people to deal with reality as it is: 'Life can be difficult, and being a Christian does not necessarily make it any easier . . . cross bearing is not fun'.[29] He also notes that this kind of eschatology promotes tolerance as it recognizes the as-yet incomplete nature of our understanding. Equally, it can promote passivity in the face of injustice, 'At worst, this is slave religion'.[30] He also notes some of the impact that a realized eschatological position has on church life: 'Positively, it can be wonderfully egalitarian and liberating'.[31] It can also empower belief that God gives us the power now to transform life in the present. He suggests that it has its negative sides too, '. . . realised eschatology easily leads to an overestimation of the innocence of insiders and the culpability of outsiders. It does not promote tolerance and empathy and may well encourage sectarianism'.[32]

---

[28] Hill, *In God's Time*, p. 189.
[29] Ibid., p. 193.
[30] Ibid.
[31] Ibid.
[32] Ibid.

The way in which eschatological visions impact the social realities of the present can also be seen in a slightly more general and social fashion than Hill's careful delineation of the impact of eschatology on church order and orientation. Paul Fiddes, in his work on eschatology, notes regarding Utopian ideas that they, 'reshape our desires, directing them to life-enhancing goals, and so Krishan Kumar is right to propose that the most interesting Utopias are not simply blueprints and designs of a good society; they enable us to *feel* what it is like to live in such a 'place' and create 'the texture of life there'.[33]

Eschatological perspectives play their part in the formation of social identities. A vision of the future offers a means to understand the present. In the terms in which we have been working, the eschatological vision of the future, coupled with the self-identity of the church in its open relationship with the world, offer a means of understanding one of the processes by which re-formation and renewal of social identity takes place. The sociologist of religion, Danièle Hervieu-Léger, notes that utopias equally function in terms of the re-formation of understandings of the past. She suggests that, 'The utopia dreamt of or put into effect subverts the imaginative projection of continuity within a given society by extending and enriching it; in this sense, it affords an opportunity to come to terms with what is new in the present. The utopian dynamic to a certain extent accords with the reality of the active dimension in tradition. . .'[34] This suggests that eschatological perspectives are significant in the process of re-formation itself, as the vision of the future provides a means by which tradition is transformed in the context of the present moment.

Eschatology, functioning as it has been suggested that utopias function, provides one of the means by which, through a re-engagement with scripture, particularly Romans, the new reality of the relationship between Israel and the church has come to be. Equally, eschatology functions as one of the means by which the *God-People of God–World* triangle finds its expression: future hope for the redemption of creation forms within Judaism, and the life of the church, concrete activities which go to form the present identity of the church.

Jürgen Moltmann, possibly more than any other theologian of recent times, has addressed the theme of eschatology as being central to, and even the

---

[33] Paul Fiddes, *The Promised End: Eschatology in Theology and Literature* (Oxford: Blackwell, 2000), p. 223.
[34] Danièle Hervieu-Léger, *Religion as a Chain of Memory* (Cambridge: Polity Press, 2000), p. 145.

starting point for, Christian theology. In his *Theology of Hope*[35] of 1964, he lays out the centrality of the theme of eschatology for the Christian faith in a fashion that has had enormous impact on subsequent theological thinking.[36] We shall, however, limit our discussion of Moltmann's thinking as it relates to our theme, to his systematic outworking of eschatology in *The Coming of Christ*, of 1995.[37] He states that

> ... there is no affirmative community between the church and Israel without the messianic hope for the kingdom. And that then means that there is no adequate Christian eschatology without millenarianism. Eschatology is more than millenarianism, but millenarianism is its historical relevance. It is only the millenarian hope in Christian eschatology which unfolds an earthly and historical future for the church and Israel. Millenarianism is the special, this worldly side of eschatology, the side turned towards experienced history; eschatology is the general side of history, the side turned towards what is beyond history. Millenarianism looks towards future history, the history of the end; eschatology looks towards the future of history, the end of history. Consequently the two sides of eschatology belong together as a goal and end, history's consummation and its rupture.[38]

Within this kind of conception of eschatology, we see that it shapes not only the relationship between the church and Israel, but that it also has a cosmic dimension, and so too is shaping the relationship between Israel, the church and the whole of creation. This future-orientated eschatology, rather than a fully realized eschatology, correlates with the ecclesial movement we identified within the New Testament. If eschatology is understood only as fully realized, ecclesiological dualisms become necessary. That which already fully is, requires the interpolation of a doctrine of the invisible church as it requires an ontology that the concrete historical church in its nature as incomplete, historically contingent and sinful, cannot provide. The millennial position Moltmann is explicating here offers both a reality, a meaning and a challenge to the historical contingency of the church. The church, as with creation as a

---

[35] Jürgen Moltmann, *Theology of Hope: On the Ground and Implication of a Christian Eschatology* (London: SCM, 1967).

[36] See Christoph Schwöbel, *Last Things First?: The Century of Eschatology in Retrospect*. In David Fergusson and Marcel Sarot (eds), *The Future as God's Gift: Explorations in Christian Eschatology* (Edinburgh: T&T Clark, 2000), p. 230ff.

[37] Jürgen Moltmann, *The Coming of God: Christian Eschatology* (London: SCM, 1996).

[38] Moltmann, *The Coming of God*, p. 197.

whole, is not yet complete; therefore, the church must orientate itself to the future and its promise of the unity of Israel and creation as a whole. Such an orientation is a prime means by which the social identity of the church is in perpetual process of re-formation, as such an orientation functions socially in the way we discussed utopias above. The understanding of history implied within this future orientation both allows God to be a living, initiating God within the historically contingent order and also to be the God who will continue to initiate within history, both in an ongoing and an ultimate sense.

It is worth exploring further the contours of Moltmann's thought as it relates to the *God-People of God-World* triangle. Moltmann addresses the question of the 'Restoration of All Things', and ultimately concludes that the most biblical and theologically satisfactory understanding of eschatology lies in the understanding of universal salvation. Within this notion rests the ultimate relationship of God, the people of God and the world, who are brought into universal relationship in the eschatological future. This must be understood as the radical future of the ecclesial movement outwards that we have noted. The ecclesial movement of the church to the whole world continues within history, but finds completion in the end of history. Moltmann traces this understanding of universal salvation, along with its predominant alternative in the Reformed tradition, the double outcome of judgement.[39] Having traced the historical origins of the two alternatives, he proceeds to address the biblical material concerned. Here, he compares different biblical passages speaking for universal salvation (Eph. 1.10, Col.1.20, Phil.2.10f., 1 Cor. 15.22ff, Rom. 11.32) and for a double outcome of judgement (Mt. 7.13f., 12.32, 25, Mk 9.45, 16.16, Lk. 16.23, Phil. 3.19; 1 Cor. 1.18; 2 Cor. 2.15). He concludes that 'Universal salvation *and* a double outcome of judgement are therefore both well attested biblically'.

Moltmann proceeds to examine the question of universal salvation theologically, suggesting that '*What speaks against a double outcome of Judgement* is the experience that God's grace is more powerful than human sin'.[40] He notes, however, that against this view is one which is concerned that grace cannot be construed as 'a compulsive power which disposes over people without asking them'.[41] Having elucidated these lines of thinking, he proceeds to suggest that

---

[39] Ibid., p. 235ff.
[40] Ibid., p. 243.
[41] Ibid., p. 244.

universal salvation is ultimately 'the expression of a boundless confidence in God: what God wants to do he can do, and will do', whereas the double outcome of Judgement is 'the expression of a tremendous self-confidence on the part of human beings . . . eternal destiny, salvation or damnation, lies in the hands of human beings'. He concludes that ultimately we must be bound to answer that God decides, and he states that, 'God *is* "for us": that has been decided once and for all in the self-surrender and raising of Christ'.[42] He then proceeds to examine the descent of Christ into hell (where he follows Luther and Calvin in understanding this as truly located before and in the crucifixion itself, exemplified in the prayer in Gethsemane). He concludes that *'The true Christian foundation for the hope of universal salvation is the theology of the cross, and the realistic consequence of the theology of the cross can only be the restoration of all things'*[43] (Moltmann's italics). What Christ demonstrated on the cross is the over-powering nature of the love of God, who in experiencing the reality of hell, and overcoming it in resurrection, giving us the assurance of salvation.

For Moltmann, universal salvation is not a simple avoidance of judgement. Rather, judgement, for Moltmann, is the cleansing of history; sin and wickedness is 'condemned and annihilated', and sinful humanity will be 'liberated and saved from their deadly perdition through transformation into their true, created being'. He suggests that: 'The eschatological doctrine about the restoration of all things has these two sides: *God's Judgment*, which puts things to rights, and *God's kingdom*, which awakens to new life'.[44]

This brief survey of Moltmann's eschatological vision is significant in understanding his ultimate vision of the relationship between Israel, the church, God and the world. In other words, it assists us in orientating ourselves to the understanding of the vocation of the church in the *God–People of God–World* triangle and also to understanding some of the implications of the historically contingent nature of the church that we have been examining. He notes the text from Revelation 21, which speaks of the Holy City and the way in which Israel's covenant formula is applied to the whole of humanity. Ultimately, in this eschatological perspective, Israel, the church and the world are united in covenant relationship with God:

---

[42] Ibid., pp. 244–5.
[43] Ibid., p. 251.
[44] Ibid., p. 255.

Behold, the dwelling of God is with men;
and he will dwell with them,
and they shall be his peoples,
and God himself will be with them
and be their God (Rev.21.3).

Ultimately, Moltmann sees a movement that works in two ways. The nations are gathered into the covenant relationship of Israel and the church, and also, that covenant is broken open and extended: 'Israel and the Church are the foundation stones for the gates and the walls of the holy city, but not for the city itself, which rises into cosmic dimensions.'[45]

Moltmann's perspective on eschatology raises highly significant themes for ecclesiology and our search for a theological account of the reform and renewal of the church. First, it shows the vocations of both Israel and the church, which find their fulfilment in the future sphere of eschatology. This fulfilment is the fulfilment of the vocation of Israel to be a light to the nations and of the church in its mission to all the nations. Ecclesiologically, what this perspective does is to correct the historic over-dependency of ecclesiology upon notions of individual salvation and the election of individuals allowing eschatological perspectives to be equally embodied within the life of the concrete historical church. The place eschatology has in this doctrinal scheme perhaps goes some way to acting as a reparative to the issues we were exploring in relation to Barth's understanding of election, time and eternity in Chapter 2. There, we noted that in Barth's relocation of the doctrine of election in Christ and the community, before the individual, one of the key doctrinal reasons why a notion of the invisible church was required had been removed. This begins to free up our understanding of the church and move it away from 'blueprint ecclesiologies' in such a way as allows for a theological account of the reform and renewal of the church. Barth reintroduces this, however, in his account of time and eternity where the in-breaking of the 'eternal moment' is the place in which the real church exists. The historical church is simply the 'semblance' of a church. Moltmann's account introduces the eschatological dimension more clearly into an account of history that allows for God's eternity to break into history, not in eternal 'moments', but rather into history itself in a millennial

---

[45] Ibid., p. 316.

fashion. History, in this account, retains its integrity as genuinely historical, and the place of God's action. This allows the historical church to be truly the church, albeit incomplete and awaiting its fulfilment. This church is then shaped by its anticipation of God's advent and in-breaking into history, while history itself in terms of the concrete historical church, retains its integrity.

Why the Church?

The kind of account that we are offering here, resting in Barth and Moltmann and their hope for a universal salvation itself, has implications for the self-understanding of the church. Put simply, it begs the question as to why the church is needed, or why one would bother with the church as all are saved anyway. Perhaps, the fact that this question springs so easily to mind demonstrates just how intrinsically difficult the idea of grace actually is. There is a Pelagian lurking in all of us waiting to emerge – human conceptions of justice seem to demand that we get something in return for our membership of the church, and all too frequently, what is demanded is that we get salvation whereas those who have not bothered with the church don't! Tom Greggs has paid this question some well-deserved attention, and his observations, through his engagement with Origen, Barth and more recently Bonhoeffer, interestingly match some of the trajectories of thinking that have been developed in this work. Greggs locates his discussion of the particularity of the Christian community within the work of the Spirit. This follows the classic creedal pattern whereby the confession of the church is located within the confession of the person of the Holy Spirit. The work of the Spirit is 'the deeply intensive work of God with particular people; He is not simply the extensive work of God that leads people into Jesus Christ'.[46] The Spirit, in this understanding, works both to bring about the intensity of sanctification within the life of the Church, as well as working beyond the immediate community in a more extensive fashion within the life of the world. The Spirit is that which realizes salvation in the midst of present life in the world, 'Salvation becomes, therefore, not something which takes place behind us in Christ and ahead of us in the *eschaton*, but something which

---

[46] Greggs, *Barth, Origin*, p. 179.

is real in the present through the Spirit who is ever present in the believer between those two events'.[47] The church is the place where salvation becomes a lived reality in the here and now, for the sake of representing this in the midst of the world, and serving the world.

Greggs' understanding correlates with the conclusions of another recent study of the work of the Spirit in election by Suzanne McDonald (in a study of election in Owen and Barth). She develops the biblical idea of election to 'representation'. Following a reading of the Old and New Testaments, and recent Christian and Jewish scholarship on election, she concludes that election is biblically understood not as a dualism of 'in' and 'out', but rather as representation. This sense of election to representation

> ... honors the utter exclusivity of election as signifying one clearly defined and distinctive community set apart to be and to do what no others can be and do, and also suggests a dynamic within which election can be seen as intrinsically for the sake of the other'.[48]

This move away from a strict correlation between membership of the church and salvation (as underpins the classic reformed understanding of the invisible church), informs our understanding of the way in which the church, through the work of the Spirit, is the community in which the eschatological hope of all is prefigured and subjectively appropriated. It also informs our understanding of the way in which the church relates to the world. Fundamentally, the church exists for the sake of the world and within the world, rather than for the sake of its members and apart from the world. Here, we can begin to see in greater depth some of the consequences of what we have termed the *God-People of God-World* triangle. It is a triadic relationship in the sense that each is related to the other. The People of God are not the world, they are called out from the world to witness and serve within the world. They are, however, fundamentally related to the world as they are within the world, and also are world, in the sense of sharing something of the brokenness of the world. They share with the world the victory that Christ has assured, and they hope on behalf of, and with, the world for the restoration that is to come. The people of God are also fundamentally related to God. It is God who has called this people, elected

---

[47] Ibid., p. 188.
[48] Suzanne McDonald, *Re-Imaging Election: Divine Election as Representing God to Other and Others to God* (Grand Rapids: Eerdmans, 2010), p. 112.

this people, brought this people into covenant relationship with God and continues to sustain and remake this people in the intensity of the work of the Holy Spirit. Further, God is in fundamental relationship with the world itself, as creator, as redeemer in the victory of Christ and in the Spirit which 'blows where it wills' (Jn. 3.8). Precisely because God is fundamentally in a covenant relationship with the whole of life in the world (the Noahide covenant), and in particular, a covenant relationship with the People of God, as Greggs puts it, 'There can be no absolute and sharp dividing line between the church and the world both because of God's freedom to work outside the bounds of the church, and because of the church's own broken and failed form. . .'[49] Each part of the triangle is fundamentally related to the other two points within it. The church lives not for the sake of its own salvation as an institution, or for the salvation of its members. Rather, it lives to mediate the salvation won in Christ for the whole of the world. It is formed into the body of Christ precisely to follow Christ and, through the work of the Spirit, to be made ever more Christ-like. In this, it follows the trajectory of Christ's ministry – one that is ultimately cross-shaped. The Church is not called to worldly success for the sake of itself and its members, but rather to fulfil the command of Christ to 'take up your cross' (Lk. 9.23).

What we have shown in this chapter is that the orientations of covenant sociality identified in the last chapter remain constant within the Christian church. These orientations, however, all find their focus in Jesus Christ. As the incarnation of the God of Israel, Christ directs the church to the historical activity of God in the people of Israel and to the historical activity of God in Jesus himself. Christ, as the divine initiator of the new covenant sociality equally orientates the church to the world through the taking to himself of the historically contingent sociality begun in the call of the disciples, which begins an ecclesial movement out into the whole of creation. Christ also orientates the church to the eschatological future of God, causing the church to actively await future divine historical activity within history and as the end of history itself. The contingent nature of the church means that the church itself is indeed a mixed community. This must not be understood as a mixed community of the saved and the unsaved, but rather as a mixed community that is both

---

[49] Tom Greggs, *Against Religion*, p. 136.

divinely initiated and upheld in the work of the Spirit, and humanly fragile and historically contingent. Salvation finds its fulfilment eschatologically and must be understood as the final divine historical event which is the end point of the extensive ecclesial movement begun in the call of the disciples (and rooted in the call of Abraham). This eschatological perspective offers us the correct understanding of the relationship of Israel and Judaism to the church. Both are the people of God, both are awaiting the same eschatological kingdom. Judaism, however, operates vicariously within the world, while the church operates in going out to all the world and calling the whole of the world into itself.

Within these orientations, the church is called to perpetual renewal precisely because it is the body of Christ who is the God who acts historically and calls into being a historically contingent sociality. It is specifically in the orientation of the church, through Christ, to the past, the present and the world that the identity of the church is formed. This, given God's choice of being active within contingent history, both in Christ and in the work of the Holy Spirit, requires that the church be perpetually re-forming its identity within these orientations. To understand the identity of the church as fixed would be to fail to be orientated to the present and future activity of God. Equally, it would be to fail to continue the ecclesial movement outwards to the world, the historically contingent world, which is divinely initiated in Christ, and divinely upheld in the work of the Spirit. We noted in the last chapter that the reform and renewal of Israel is understood in biblical perspective to be repetition with variation of the covenant mediated by practices, and the renewal of those practices in specific contexts. We need to move now to an exploration of how it is that practices uphold the reform and renewal of the church as the mediation of the repetition with variation of God's covenant.

7

The Practices of Identity Renewal

The mediation of social identity: The contribution of 'collective memory'

We have begun to build a complex understanding of various related elements which help us understand the reform and renewal of the life of the church. We have seen that theologically, it is necessary to understand the visible, historical church as *the* church, and to move away from the dualisms of visible and invisible. This creates a theological space in which it becomes possible to understand the way in which the church exists in historical contingency. We've also seen that this is always mediated in the set of relationships the church finds itself in, which we have characterized as the *God-People of God-World* triadic relationship. It is this that is the relational environment in which the sociality of the church is continually being formed and re-formed. Within this relational context, we have seen that the reading and re-reading of scripture is fundamental to the formation of the social identity of the church, seen both in the reformation of doctrine as it concerns the relationship of the church to Israel, but also in terms of the way in which scripture itself presents the renewal of social identity in the renewal of the covenant. We have also seen that that covenant, and the election of the People of God is precisely for the sake of the world, and has a representative function within the world, and that alongside this, God too is in immediate relationship with that world. The context of the world as the place of the witness of the church by definition has to inform the form that church life takes as it fulfils its vocation. We have also seen that the renewal of covenantal identity is mediated through the practices of communal life. The covenant is always renewed in some sense in the context of the renewal of practice, and this happens in a form of repetition with variation.

The one eternal covenant is renewed and upheld in the renewal of practice. We need now to begin to offer some account of the way in which the practices of church life fulfil this function of reform and renewal, identifying what some of those practices are, and how it is that practice mediates covenantal identity and its renewal. This is obviously a vast topic, and one that could be approached in many ways. All that is possible to do is offer some brief reflections on how this might be understood.

In attempting to understand the functioning of practices as the mediators of reform and renewal, we shall first examine the contribution that memory plays in the formation of identity from a discipline outside theology. Throughout this work, memory has been a theme which recurs, but memory itself is not a static thing; rather, memory itself is mediated in practices. Theories of collective memory have been developed within the field of sociology, which will assist us in understanding how memory – and the practices of the church – act to form and reform social identities.

Mary Curruthers' work, *The Book of Memory*[1] and Frances Yates in *The Art of Memory*[2] examine the development of notions of memory with respect to literature and art history, respectively, examining classical notions of the training of memory through education. Memory in contemporary society is something largely taken for granted; it is construed individually and, more often than not, we are concerned with the size of the memory of our computers rather than our own, often fallible, memories. Notions of communal memory are not common in day-to-day life, and the impact that such communal memories have in the life of the church are largely ignored when thinking of the formation of the identity of the church. Curruthers notes this when she states that, 'Where classical and medieval rhetorical pragmatism diverges from modern is in assigning a crucial role to a notion of communal memory, accessed by an individual through education, which acts to "complete" uninformed individual experience'.[3] This notion of memory accurately reflects the notion of memory which under-girds the process of covenantal people formation. The individual, through access to social norms (law) and religious practices

---

[1]   Mary Curruthers, *The Book of Memory* (Cambridge: Cambridge University Press, 1990).
[2]   Frances Yates, *The Art of Memory* (London: ARK Paperbacks, 1966/84).
[3]   Curruthers, *Memory*, p. 24.

(cultic activity) becomes a bearer of a communal memory, participating in such a memory, and forming it in a dialectical process.

Modern sociological perspectives on memory emerged primarily in the work of Maurice Halbwachs' in the early twentieth century. His primary work on the subject, *On Collective Memory*,[4] argues that all memory is essentially social and that without social interaction there is no such thing as memory. He suggests that all memory is to some extent in fact social memory, in that each individual forms his memory from thoughts that come to him from the social milieu. In each individual act of memory, we are perceiving ourselves as others might perceive us, '. . . the framework of collective memory confines and binds our most intimate remembrances to each other.'[5] From this perspective, he locates social memory primarily in the family unit, arguing that families create a collective memory, which gives them their identity. Such family memories, however, are not the same thing as a simple history. Halbwachs states that the family memory is, '. . . constituted by facts that can be dated – by images that last only for a certain span of time, as one finds in it judgements that the family and those surrounding it have expressed about themselves – it partakes of the nature of those collective notions that cannot be placed in a particular place or at a definitive moment, and that seem to dominate the course of time.'[6] Family memories are both historical in the sense of Halbwachs' reference to 'facts that can be dated', but equally, he is acknowledging that family memories have a more amorphous quality, which one might even characterize as 'myth'. Such memories may or may not relate to a specific event, or a conflagration of events, but serve to inform the family identity by virtue of their existence as memory. Such family memories are, however, affected by the social norms and expectations of society as a whole, whereby the interplay of the family with wider society impacts either positively or in a reactionary fashion, the collective memory and identity of the family group.[7]

The question of the relationship between memory and history is an interesting one, and one considered by Aleida Assmann in her seminal work, *Cultural Memory and Western Civilization*. She develops a typology of the difference and

---

[4] Maurice Halbwachs, *On Collective Memory* (Lewis A. Coser (ed.), Chicago: University of Chicago Press, 1992).
[5] Halbwachs, *Collective Memory*, p. 53.
[6] Ibid., p. 59.
[7] Ibid., p. 74.

relationship between memory and history in the terms of 'inhabited memory' and 'uninhabited memory'.[8] Inhabited memory is that which has a connection with the 'carrier' of the memory, which might be an individual, institution or group; it connects the past, present and the future; it 'proceeds selectively by remembering and forgetting' and it 'provides values that can support identity and norms'.[9] This relates to what we might consider memory rather than history. Uninhabited memory, however, is not owned in the sense of having a particular carrier, relates only to the past, rather than integrating the present and the future, 'is interested in everything and everything is equally important' and 'seeks to establish truth and suspends behavioural norms and values'.[10] It is possible to see from these descriptions how the one shapes identity in the way that the other does not directly. We are formed by what we remember, not by what 'actually' happened, as it were. However, Assmann wants to see a rather more complex relationship between the two. She sees the former as 'functional' memories, and the latter as 'storage' memories. Storage memories are 'memories of past memories', and are what one might find in archives, and what historians engage with. What is very interesting is the suggestion that storage memories can at times be reconnected with functional, identity forming memories: 'it is possible for historical knowledge to reclaim some of these disembodied relics and abandoned materials and perhaps even reconnect them with the functional dimension of cultural memory'.[11] This idea intersects with the way in which the canon of scripture functions. We will reflect further on the canon below, but what is interesting to note here is that, in this typology, one could say that not all of the canon at any one time is acting as inhabited memory, functionally forming identity. Some of it is acting as storage memory. In this way, reengaging with the canon may at times release parts of storage memory that have been functionally forgotten, and reintegrate them into inhabited, identity forming memory. It is possible that in some senses this is what has happened in the twentieth century with the retrieval of readings of Romans 9–11 in the case of the Jewish–Christian dialogue.

---

[8] Aleida Assmann, *Cultural Memory and Western Civilization: Functions, Media, Archives* (Cambridge/ New York: Cambridge University Press, 2011), p. 123.

[9] Aleida Assmann, *Cultural Memory*, p. 123.

[10] Ibid.

[11] Ibid., p. 124.

While later developments have, as in Assmann, developed Halbwach's understandings further, he himself was very interested in religion as collective memory, which he understands in a way analogous to the family. While operating from a pre-Vatican II context of French Catholicism (perhaps better expressed as post-Vatican I), his arguments provide the foundation for later work on collective memory concerning religion. His argument is that Christianity operates as a collective memory, which is perpetually recalling the life of Christ and the early church, but is, however, open to transformation, a role he prescribes particularly to the mystics within the history of the church. Regarding the role of mystics, Halbwachs suggests that they were able to expand and enlarge the picture of early Christaintiy, and therefore to change the understanding of the faith. They were able to 'attract the attention of believers to certain facts and persons in the Gospels that were initially neglected, poorly known, or little noticed'. This, in turn, was able to lead 'to a new direction of religions memory fashioned to recover such aspects of evangelical history that until now had been neglected'.[12] Halbwachs' argument is interesting not simply because of the role he ascribes to mystics, but rather the process itself. The idea that innovation is normally achieved through an expanding of the original memory framework rather than through the revolutionary accession of a completely new idea reflects well what we see in church history. Most major moments of reformation are not seeking to break with the past, but rather to rediscover the past in such a way as the present can be reformed to better embody the tradition. Thus, Luther and Calvin were not attempting revolution, but rather to at once return to a lost memory framework, and also to repaint in more lively colours the existing memory. For example, notions of priesthood were not overturned, but rather transformed, meeting the need of what was perceived as the moribund state of the ordained ministry in the period preceding the reformation. Equally, the need for an apologetic to meet new forms of humanist scholarship can be seen as resulting in the readjustment of the framework of memory, calling upon forgotten aspects of the scriptures and the teachings of the Fathers.

---

[12] Halbwachs, *Collective Memory*, p. 106.

In the process of the re-forging of the framework of Christian memory, Halbwachs suggests that what has resulted is various Christian memories that have arisen to meet the societal needs of the time, emphasizing different areas of doctrine and different practices. Therefore, he claims that 'In the core of Christian collective memory there are many collective memories, each of which claims to reproduce more faithfully than any other that which is their common object: the life and teachings of Christ'.[13] Hence, within the Christian tradition, there are a variety of rich memory traditions which can be drawn upon by groups and individuals and enlarged to meet the needs of the contemporary moment. Halbwachs concludes his section on the church by saying, and it is worth quoting at length here:

> . . . the religion of today is not only the commemoration of the past for believers; since his resurrection Christ is present in the church at every moment and in all places. The church can hence allow without apparent contradiction that new revelations occur. But it tries nevertheless to link these new data to the ancient data and to place them within the body of its doctrine, that is, of its tradition. In other words, the Church does not acknowledge that these data are really new; it prefers to conjecture that the full content of the early revelation was not immediately perceived. In this sense the Church completes and illuminates its earlier remembrance through representations which, even though they have only recently attracted its attention are themselves also remembrances. In this way, although religious memory attempts to isolate itself from temporal society, it obeys those same laws as every collective memory: it does not preserve the past but reconstructs it with the aid of the material traces, rites, texts, and traditions left behind by that past, and with the aid moreover of recent psychological and social data, that is today, with the present.[14]

Here, we have an extremely interesting account of the reformation of the church. The idea that the church is accepting new ideas, while denying their innovative quality to ensure a continuation of established memory frameworks, provides considerable illumination on the way the concrete church functions. Through its rituals and traditions, as well as through its body of teaching, the church

---

[13] Ibid., p. 115.
[14] Ibid., p. 119.

propagates a memory framework which allows for its own perpetuation. Equally, the church allows itself to re-remember its traditions as it seeks to find its place within shifting societal patterns. This correlates very well with the process of covenantal re-formation that emerged in our study of the Hebrew scriptures, and even with the way we saw that the canon itself re-receives and reforms even the Torah itself at times.

Social theorists posit that collective and cultural memory is not, however, simply communicated through texts. Rather, it is communicated through various practices. Paul Connerton, in his work *How Societies Remember*, examines two broad exemplars of how this happens – commemorative ceremonies, and bodily practices. He examines various commemorative ceremonies from parades and 'festivals' that accompanied Hitler's National Socialist rule in Germany in the 1930s and the 1940s[15] through to Jewish commemorative festivals[16] and analyses them in psychoanalytical, sociological and historical perspectives. Ultimately, Connerton concludes in answer to the question concerning what it is that is being remembered in commemorative ceremonies that 'a community is reminded of its identity as represented by and told in a master narrative' and that 'this is conveyed and sustained by ritual performances'.[17] This process he terms a 'performative' process, which usually manifests itself in ritual. This, however, is not simply a commemorative enactment. He states that 'Performative memory is bodily. Therefore, I want to argue, there is an aspect of social memory which has been greatly neglected but is absolutely essential: bodily social memory'.[18] In terms of bodily practices, he then considers this in two categories – 'incorporating practices' and 'inscribing practices'.[19] He illustrates the former through practices such as gestures, which might be as simple as a handshake[20] or complex bodily gestures that communicate status and class in terms of how we relate within social groups.[21] 'Inscribing' practices are his way of speaking of practices of memory storage, such as writing, indexes, photographs etc.[22] It is interesting that Connerton sees

[15] Connerton, *How Societies Remember* (Cambridge: Cambridge University Press, 1989), p. 41.
[16] Connerton, *How Societies Remember*, pp. 45–6.
[17] Ibid., p. 70.
[18] Ibid., p. 71.
[19] Ibid., pp. 72–3.
[20] Ibid., p. 72.
[21] Ibid., p. 74.
[22] Ibid., p. 73.

both the commemorative ceremonies and the bodily practices as inherently conservative. They preserve memory without necessarily resulting in cognitive awareness of what is being preserved, 'Every group, then, will entrust to bodily automatisms the values and categories which they are most anxious to conserve. They will know how well the past can be kept in mind by a habitual memory sedimented in the body'.[23]

The inherent conservatism that Connerton notes in commemorative and bodily practices is revealing in two different ways. First, it demonstrates well the way in which practices form and maintain memory. Practices are indeed a means of preserving continuity of is embedded within. It also suggests that the renewal of the practice, or its reformation, can fundamentally shift what is being remembered. Thus, reformation of practice constitutes both continuity and discontinuity – a means of perpetuating the memory, and also of shifting the memory. If nothing else, this observation suggests a very great significance for practices – what we do. What we do forms who we are – what we do communicates our fundamental beliefs, convictions and values, and holds those within our communities. A self-conscious reflection on what the practices of the church are indeed embodying is perhaps one of the functions of the practice of theology. Are practices of church life congruent with the memory of the church as held within its canon of scripture and within its historic tradition, or is church practice now, in reality, embodying something different? Our reading of the scriptural understanding of social identity formation of the people of God leads us to suggest that the renewal of practices is at times essential for the maintenance both of the covenantal identity of the People of God itself, but also in terms of upholding the right relationality between God, the People of God and the world. Simply to keep doing the same thing over and over again may well ultimately mean that you are no longer in fact communicating the original intention, but rather that one is communicating something different precisely because the context of the world which the people of God is called to witness to and within has shifted. We shall return to this thought in the final chapter.

---

[23] Ibid., p. 102.

Practices of remembrance: Collective memory in the Deuteronomic tradition

Following this outline of the role and function of social memories, we now need to return to the Hebrew scriptures to understand the way in which the law and cultic practices serve to create, inform, maintain and reform the collective memory of the people of Israel. We noted in Chapter 5 that, particularly with reference to the accounts of the Sinai covenant, the law was the essential context for the covenant. Within the Deuteronomic account of that covenant and the law, the notion of memory plays a significant role. This has been detailed particularly by Brevard Childs from the perspective of a study on the verb *zkr*,[24] to remember, and also by Jan Assmann, an Egyptologist who has produced particular work concerning the role of collective memory within religion. Assmann too has been influenced by Halbwachs, and the sociological schools of thought surrounding notions of religion and collective memory.

Assmann labels the story of the finding of the book of Deuteronomy as 'the shock of forgetting'.[25] Following Assmann, we shall not concern ourselves at this moment with the historicity of these texts in terms of historical reality (*"geschichtlichen Wirklichkeit"*[26]) as his fundamental point concerns the significance of the Deuteronomic texts and Josianic reforms as in terms of the recovering of a central memory of identity. We have already noted in Chapter 5 the significance of the use of Deuteronomy in the re-establishment of the covenant in the period of the Josianic reforms. We are now in a position to understand more exactly how these reforms, and the Deuteronomic law, serve as a set of practices which create a specific collective memory and sense of social identity.

It is possibly not surprising that in the context of a 'lost' book of the law being 'found', memory plays such a significant part in the Deuteronomic reading of history, law and cultic activity. Childs lists the objects of Israel's remembrance as they fall into categories: 'the great acts of Yahweh (*circa* 22 X), Yahweh

---

[24] Brevard S. Childs, *Memory and Tradition in Israel* (London: SCM, 1967).

[25] Jan Assmann, *Cultural Memory and Early Civilization: Writing, Remembrance, and Political Imagination* (Cambridge/New York: Cambridge University Press, 2011), p. 193.

[26] Assmann, *Cultural Memory*, p. 216.

himself (17 X), his commandments (9 X), sins (7 X), special days (3 X)' He also notes, that 'In marked contrast with the usage with God as subject, nowhere does Israel remember the covenant (*berith*). This is interesting, since Israel can forget the covenant (Deut. 4.23)'.[27]

Childs identifies memory as historical memory of past events.[28] Deuteronomy 8:2 provides a key example:

> Remember the long way that the LORD your God has led you these forty years in the wilderness, in order to humble you, testing you to know what was in your heart, whether or not you would keep his commands. (Deut. 8.2)

In this passage, the memory of the Exodus experience is the ground for the present significance of the law. The past testing of Israel is the key to understanding the present necessity of the keeping of the law. He suggests that, 'The covenant history of Yahweh with his people continues. The role of Israel's memory here is not to relive the past, because much of what is remembered is painful, but to emphasize obedience in the future. Memory serves to link the present commandments as events with the covenant history of the past'.[29] This use of memory, to relate the past with present necessity is a recurring theme in Deuteronomy. Childs evidences Deut. 7.18; 9.7; 24.9; 25.17,[30] as examples of this use of memory. Particularly interesting among these examples is 7:18, where the past memory of what God did to the Egyptians serves to offer the hope for the future that God will act similarly again against Israel's enemies. The past history is offering both a means to comprehend the present situation and a future hope.

A closely related but somewhat different use of memory appears in the account of festivals within the Deuteronomic legal code. Deuteronomy 5:15 reads,

> Remember that you were a slave in the land of Egypt, and the LORD your God brought you out from there with a mighty hand and an outstretched arm; therefore the LORD your God commanded you to keep the Sabbath day. (Deut. 5.15)

---

[27] Childs, *Memory*, p. 46.
[28] Ibid., p. 50.
[29] Ibid., p. 51.
[30] Ibid.

Childs notes the position of 'therefore'.[31] It is because of the need to remember the slavery in Egypt that the Sabbath is kept. A similar use of memory occurs in 16.3 concerning the Passover festival:

> For seven days you shall not eat unleavened bread with it – the bread of affliction – because you came out of the land of Egypt in great haste, so that all the days of your life you may remember the day of your departure from the land of Egypt. (Deut. 16:3)

Once again, the festival, which is a form of re-enactment, is for the sake of memory – memory of the Exodus. Childs argues that this is more than a simple act of remembrance, but rather that it is functioning as an actualization of the past; that in the keeping of the Sabbath and the Passover, present-day Israel is participating in the Exodus event itself.[32] The memory, in this sense, is about present social formation, it is serving as a realization of the past within present social structures, it is functioning as *anamnesis*. This notion is still current within Jewish thought. David Novak points out that the first Passover was celebrated in anticipation of redemption, rather than after the fact, and therefore, the Passover is 'as much a celebration of the past as it is an anticipation of the future. As such, its meaning is essentially present before it is either past or future'.[33] He goes on to point out that therefore it is not simply a re-enactment; the point is not to replicate every detail of the original. Placed next to Child's account of memory in the Deuteronomic tradition, we note the way the Passover is essentially orientated to the formation of the contemporary social entity. The account of the past, even to the extent that one can say the event of the past itself, exists and is remembered for the sake of the present. The future orientation is equally present within the Passover; the calling to mind (remembrance) of the future. It is an event, celebrated annually, which physically manifests a remembrance of both the past and a calling to mind of the future in a fashion that forms the social identity of the people in the present context within the world and within history.

It is worth quoting in full Childs' summary of his discussion of Deuteronomy as it expresses the problem faced by the writer of Deuteronomy and equally applies to concrete social religious entities today:

---

[31] Childs, *Memory*, p. 53.
[32] Ibid.
[33] Novak, *Election of Israel*, p. 152.

The writer has as his chief problem the relating of the new generation of Israel to the tradition of Moses. No longer has Israel direct access to the redemptive events of the past. Now memory takes on central theological significance. Present Israel has not been cut off from redemptive history, but she encounters the same covenant God through a living tradition. Memory provides the link between past and present. The Deuteronomist is acutely aware that Israel's redemptive history has not ceased. Her history continues only as present Israel established her continuity with the past through memory. The divine commands as event meet each successive generation through her tradition calling forth a decision, and in obedience Israel shares in the same redemption as her forefathers.[34]

Through the remembrance of God's activity and through the re-creation in cultic actions of the same, Israel as a social entity is formed. It is through this process of remembrance that the law becomes a living covenantal reality that binds the people together. Returning to the context of the Josianic reforms, it becomes possible to see how this is recounted as operating in the case of a radical forgetting of the tradition. We have already noted the immediacy of the covenant statements in Deuteronomy and the effect this might have wrought on the people assembled for the reading of the 'found' scroll. This, however, is extended into cultic activity in the way that Childs described. In the context of the radical reforms concerning idolatry, priestly activity etc., we find the reinstatement of the Passover. 2 Kings 23:21 recalls that:

> The king commanded all the people, "Keep the Passover to the Lord your God as prescribed in this book of the covenant." No such Passover had been kept since the days of the judges who judged Israel or of the kings of Judah; but in the eighteenth year of the King Josiah this Passover was kept to the Lord in Jerusalem. (2 Kings 23. 21–23)

The traditions of memory, or rather, the cultic forms which made that memory present were re-established. Central to Josiah's attempt to re-form the people of Israel was the festival of memory. Similarly, the cultic practices of memory are equally important in the post-exilic accounts of Ezra-Nehemiah, where the re-establishment of the Passover and the festival of Booths are key events in the re-establishment of the people in the land (Ezra 6.19–22, Neh. 8.13–18).

---

[34] Childs, *Memory*, pp. 55–6.

Significantly, the account of the celebration of the festival of Booths comes between Ezra's reading of the law and the act of national confession and the re-establishment of the covenant. The reading of the law and the national confession are both acts of historical remembrance – between the two acts comes the actualization of that remembrance in the festival. This serves to underline the point made by Childs – at the heart of being the present people of God lies the actualization, through memory, of history.

Jan Assmann offers a complementary account of the means of transmission of memory in such a way as it becomes realized in the process of social formation. Assmann uses the term '*kollektiver Mnemotechnik*' to describe the process of active memory which is the foundation of social formation. Assmann states that 40 years represents the circle of collective memory. Thereafter, 'if this account was not to be lost, it had to be transformed from biographical to cultural memory. The means used were collective mnemotechniques, and Deuteronomy names no fewer than eight different techniques of cultural memory'.[35] The notion that what the Deuteronomic texts offer are a means and a practice by which a cultural memory can be held begins to help us understand the means by which a society begins to own its history. It will be useful to summarize the eight examples of the formation of cultural memory that Assmann identifies.[36] The first is self-consciousness, which he understands as being concerned with raising the awareness of individuals by commands such as that in Deut.6.6 to 'Keep these words that I am commanding you today in your heart'. 'These words' in this context are 'The LORD is our God, the LORD alone' (Deut. 6. 28), the first part of the *Shama* prayer. Secondly, there is the notion that the history of the past must be communicated and circulated to the following generations (6.7, 11.20). This is closely linked to his third and fourth points, which concern binding 'these words' which are to be bound as a sign to the hand and forehead and written on the doorposts of houses. His fifth point is the setting up of stones containing the words of the law, to be set up after crossing into the promised land. Sixth comes the three festivals of collective remembrance. Assmann's seventh 'collective mnemotechnique' concerns the command to learn the song of Moses which closes the Pentateuch. This song

---

[35] Assmann, *Cultural Memory*, p. 196.
[36] Ibid.

contains a summary, as it were, of the history of Israel, and is to be taught to the Israelites: 'put it in their mouths, in order that this song may be a witness for me against the Israelites'. The last point listed concerns the canonization of the texts of the Pentateuch when Moses 'wrote down this law and gave it to the priests' (Deut. 31.9), along with the command to:

> Every seventh year, in the scheduled year of remission, during the festival of Booths, when all Israel comes to appear before the LORD your God at the place that he will choose, you shall read this law before Israel in their hearing . . . and so that their children, who have not known it, may hear and learn to fear the LORD your God, as long as you live in the land that you are crossing over the Jordan to possess. (Deut. 31:9–13)

Thus, the text itself becomes a fundamental means of encountering the memory of God's dealings with Israel. In these eight points, Assmann identifies clear, differentiated ways in which the history of God's activity within Israel is to be remembered. The remembrance is not simply a theological construct, but rather a theological practice. It is in the means of communicating the cultural history of this people that they become a people with one foundational story, which binds them together. The process of social formation is inextricable from history. Equally, the history itself becomes inextricable from the practice of the people – history becomes actualized in ethics (the observance of the law) and in cultic practice. Ultimately, history becomes actualized in the creation of a people, a social entity.

It must be emphasized that the process of calling to mind the past in such a way as it informs the present also cannot be separated from the calling to mind of the future. This is a point that Novak emphasizes, and is also a point made by Hervieu-Léger from a sociological perspective. She states that:

> The remark has been made that any tradition in its relationship to a past, given actuality in the present, always incorporates an imaginative strain. The memory it invokes is always, in part at least, a reinvention. This reinvention is most often effected through successive readjustments of memory, readjustments that are often minute or invisible, above all readjustments that are almost invariably denied on the score of the absolute and necessary permanence of tradition. What is specific to utopia as compared with the ongoing exertion of memory on itself is that it makes of the complete and total break with the old order the condition of access to a new one, which

is glimpsed by means of a memory that has been replenished at a source for which greater authenticity is claimed. Utopia contains the proposition to install, in place of an official memory that has become corrupted or misappropriated, a new order of memory (hence a new imaginative order) on the basis of which it is possible to redefine the way that society operates in terms of its economic, political, symbolic and other functions.[37]

Traditional practices are not, in this understanding, static. Rather, whether the community wishes to accept it or not, traditional practices in the context of a future vision are always subject to reformation. The cultic practices re-form their meaning and re-form the social entity each time they are performed. This allows for what Novak calls the 'lived present'. The practices of memory, be they in biblical or contemporary sociological perspective, are always repetition with variation. Theologically, we would want to correlate that with the functioning of the work of the Spirit that we identified in the previous chapter. Theologically, we might wish to speak of the practice of theology as being to act as a measure of such variation, ensuring that it is indeed repetition with variation of the formation of the covenant identity of the people of God, not the formation of something totally new, and far removed from what it is to be God's people in and for the world.

We see embodied in these practices what we have termed the three means by which reformation takes place – a returning to scripture, the impact of the present context and the mediation of practice. These practices are those that mediate, and in the case of the festivals, the marks of separation and the reading of scripture – all of which Assmann identifies as practices of collective memory, we see the centrality of scripture along with the space identified by Novak for the present contextual reality to differing degrees in differing cases.

Throughout this work, we have taken, by and large, a canonical view of scripture. We have addressed scripture as theological text, rather than enquired after historical textual formation. The very existence of a canon, however, is a form of cultural memory. The fact that a set of texts has been given an authoritative status, and that those texts have remained stable as canon for millennia, offers one very visible point of continuity within the tradition. As has become clear, however, such diversity of texts and the changing contexts

---

[37] Hervieu-Léger, *Religion*, p. 145.

in which those texts are read mean that there is a continuing shift in the interpretation and meaning that those texts carry. The re-reading of the New Testament regarding the theological position of Israel is simply one example of this process. However, the canon itself comprises a set of texts that, in and of themselves, do have a particular history and were written to serve a particular function.

One of the more controversial movements in biblical studies at the moment is the 'minimalist' school of the history of Israel.[38] This supposes that the vast majority of the biblical texts of the Hebrew scriptures arise out of the Persian period, reflecting the particular situation of a post-exilic people to the extent that any kind of knowledge of the history of the real historical Israel before this time is impossible.[39] Paula McNutt points out that within this post-exilic context the creation, or re-creation, of a social identity was one of the priorities reflected in the text,[40] which includes the creation of a unified 'history' that reflects the social needs of the time (particularly of the literary classes).[41] While precise questions of the historicity or otherwise of the Hebrew Scriptures need not concern us (what is of far greater concern is how the texts as we have them today form and re-form the identity of the church), it is simply interesting to note the likelihood that these texts were written precisely for the purposes of fashioning a social identity, with a common history and cultic expression. It should come as no surprise therefore, that if these texts were written precisely to be such social identity-forming documents that they continue to serve this purpose so powerfully in the present.

What the understandings of collective memory, specifically understood in the light of the Deuteronomic material, reveal is the way in which the historicality, in terms of the present understood through the past and the future, is mediated through practices that form collective identities. Memory mediates identity through mediating history (in the sense of the remembrance of the past) and through mediating future expectation, and all of this takes place in the context of the orientation of the people to the immediate context

---

[38] For representatives of this 'school', see Philip R. Davies, *In Search of 'Ancient Israel'* (Sheffield: JSOTS, 1992); Keith W. Whitelam, *The invention of Ancient Israel: The Silencing of Palestinian History* (London: Routledge, 1996); Paula McNutt, *Reconstructing the Society of Ancient Israel* (London: SPCK, 1999); Niels Peter Lemche, *The Israelites in History and Tradition* (London: SPCK, 1998).

[39] Davies, *In Search of Ancient Israel*, p. 94.

[40] McNutt, *Ancient Israel*, p. 182.

[41] Ibid.

of the world. Through this process, it is possible to see how the people of God can be understood as being formed and upheld through practice. The divine initiative, sustaining and reformation of identity in terms of the past and future historical activity of God is a process of holding together the orientations of past, future and world through the practices themselves. This process assists us in understanding how it is that re-formation and renewal of social identities is both possible and necessary. It also assists us in understanding how the maintenance of a divine social identity is mediated and upheld within the context of historical contingency.

The reformatory practices of the Church

The same processes we have identified thus far in this chapter are equally at work within Christian worship. What differentiates it from the Jewish context is, as we have seen, the specific relationship of the Christian church to the world – one of openness not separation. Rather than a body of doctrinal beliefs forming identity, or even scripture alone forming identity, the identity of the church is formed through its practices embedded within which are both doctrine and scripture in a dialectical relationship – doctrine and scripture form the practice, as the practice then embodies the doctrine and scripture, which in turn forms the community. These practices, as with the corresponding Jewish practices, find their origin in scripture and seek to embody scripture in practise. Identity, however, is formed through the mediation of that practice, not simply through a direct correlation of either beliefs or texts to social identity.

Lawrence Hoffman notes that:

Both Jewish and Christian services look forward and backward simultaneously, collapsing time into a single worship moment – that is, they remember time past when a covenant was initiated and look ahead to a messianic future when the covenantal promise will be realized. Both demand a certain structural order – in fact, Christians describe their worship as an *ordo*, the Latin equivalent for *seder* or *siddur* (order), the word customarily used for the Jewish service.[42]

---

[42] Frymer-Kensky et al., *Christianity in Jewish Terms*, pp. 175–6.

This observation concerning Christian worship from a Jewish perspective offers the contours of an understanding of the practice of Christian worship and how it forms and re-forms social identity. It must be acknowledged that there are many practices of the church, not least in terms of its polity, that all play their part in forming and reforming social identity. Worship, however, lies at the heart of the process. This is so not least because it is worship that takes us to the heart of the way the church orientates itself to past, future and the world at its most basic level, the congregational level. It will assist us to examine, briefly, the overall structure, the order, of Christian worship.

To examine the nature of worship is intrinsically almost an impossible task, particularly within the reformed tradition, as it is a context in which there is no set order or liturgy. Reformed worship is not structured around a prayer book or missal. There is, however, a generally accepted structure, within which liturgical freedom then expresses itself, and reformed churches do use books of liturgy. The position is made clear in the Introduction to *Worship: from the United Reformed Church*, which is the current service book of the URC. It states that, 'The orders found here are not prescribed. It is not expected that they will be used in our churches to the exclusion of others. Yet we believe most of these services reflect the ethos of our Church and its inherited traditions.'[43]

In what follows, we shall outline what might be the content of a reformed order of worship (in as much as there is a typical example), drawing on particular examples from particular liturgies where they are useful. The purpose of this is to show how the practice of worship can, and in one received expression of it, perhaps is, forming the identity of the church. This is necessarily a very limited exercise as the practices of worship can never be fully appreciated simply in the words that are said. However, it is hoped that reflection based upon liturgical texts will illustrate the intent and the reality of what can occur in worship.

Worship begins with a 'call to worship', sometimes as simple as the phrase 'Let us worship God', coupled with this will be a 'scripture sentence'. The call to worship acts as a moment of separation. Something has begun which is of significance, we are coming consciously into the presence of God. This, coupled with a scripture sentence, acts immediately as a mediator of memory. Implicit within the call to worship is the notion of continuity that God's people

---

[43] United Reformed Church, *Worship: From the United Reformed Church* (London: United Reformed Church, 2003) from the Foreword.

are gathering again as they have done for millennia. Equally, the scripture sentence makes present the canonized collective memory which is scripture. While it is not always the case, it is interesting to note that the *Second Order of Holy Communion* from the URC begins with the sentence: 'The time is fulfilled, and the kingdom of God has come near; repent, and believe in the good news'.[44] In this particular instance, right at the start, not only is there an orientation to the past through the reading of canonized scripture, but in that reading, the act of worship is also immediately orientated towards the future, richly suggestive of a proleptic understanding of the presence of the kingdom; the future is made present at that moment through anticipation.

Throughout reformed worship, and the worship of the Christian church in general, music plays a significant role, particularly within the reformed tradition congregational hymn singing. It is impossible to engage at this juncture with an understanding of hymnology and the functioning of congregational singing, but it serves as an interesting illustration. Hymn singing is a collective act, social in nature. Bonhoeffer characterizes hymn singing thus:

> Why do Christians sing when they are together? The reason is quite simply, because in singing together it is possible for them to speak and pray the same Word at the same time; in other words, because here they can unite in the Word. All devotion, all attention should be concentrated upon the Word in the hymn. The fact that we do not speak it but sing it only expresses the fact that our spoken words are inadequate to express what we want to say, that the burden of our song goes far beyond all human words.[45]

He goes on to suggest that all singing should truly be in unison, to reflect the unity of the activity. The singing of hymns, then, reflects the social nature of the people of God; they act and speak corporately in song. As such, hymn singing can be understood as part of the process by which sociality is upheld. Hymns provide another interesting insight – the publication of hymn books by churches provide what could be understood as a secondary canon. By virtue of their collation and publication by church authorities, they take on an authoritative status. Hymn books function similarly to a canon, providing a textual collective memory of the tradition of the church. Equally, hymn

---

[44] URC, *Worship from*, p. 18.
[45] Bonhoeffer, Dietrich, *Living Together* (London: SCM Press, 1954), p. 43.

books are examples of the reformation of the church. The Church of Scotland has recently published its *Church Hymnary Four*,[46] the very title of which is indicative of reformation. New hymns are added to the canon of hymnody, expressing in new ways the being of the church.

Frequently, hymns will be settings of Psalms, or based upon the Psalter, and Psalms have always taken a central part in the worship of the church. This too is an example of the manifestation of the collective memory of the church. In the reading or singing of psalms, the past experience of the people of God is made present. The diversity of psalmody, in terms of praise, confession, lament, hope and all of the varying varieties of psalm, means that not only are they a manifestation of collective memory, but frequently call to mind the contextual situation of the people of God and equally, at times, call us to a vision of future hope.

Following a call to worship, scripture sentences and congregational singing, prayers of adoration, confession and the assurance of pardon (or absolution) follow. In adoration, the church is expressing its dependency on God. It is God who has called the church into being, and it is God who is praised. Adoration serves to demonstrate the origin of all things in terms of both creation and of the calling of the people present. An example of the prayer of adoration from the *Third Morning Service* from the Church of Scotland illustrates the point well:

> Lord God,
> the wonders of your creation,
> the splendour of the heavens,
> the beauty of the earth,
> the order and richness of nature,
> all speak to us of your glory.
> The coming of your Son,
> the presence of your Spirit,
> the fellowship of your Church,
> show us the marvel of your love.
> We worship and adore you,
> God of grace and glory,
> through Jesus Christ our Lord. **Amen**.[47]

---

[46] Church of Scotland, *Church Hymnary – Fourth Edition* (Norwich: Canterbury Press, 2005).
[47] Church of Scotland, *Book of Common Order* (Edinburgh: Saint Andrew Press, 1994), p. 29.

Here, we clearly see the origin of not only the gathered community ('the fellowship of your love'), but also the origin and dependency of the whole of creation on God. Such a prayer orientates the community both to God, Father, Son and Spirit, but also to the world. The gathered congregation is confronted at once with an orientation to the world through the praise of the creator, God.

In the confession of sin, one thing we clearly manifest is, as we noted in the first part of this thesis, the incompleteness of the church. In confession, the church admits its faults and failings in such a way as to confess that it is, at present, not complete. The confession of sin serves equally as a confession that the church is *not* the kingdom. As such, confession is rooted in the present reality of the church, but equally is orientated towards the future; it is the recognition that the future kingdom of God will bring a redemption that is not yet. Equally, confession frequently contains an orientation to the world, particularly where the church confesses its part in the sin of the whole of creation (the confession of what one might term 'structural sin'), or even at times, confesses vicariously on behalf of the world. This can be well illustrated from the confession in the *Second Order of Holy Communion* of the United Reformed Church:

> God of justice and forgiveness,
> we confess that we live in a world
> in which some are hungry even for bread,
> many people are sad or hurt,
> and there is much that is unfair and unjust.
> We confess that in our own lives
> we do not always do what is right
> or turn away from what is wrong.
> We ask your forgiveness,
> we claim your love and mercy,
> and we ask for courage to make a new beginning.
> In the name of Jesus Christ. **Amen.**[48]

In this example, the incompleteness of the church is very clearly manifest (along with the brokenness of the world), and the prayer includes a petition asking for a new beginning. Here, we see a liturgical expression of the centrality of

---

[48] URC, *Worship*, pp. 19–20.

reformation within the life of the church. The church is seeking in its confession to re-form, to begin anew. Equally, in this specific prayer, the orientation to the world is clearly manifest, inherent within this is an understanding of the present in the light of a future orientation – the kingdom is not yet fully here, therefore the world is broken as we are, and hence forgiveness is required. The assurance of pardon following this prayer of confession within this particular liturgy (which, in this instance, is called the *Prayer for Grace*) is equally interesting:

> Jesus said, 'Your sins are forgiven'.   Mark 2:9
> He also said, 'Whoever does the will of God   Mark 3:3
> is my brother and sister and mother'.
> Eternal God,
> we believe the good news
> of your mercy and love,
> and rejoice that we are forgiven and free.
> Receive us as your children,
> as brothers and sisters of Jesus,
> part of your new community of love,
> and give us strength to do your will
> today and always. **Amen.**[49]

Here, in the context of the assurance of pardon, the use of scripture is drawing on the authoritative canonized collective memory of the church. Following this, the prayer emphasizes the social nature of the church, drawing on the Markan familial imagery to speak of a new community. This sociality is then placed in the context of a time reference, 'today and always', which emphasizes the historical location of the people of God, and also echoes the Hebraic form, 'the day today', which we noted above, holds within it the significance of being the day in which God acts.

From out of this context of approach, adoration and confession arises the proclamation of the Word, the public reading of scripture and the act of preaching. The public reading of scripture calls to mind the commandment in Deuteronomy 31 concerning the reading of the whole law. While there, it is presented as a seven-year festival, week by week, in both churches and synagogues, scripture is read aloud before the gathered congregation. This

---

[49] Ibid., p. 20.

returns us to the centrality of the canon as a means of affirming continuity (the canon is closed), but in the re-reading of scripture (as exemplified in the shift in Jewish–Christian relations) also a catalyst for reform and renewal. However, the reading of scripture in public worship is a selective affair. Frequently, local churches follow a lectionary, the most common of which at present is the Revised Common Lectionary (followed by most of the Western church traditions). This, however, begs the question of what is included in the lectionary. John Goldingay expresses the point well, 'Revising the lectionary might seem an esoteric and marginal enterprise until one takes account of the fact that for many ordinary Christians the readings in church are the one way they come across the scriptures'.[50]

The use of a lectionary (or indeed, any means of selecting biblical material for use in worship that excludes portions of the canon) offers what we might call a mutated memory. The form of the Revised Common Lectionary is as a three-year lectionary, with a (practically) continuous reading of each of the synoptic gospels within each year, with selected 'old' testament and epistle readings to complement the gospel. Goldingay notes that this causes a number of problems. In allowing the gospel always to dominate the choice of readings, other readings – the 'old' testament particularly – lose a sense of their own 'voice' and continuity.[51] Goldingay also notes the limited coverage of material, particularly with reference to the psalms, where 40 are not utilized in the three-year cycle, 32 of which are psalms of lament, leading to a misleading impression of the Psalter overall.[52] Goldingay also notes that:

> . . . we never read God's words of judgement on Adam and Eve in Gen 3:16–24 or the story of Cain and Abel, or most of those Old Testament stories which *Patterns for Worship* misses from JLG [listed as: Lot, Hagar, Ishmael, Isaac, Joseph, Moses in the bulrushes, the spies in Canaan, the fall of Jericho, Achan, Deborah, Barak and Samson, Mary and Martha, the man born blind, Jesus calming the storm, Legion, the pool of Bethseda and the story of the rich fool] . . . Astonishingly, it incorporates not one passage from Chronicles. It offers no stories about Daniel.[53]

---

[50] Goldingay, John, 'Canon and lection', in Bryan D. Spinks and Iain R. Torrance (eds), *To Glorify God: Essays on Modern Reformed Liturgy* (Edinburgh: T&T Clark, 1999), p. 85.
[51] Spinks, *To Glorify God*, pp. 94–5.
[52] Ibid., p. 95.
[53] Ibid., pp. 96–7.

This alarming list suggests that a highly selective form of memory is being offered to congregations.

With the caveat noted concerning some of the weaknesses of the lectionary, we can still make the valid point that the foundational stories of faith that serve to underlie the collective memory of the church are presented week by week within the church. Scripture, in its reading, forces us to both look back (in the double sense of scripture itself being 'ancient', and it recalling 'history' in a narrative fashion) and forward, in terms of the explicitly eschatological and apocalyptic literature and themes within the canon.

At the heart of the act of worship lies the preaching of the Word. Any full exposition of the theology of preaching lies well outside the scope of this book, but a few remarks are in order. It is perhaps to be lamented that in the contemporary church, much consideration is given to how one might preach, but relatively little attention is given to what, in theological terms, preaching actually is. Preaching is first and foremost an exposition of the Word of scripture; however, it is also intrinsically a reformatory activity. The sermon engages both with the text and the context, the immediate context of the gathered worshipping community and the wider context of life in the world. Through its engagement with canonical scripture, preaching should be properly understood as an anamnestic practice. The words of scripture are not simply recounted, but are made present in the immediate context. Preaching is also essentially a social activity. Too often, preaching is considered to be something that the preacher does. However, in both the preaching and the hearing, the whole gathered congregation is active. Preaching serves to revivify the collective memory of the church regarding its foundational texts, drawing on the rich seam of collective memory manifest in the history of the church and the history of biblical interpretation.

Preaching is also a proleptic practice. It serves to draw the eschatological vision of the future into the present. It is not simply a case that this happens solely when particular texts with an eschatological focus are serving as the basis of the sermon. Rather, preaching is a proleptic activity in its own right, anticipating the kingdom of God in the act of proclamation and active hearing itself. The sermon draws on collective memory and collective anticipation in the terms of eschatological hope in such a way that the immediate identity of the gathered congregation is formed and renewed.

The context of the sermon, and the way preaching engages with this context, is its orientation to the world. In preaching, the canon of scripture is orientated towards the world, seeking a social orientation in terms of ethics and practices by the people of God within the world. As such, preaching as an activity is foundational to the formation and re-formation of the social identity of God's people in that it encapsulates the anamenstic, the proleptic and the orientation of the church to the world. It is where the church is continually confronted with the reality that it exists for the world, not for itself.

Following the sermon, the church orientates itself more self-consciously to both the formation of its own identity and the concerns of the world in the prayers of intercession. Individuals, the church itself, the immediate community, the needs of the world and the faithful departed are upheld in prayer. In doing so, the sociality of the church is proclaimed in expressing the needs of the individual members of the community and, frequently, the church itself (with reference to both its immediate local manifestation, and the wider manifestation of the church throughout the world) is brought before God, often in terms of petition for the upholding of the sociality and the renewal of the sociality. The prayers of intercession orientate the church both to itself and to the needs of the world in such a way that the anamnesitic and proleptic lives of the church are orientated towards the life of the world in its brokenness. Intrinsic to this process is the eschatological vision of hope for the whole of creation.

The Lord's prayer also takes a significant place within the regular worshiping life of the community (its position within the 'order' can vary significantly). This is a very particular form of collective memory finding its origin in Christ. In the offering of this prayer, the church is orientating itself as the body to its head, Christ. The fact that it is prayed collectively serves to underline its centrality in the formation of the sociality of the church, and it orientates the church to its origin (Our Father) and its goal (your Kingdom come), while maintaining the orientation to the world (on earth as it is in heaven).

It is in the sacrament of Holy Communion (or the Eucharist) that many of our themes relating to the orientations of the people of God are most clearly united in what, in the very physical sense of the term, is a practice. The gathering of the church around the table of the Lord is a very specific act that orientates the church, through Christ and in the power of the Holy Spirit, to the past, the future and the world. Specific and precise orders of the Holy

Communion vary within individual denominations, even within the reformed tradition, so once again, I shall select specific examples to illustrate the way in which the act of Holy Communion orientates the church.

The prayer of thanksgiving, or Eucharistic prayer, recalls salvation history, the activity of God within history. A clear example comes from the *First Order of Holy Communion* of the United Reformed Church, which reads:

> We offer you thanks, Creator, Saviour, Giver of Life.
> From the beginning you have made yourself known:
> the heavens proclaim your glory and the earth sings your praise.
> In wisdom you made all that is
> and you bless us with earth's fruitfulness.
> you are merciful and gracious, and abounding in love.
> Yet from our first days we have disobeyed your will.
> Long ago you called to yourself a people
> to shine as light to guide all nations to your presence.
> You led them to freedom;
> you revealed to them your Law
> and taught them through your prophets.
> Finally you sent your promised Son, Jesus Christ,
> who shared our human nature and understood our weakness.
> Born of Mary, he showed forth your love by word and sign.[54]

God's historical divine activity of creation and its correlation in initiating a covenant people are called to mind, and the prayer reaches its climax at this point in the memory of Christ. The orientation is clearly to the past. The gathered congregation in one time and place is recalling its origins in the divine initiative within history. This, as with all the interconnecting themes in the sacrament, is most clearly present in the 'Narrative of the Institution', with the words '. . . the Lord Jesus on the night that he was betrayed took a loaf of bread, and when he had given thanks, he broke it and said, "This is my body which is broken for you. Do this in remembrance of me."' (1 Cor. 11.23–24) The remembrance is a divine command. The nature of the remembrance must be understood in the context of the way memory functions as anamnesis and as collective memory. The understanding of the 'Last Supper' as intrinsically bound up with the celebration of the Jewish Passover leads us to understand the

---

[54] URC, *Worship from . . .*, p. 9.

way this particular remembrance functions to enable the gathered congregation to participate in the events of the past in such a way that the collective identity of the people is formed and re-formed. Welker puts the point this way:

> The "memorial" that Jesus institutes by the celebration of the Supper makes the canonical memory based upon the biblical traditions focused, concrete, and existential. It weaves those who celebrate the Supper into the memory of Christ in a more basic way than is possible for interpretation and proclamation. The Emmaus disciples recognize the risen Christ in the breaking of the bread – only in hindsight does it become clear to them that their hearts were already burning within them while he was opening the scriptures to them![55]

What emerges here is the significance of the fact that the identity forming 'memorial' is centred precisely in a practice. It is in the fact that the Eucharist is a sacrament, something physical, which involves a doing, the sharing of a common meal in bread and wine, which is so significant. What is happening is not solely theoretical, or to be understood only in an intellectualized sense. Rather, it is concrete; it is an activity. Welker goes on to unpack more clearly what the 'memorial' is actually doing:

> The celebration of the meal creates a memorial for Jesus Christ. Jesus' life, death, and resurrection are not simply internalized individually and communally. They are publicly proclaimed, so that the memory of Christ is carried further and spread aboard. The memory of Christ is cultivated and spread as a living cultural memory, a canonical memory. This living cultural and canonical memory is at work in the midst of the fluid communicative memory that human societies continually vary, supplement, reconstruct, and re-layer (Jan Assmann). The living cultural and canonical memory imposes meaning-bearing forms on recollections, experiences, and expectations.[56]

Here, we begin to see the dynamic in which the practice of the sacrament forms and upholds the divine sociality of the church within and through the historical contingency of life in the world. The social identity, rooted in a dynamic and social memory, is formed through being orientated to Christ. This orientation then orders the multilayered cultural memories, experiences of the world and

---

[55] Welker, Michael, *What Happens in Holy Communion?* (Grand Rapids: Eerdmans, 2000), p. 130.
[56] Welker, *Holy Communion*, p. 133.

future expectations in such a way as the divine historical activity of God takes to itself the historical contingency of the church's life in the world. The divine activity itself remains historical, in the sense of being activity within historical contingency, and the church too remains formed and re-formed within the historically contingent order. The divine identity of the church, as formed through divine initiative and upheld in the gift of divinely initiated practices, continually re-creates what we can now truly understand as the Body of Christ within and for historical, contingent and worldly existence.

The practice of the Holy Communion must also be understood as particularly rooted in the work of the Holy Spirit. The prayer of thanks giving continues with an invocation of the Spirit (epiclesis). Welker states that, 'It is a gift of the Holy Spirit, who calls and binds together the faithful, and makes it possible for Christ himself to act among them'.[57] This is clearly expressed in the *Second Order for Holy Communion* of the Church of Scotland:

> Send down your Holy Spirit on us
> and on these gifts of bread and wine;
> that they may become for us
> the body and blood of your most dear Son,
> and that we may become for you his living body,
> loving and caring for the world
> until the dawning of the perfect day.[58]

The role of the Spirit in the formation of the community as the body of Christ within the life of the world is clearly explicated here. The Trinitarian dimension is also clear. The Spirit makes present Christ for the community, but more than this, it forms the people in their identity as the body of Christ, being the continuation of Christ's ministry, a ministry the first disciples were called to share, within the historically contingent order. More than this, however, the being of the people as the body of Christ intrinsically carries with it the future hope and expectation for the whole of creation. Welker states that:

> As long as the Supper is celebrated in a particular time and world and in a concrete community, we orient ourselves in expectation and hope toward the complete presence of Christ. On the one hand, we experience the world's

---

[57] Ibid.
[58] Church of Scotland, *Common Order*, p. 152.

imperfection, its condition of being threatened by the power of sin, and the still relative absence of Christ. On the other hand, we await the coming of the exalted Christ, his assumption of complete sovereignty.[59]

Here, we see the essential dynamic relatedness of the orientations we have identified in the process of identity formation through practice. The orientation to Christ, the historical activity of the one who called the church into being, equally orientates us simultaneously to the future expectation of the ultimate rule of Christ. This too, simultaneously orientates the community to the world through the understanding of the rule of Christ over the whole world.

This brief overview of the parts of Christian worship, particularly in Holy Communion, serves to illustrate the dynamic of practice as it forms the identity of the church. The worshipping life of the church seeks to uphold and re-form the collective memory of the church through the activity of the living God, who initiates and upholds the church's divine sociality within concrete historical life in the world. Worship forms our identity as the body of Christ and simultaneously locates us within history. The past activity of God is experienced through memory and the dynamic of anamnesis, the current activity of God within history in the work of the Spirit orientates us to Christ forming our identity as his body in the here and now in our present historical worldly context. Equally, the future historical activity of God is pre-empted in the proleptic movement within worship, forging our identity through hope in future promise and fulfilment.

It is in the gathering and doing of worship, in its happening as a practice that these processes and dynamics are all brought into interrelationship in such a way as the social identity of the church as church happens. We must bear in mind that while worship is central to this, it does not happen exclusively in worship. Equally, the practices of the life of the church in terms of its social activity outside worship form part of the overall dynamic. It is beyond our scope to examine these, but to do so would be to pay attention to the structures and decision making processes within the church. It would also need careful examination of all activities of church life in terms of service and work.

In our concentration in the latter part of this chapter on worship, we have followed a very traditional model of worship, rooted in particular liturgical

---

[59] Welker, *Holy Communion*, p. 124.

texts from the reformed tradition. This has been simply one means (and the most easily identifiable) of perceiving how the orientations of re-formation are realized in the practices of worship. It must be understood, however, that it is the orientations themselves becoming manifest within practice that is of significance. The precise practices themselves can, do and must vary. We noted in the introduction the varied manifestations of the worshipping life of the church. What all of these exemplify, or should seek consciously to exemplify, are the making manifest the orientations necessary for the formation of the identity of the People of God within history. This may happen in silence, in music, in art, in dance, through activity; it is not necessary for this to happen in formalized articulated language, as in the examples we have drawn upon. One of the most interesting worshipping communities known to me is a Methodist church in Liverpool city centre. It gathers around the baking of bread. From this simple social activity, a church has emerged, which looks very little like a traditional church. It gathers in a rented room above a shop, and is equipped not with communion table and pulpit, but bread ovens. Out of the immediate bread-baking community, worship emerges, as have 'faith development' sessions, and bible study. It is a community in which the three orientations we have identified, are all held in tension. This is but one example of how the identity of the church might form and re-form itself, and serves as an illustration at this point simply to demonstrate that it is the fact of practice upholding the orientations of church life which is the significant point, not the precise nature of that practice.[60]

What is essential is that the process of upholding the orientations of church life in practice happens. It is essential that worship is understood and practised as the process which orientates us, through Christ and in the work of the Spirit, to the past activity of God within history, to the contemporary moment of life in the world within history, and to the future activity of God within history. When this happens, and these three orientations are held in creative tension within the practice of the church, the identity of the church is re-formed and renewed to be the very body of Christ, continuing the ministry of Jesus within the historically contingent life of the world.

---

[60] For an account of the development and life of this particular church community, see Barbara Glasson, *I am Somewhere Else: A Gospel Reflection on an Emerging Church* (London: DLT, 2005).

8

Toward the Reformation of the Church

The Church and the world

The church exists for the world. This statement is not a particularly radical one, but it is one that has massive consequences for the reform and renewal of the church. It is the consequence of an understanding of election which follows Barth's move and places this firmly in Christ, and thereafter in the community that is 'in' Christ. This means it is incoherent to speak of the invisible church in the way that the classical reformation did, particularly in Calvin. The 'true' church is not the sum of elect individuals; it is rather the concrete historical church. It is that, in all its historical contingency and fallibility, which is the body of Christ. It is that which is united to Christ by the work of the Spirit. It is that which, along with Israel, is the people of God, in and for the world. It is that church which carries its representative role, bearing witness and making present Christ's victory on our behalf, and being a community of reconciliation – reconciliation between God and humanity, and within the manifold diversity of human life in the world. The church does not exist for the sake of the salvation of its members. It exists because of the salvation God sends the church to bear witness to in and for the world.

If it is true that the church exists for the world, along with various other key theological statements, such as God being creator, God being sovereign, and Christ being God incarnate in the midst of the world, then the church is called to take the world very seriously. It is precisely this that the church is struggling to do at this moment in the West. The mainstream inherited churches feel lost and are searching for a form and expression that enables them faithfully to fulfil its vocation to witness to, and serve, the world. In the introduction, we sketched some of the features of contemporary western life, which is the context in which the church lives at present. It will repay us, following the theological journey we have been on throughout this work, to revisit some of the key issues, but hopefully thrown into a new light.

We have seen that the identity of the church as the people of God, the body of Christ, is formed to a significant degree through being a community of memory. Our exegesis of the renewal of the covenant shows that the covenant people are always renewed by being called back to the memory of the initiative of God to call God's people into being in the midst of, and for the world. It does this in the immediate present context in which God's people find themselves, and it does so in hope of the future transformation of life in the world. So, how do we understand this present moment in which we are attempting to be the church?

Paul Connerton has written a book, something of a companion to his work on how societies remember, called *How Modernity Forgets*.[1] In this work, Connerton argues that forgetting is becoming one of the key features of life within late modernity. He speaks of that which is being forgotten in terms of, 'the human-scale-ness of life, the experience of living and working in a world of social relationships that are known'. This then is the cause of 'some kind of deep transformation in what might be described as the meaning of life based on shared memories, and that meaning is eroded by a structural transformation in the life-spaces of modernity'.[2] He expounds this thesis with reference to received understandings of how memory functions, particularly with regard to the sense of place. He compares two different kinds of memory-place – the memorial and the locus. The former is a specific kind of memory bearer, but the latter is formed from everyday experiences of space, such as the street or the layout of the city. It is just this kind of place which functions as a site of memory, but in a very indirect way and with 'a certain matter-of-factness, a *taken for grantedness*'.[3] He goes on to analyse the way in which the locus has changed within modernity. Its sheer scale has grown beyond the human,[4] the speed with which we experience it has grown exponentially with contemporary forms of travel,[5] and the locus is repeatedly intentionally

---

[1]   Paul Connerton, *How Modernity Forgets* (Cambridge: Cambridge University Press, 2009).
[2]   Paul Connerton, *How Modernity Forgets*, p. 5.
[3]   Ibid., p. 34.
[4]   Ibid., pp. 100–8.
[5]   Ibid., pp. 108–17.

destroyed and rebuilt.[6] These factors, taken together, he argues, 'generate a diffuse yet all-encompassing and powerful cultural amnesia; and they are in their turn generated by the capitalist process of production.'[7] Alongside this, he identifies shifts in the experience of time as well, which happen in the separation of the labour process from consumption, the processes of consumption themselves, shifts in the patterns of working life away from the permanent and developed career, and the speed and flow of information as we experience it within the media.[8] The combined effect of shifts in the human experience of place and time, leads to a situation where the continual flood of new information, in terms of our lived experience of always being in space which is not intimately known to us, and being surrounded by information which overwhelms our ability to order it, means that we live with a constant forgetting. He concludes:

> The paradox of a culture which manifests so many symptoms of hypermnesia and which yet at the same time is *post-mnemonic* is a paradox that is resolvable once we see the causal relationship between these two features. Our world is hypermnesic in many of its cultural manifestations, and post-mnemonic in the structures of the political economy. The cultural symptoms of hypermnesia are caused by a political-economic system which systemically generates a post-mnemonic culture – a modernity which forgets.[9]

The sheer quantity of cultural media that we engage with is the flip side of a society in which the places and times upon which our memories depend have become such that the 'hooks' that they hang upon have been removed. This view is the one that is shared by Danièle Hervieu-Léger whose work we were engaged with earlier. She addresses the question of transmission of information and knowledge within culture and argues that whereas the issue can be seen as the failure of educational methods to transmit cultural knowledge, in actual fact, it is 'structurally linked to the collapse of the framework of collective memory which provided every individual with the possibility of a link between what comes before and his or her own actual experience.'[10] She understands

---

[6] Ibid., pp. 117–24.
[7] Ibid., p. 125
[8] Ibid., pp. 40–94.
[9] Ibid., pp. 146–7.
[10] Hervieu-Léger, *Religion*, p. 130.

secularization as being a 'break in the chain' of religious memory, in the context of new ways in which society functions.[11]

Alongside this shift in the way in which collective memory functions within contemporary society, it is illuminating to examine Anthony Gidden's argument about the location of trust within modern societies.[12] He characterizes this in relationship to the situation in pre-modern societies, where trust was localized in terms of place, and expressed primarily in kin-relations.[13] This, he argues, has shifted, and trust is now placed in abstract systems (he uses the example of boarding a plane, and the trust in the systems that are required to process the journey and ensure that you arrive at your destination) and in personal relationships we choose to enter.[14] This has had marked consequences for personal relations, where friendship, for example, is no longer institutionalized, and friends are no longer those who are the opposite of 'enemies', but rather friendships, and intimate sexual relationships, are chosen and places where we gradually disclose trust to the other person.[15] He also develops his argument in terms of a shift away from tradition and the past as being locations of trust, to a fundamentally future-orientated approach where we are striving after a vision of what the future could be.[16] This has all affected the way in which we perceive ourselves as being human, and in terms of our relationships with others, has led us on the quest for 'self-identity'.[17]

The analyses of both Connerton and Giddens begin to point to why it is so very difficult to be the church in this present moment in time. If the church is indeed a community of memory, and the social identity of the church is formed and re-formed through the re-appropriation of the past, and the anticipation of the future through practices of memory in the present, it is easy to see why it is that our mediating practices seem to be failing us in the midst of God's world as we experience it presently. Equally, if personal relationships are now formed fundamentally differently from a period in which they were formed through one particular location and through kinship ties, it is again easy to see how forms of church life rooted in the Parish or in extended family-style

[11] Ibid., pp. 121–40.
[12] Anthony Giddens, *The Consequences of Modernity* (Cambridge: Polity Press, 1990).
[13] Giddens, *Modernity*, p. 102.
[14] Ibid., p. 112.
[15] Ibid., pp. 117–21.
[16] Ibid., p. 102.
[17] Ibid., p. 122.

networks appear to be failing in this context. The very notion of being baptized into a new people, which fundamentally shifts one's identity to that given by the new group, is one which becomes almost nonsensical. Fundamental to the understanding of the church has always been Paul's statement in the letter to the Galatians:

> As many of you as were baptized into Christ have clothed yourself with Christ. There is no longer Jew or Greek, there is no longer slave or free, there is no longer male and female; for all of you are one in Christ Jesus. And if you belong to Christ, then you are Abraham's offspring, heirs according to the promise. (Ga. 3.27–29)

Intrinsic to Christian identity is the fact that one takes on one's primary identity from the sociality which is the church, which one enters in baptism. Our biological, cultural, ethnic and social identities remain, but are radically relativized through our entry into the Christian community. The work of Dunn and N. T. Wright that we examined earlier marks a significant shift back towards understanding Paul's primary theology being precisely about incorporation into the body of Christ, rather than assent to a propositional or experiential understanding of the nature of faith. This whole notion, however, seems entirely antithetical to the situation in which the church now finds itself in the West. Increasingly, church growth actually only masks the fact that people are moving from one church to another, or is emerging through patterns of immigration where the maintenance of an ethnic identity is actually primarily forming the identity of the church. The result is the steep decline that we see continuing across Europe, and that many perceive within North America. Western Europeans, and many North Americans, simply do not understand themselves as being formed by the socialites to which they belong. Just as, in Gidden's analysis, we are not formed by our kinship groups in the same way, but rather take personal decisions to disclose trust to those with whom we wish to be intimate, so we are not formed by the church functioning as a kinship group. We determine whether or not we will join it and place our individual trust within its social structure and identity narratives (this is what we noted in Charles Taylor's work and his observation that the conditions of belief have altered in the modern period).[18]

---

[18] See above pp. 12–13.

The danger is that the church attempts to go back, to recreate a world in which we no longer live. Here, we have to be careful in exactly what we say, for equally, we must learn from history that it is always dangerous simply to baptize the prevailing culture – we must not be scared of taking a prophetic stand where we are called to. It is worth noting the warning of Martin Stringer in the conclusion of his sociological history of Christian worship, that 'the form and pattern of worship is rooted in the social and political situation of the church at each specific time and place. No time is like the present, and no time should be recreated'.[19] The question for the church in the present moment is exactly the same as it has been in every other moment: how do we become the church in this time and place such that we exist for the sake of the world?

Finding our orientations

There have been two sets of triadic relationships that have emerged in the course of this work. The first has been the *God–People of God–World*, triad, and the other has been the triad of the past, present life in the world and the future. Our exploration of covenantal identity formation held these two triads in tension. God is always at work, calling a covenant people into existence for the sake of the world, and this is always done through the memory of the activity of God in the formation of the covenant, and the future expectation of the work of God in the outworking of that covenant for the sake of the world. All of that happens in the present moment within life in the world. We have argued that this is presented biblically as being mediated through practices. In this conclusion, we opened by taking our orientation from the *God–People of God–World*, triad, and have attempted to situate these reflections on the future reformation of the church in the context of contemporary life in the world. The form in which that happens needs to be informed by the other triangle, that of past, present and future.

In Chapter 6, we noted that the orientation of the Church to Christ orientates the Church through Christ in these three distinct directions, giving

---

[19] Martin D. Stringer, *A Sociological History of Christian Worship* (Cambridge: Cambridge University Press, 2005), p. 237.

us a greater understanding of the implications of being the body of Christ. What in fact these orientations are, are to historical divine activity within the world. In the past, the present and the future, the Church seeks to discern the historical activity of God within the whole of creation. It is in the past activity of God in creation that the Church finds its origin, and the beginning point of its identity. It is in the world as God's creation, and with 'all living flesh' with whom God is in pre-existing covenant, that the arena of God's historical activity is perceived. It is in the hope of the redemption of the whole of creation that equally our orientation to the world is formed. Equally, it is in the hope, expectation and awaiting of God's future activity within this historical world that identity is filled with a vision for the future which informs the past, and a true sense of the living God who has yet new things to do.

Given this understanding of these fundamental orientations, what are their specific impacts on Church life? The Church is called to live as the central point of these three perspectives, and if the activity of God within the historical contingency of the world is to be perceived and the identity of the Church to be perpetually reformed in the light of this activity, all three of these orientations have to be held in tension. The significance of doing so is perhaps best understood in the light of the consequences of not doing so. The Church is prone to either emphasizing one of these orientations over and against the others, or at times to lose sight altogether of one of them. When such situations occur, the Church is in grave danger of failing to discern the very activity of God that continues to create and recreate the identity of the Church.

The orientation to the past can become unduly prevalent very easily. The significance of tradition, when not held within the perspective of the other orientations, prevents the Church from perceiving its context in the world and stops the Church expecting any new activity of God. The danger of this is clear. Churches beset by this problem find change almost impossible. By failing to appreciate that God continues to be active within creation, and that God will, in the future, still be active within the historical sphere, changes in the surrounding society and changes within the life of the Church itself become highly frightening. If God can only be perceived in the past, then things can only be as they are. Any notion that God continues to be in covenant relationship with the whole of creation and God's Spirit might be actively at work within that creation becomes an impossibility. In such situations, other ecclesial bodies are viewed with deep suspicion for having 'sold out' to the prevailing culture, in having left behind the customs and thought forms of the past.

Another equally problematic expression of an over-emphasis on the past lies in the understanding of scripture. Scripture is seen only as a historic text, which binds to contemporary life the past context of the composition of those texts. Forms of biblical fundamentalism arise, which frequently do not so much emphasize the authority of scripture itself, but rather the interpretation of scripture of a particular past era. Frequently, doctrinal perspectives on the faith arising within the eighteenth and nineteenth centuries are actually the part of the past that becomes normative in fundamentalist positions. Such positions do not allow for the re-reading of scripture in the way we noted was so significant in the reformation of the Church regarding its understanding of Israel. Scripture cannot be inspired in the reading community in the present by the Spirit. The work of the Spirit in this sense is limited only to the past. God cannot and will not do anything new. It is a fear of this kind of problem which prompts movements like the Emerging Church movement and Fresh Expressions to critique the inherited forms of church life. They fear that such forms of church life have actually baptized a particular period of cultural history in which the identity of the church was formed, and that the church has ceased, therefore, to be concerned with God's world as it is now, or embody its life in such a way that enables the church to be for the world in the present context.

The orientation to the world equally can become emphasized at the expense of the other two orientations. When this arises, the distinctiveness of the Church becomes threatened, and any sense of identity is easily eroded. Such churches often come to express their lives in forms of social service, which are seen primarily in the terms of being and doing good. Without a secure perspective on the activity of God in the past, church life easily becomes only a perpetual meeting of the needs of the world. When this orientation receives such extensive emphasis, the church essentially loses its memory. As with the person suffering from amnesia after a bang to the head, the Church loses all sense of its identity and location within the past or future activity of God. The fundamental story of the people of God becomes lost amidst the competing collective memories of the surrounding culture.

When the Church becomes totally orientated to the world around it, rather than to the historical activity of God in past and future, the Church equally easily loses hope. The endless stream of needs to be met becomes overwhelming without the possibility of the in-breaking of God into this historical life. Equally, any sense of moral or ethical positions offered by either the past or future activity and judgement of God becomes impossible. At worst, the orientation to the world becomes totally prescribed by the prevailing culture, even if that is the fascist Nazi culture of the 'German Christian' movement under the third Reich. In a far less extreme fashion, some of the critics of Emerging Church and Fresh Expressions movements see this danger within them. They fear that what is happening is precisely the baptism of a consumer society, or the church having lost its prophetic edge in failing to offer critiques of injustice within the life of the world. To have a distinctive and Godly orientation to the world requires the calling to mind, the remembrance, of both past and future.

Perhaps the most extreme version of future orientations are exemplified in churches focused almost exclusively millennially. The immediate concerns of the world around become totally lost, as does any sense in which the past might forge present identity. In such situations, the past and present tend to function solely in attempts to predict both what and when the millennial moment will be. In such situations, the Church becomes very much concerned with questions of belonging and salvation. Who is in, and who is out, is of ultimate concern, as the Church is desiring to manifest the end before the end has come. At times, present moral concern, particularly within the political sphere, becomes repressed in favour of self-centred morality, with the only concern being what will happen to the individual at the millennial moment.

In less extreme cases, an undue orientation to the future provides other problems for Church life. Churches in this situation emphasize change more than continuity, and a confusion of new ideas and practices becomes the norm, and seen as filled with future promise. The reading of scripture equally can become totally detached from readings offered by past generations. There is no check on interpretative innovation as innovation is simply a good thing in its own right.

This brief overview of some of the implications of the Church failing to hold in tension the orientations of identity formation serve to illustrate their significance. When the Church does succeed in holding these in tension, it finds itself perpetually called to re-formation as it is perpetually called afresh into being by the living God who is active within history. When the Church holds these orientations in tension, it both retains the collective memory required to have an identity as the people of God and the body of Christ, but it also is constantly awake for the new thing that God might be doing. Equally, it concerns itself not so much with a simple perpetuation of its own past identity, but with God's concern for the whole of creation.

Reforming and renewing scriptural practices

In Chapter 2, we noted the way in which Colin Gunton had sought to move the doctrinal understanding of the church away from the visible/invisible divide. He moved our thinking towards the way in which the church is formed in the proclamation of the Word and the sacraments of the Eucharist and Baptism. We were left at that point, with the question as to how it is that these kinds of practice form and reform the church. Hopefully, we are now in a better position to give a more fully worked out answer to that question. We have seen throughout this work the way in which returning to scripture and the fundamental narrative of God's covenant relationship with the world, and particularly the people of God within the world, the reading and re-reading of scripture is a central activity. What we have been attempting to tease out is implicit within Robinson's farewell sermon to those who set sail for the New World: 'the Lord hath more truth and light yet to break forth from His holy word'. We have seen how that has functioned within the reading and rereading of scripture in the light of the Jewish-Christian dialogue; we have seen how this works in the accounts of covenantal renewal within the life of Israel and in the formation of the 'new' covenant of the church. We have seen how scripture itself reads and rereads itself in terms of the development of the canon, and we have seen how the reading and rereading of scripture becomes embodied in the practices of the church, particularly in its worship. There can be no doubt that continued fresh engagement with scripture within the life of the church is one of the prime drivers of reform and renewal.

In our account of an idealized act of worship, we reflected on what happens in our engagement with scripture within preaching. It is vital that when preaching happens, it happens well. There can be no room within the church for bad preaching – for this is the mishandling of our scriptures. Too often, preaching is dull, lacking in engagement with the text of scripture, and primarily concerned with the church for its own sake rather than with building the church up in its vocation of being for the world. The sermon must never be simply an ethical injunction around the lives of the congregation – that is, to misunderstand grace, to fall into the practice of works righteousness and to deny the reality that the election of the covenant community is for the sake of the world. We must, of course, note that preaching is one practice, but there are many others in which scripture is engaged within the life of the church, and it may be that in the contemporary world these need greater exploration than they have hitherto received. Scripture is handled in conversation, in art, in architecture, in movement, in music, in digital image and sound. When Fresh Expressions and Alternative Worship movements seek to explore the ways in which scripture is engaged in these different media, they engage in something vitally important for the health of the whole body of Christ. The point is that scripture itself must be engaged. One cannot extrapolate a 'message' from scripture, which is then turned into another form of communication. That is to assume that doctrinal propositional statements form the church, not the practice of engagement with scripture itself.

The sacraments of Baptism and the Eucharist also become clearer to us in terms of how they function as practices of the church that form identity. The shear bodily physicality of the sacraments is vital for the way in which they embody the narrative of the faith. We take bread and wine and water, and our bodies are touched and transformed through them. The worry is that these practices have become desperately thin. They all too often become matters of course, or actually embody something very different from the intention. Within non-conformist traditions, the use of individual little cups for communion embodies nineteenth century concerns about hygiene and a desire to express our faith individually, which is absolutely antithetical to a practice that is precisely about our incorporation into one another and into Christ. Equally, the working assumption is always that words are the predominant media within which the Eucharist and Baptism are celebrated. Words are an excellent media in which to do this, but they alone are not its significance (and here, we see the limitations of attempting to examine liturgical texts to understand the practice as we did in Chapter 7). Again, connecting with the visual, the kinaesthetic, the aural, the whole range of bodily senses are significant for the celebrating of these central scriptural practices which are about our whole bodies, our whole being and our interdependence. It is clearly not simply in the dominical sacraments, but in all kinds of practices which concern our life together, that this process is happening.

Some Christian traditions do not celebrate sacraments (the Friends and the Salvation Army, for example), but nevertheless, within their common life together, adopt scriptural practices which function in the way we are understanding them. Most Christian traditions world-wide place these sacramental practices centrally within the life of the church, and I would want to challenge those that do not to rethink whether their life together might not be enriched if they were to adopt them. I do not, though, want in any way to suggest that what I'm saying 'de-churches' them for the lack of these practices. Equally, those of us for whom sacraments seem vital might well be challenged by these traditions to think about the way the totality of our Christian life together embodies what we see happening specifically in these sacramental activities.

Baptism and the Eucharist, in my understanding, and that of the tradition out of which I am writing, take a very specific and central place within the reform and renewal of the life of the church precisely because they are the practices that we were given as gracious gift by Christ. These are the practices which Jesus gave to his disciples to offer to the communities they would form as the means of uniting them with himself and with one another. They are continually renewing and reforming the Christian community, but also, they themselves are renewed and reformed. Neither Baptism nor Eucharist are about an identical repetition of New Testament practices. We are not all called to baptize, like John the Baptist, in the Jordan, or gather in an upper room in the midst of the Passover festival in an attempt to identically repeat the Last Supper. These sacraments are utterly central to the life of the church, but this does not mean they must always be celebrated in the form in which we have received them. It does mean that it is difficult to understand reform and renewal movements without these sacraments as being a fully rich and engaged form of the life of the church. In short, Emerging Churches or Fresh Expressions that do not gather around these sacraments are deeply lacking. It is precisely in these practices that the identity of the Church as the people of God and the body of Christ are formed.

Taking seriously the reality of the visible church as the true church causes the reformed tradition (and others) to take very much more seriously the practices of church life. Too often, the faithfulness of the church has been measured according to doctrinal standards. Faith has been understood primarily as assent to propositional statements which are very much a product of the modern period. What we have seen is that propositional statements do not themselves form and reform social identity. In the biblical understanding we have developed, along with insights from cultural and social theorists, it becomes clear that social identity is formed in the structures and practices of social life together, not purely in structures of belief. It is not that structures of belief, or, in theological terms, doctrine, is secondary, it is that structures and patterns of doctrine are embedded within the form and practice of the church, and identity is formed by those practices. That reality causes us to consider briefly what the place of the practice of theology is within the reform and renewal of the church.

Throughout this work, we have referred to theology as one of the practices of the church. Doctrine is one part of the functioning of that practice. This book is not attempting to offer a fully fledged account of the nature of doctrine, or the theological enterprise. The account of George Lindbeck of the *Nature of Doctrine* offers a good starting point in naming some of the presuppositions that have been in play within this work. Lindbeck identifies three different ways in which doctrines are understood and function. First, a 'propositional' approach that turns doctrine into cognitive truth claims that either are or are not true. Secondly, 'experimental-expressive' approaches that use doctrinal statements as a way of speaking of feelings, emotions or attitudes. Thirdly, what Lindbeck calls 'experiential-expressive' approaches, where 'religiously significant meanings can vary while doctrines can alter without change of meaning'.[20] Lindbeck goes on to propose his own model, which he terms a 'cultural-linguistic' approach. This treats religion as primarily a social reality which can be understood best in cultural or linguistic terms. 'It comprises a

---

[20] George A. Lindbeck, *The Nature of Doctrine: Religion and Theology in a Postliberal Age* (London: SPCK, 1984), pp. 16–17.

vocabulary or grammar in terms of which this vocabulary can be meaningfully deployed'.[21] Doctrine functions in a sense like the 'rules' or 'grammar' of a language: 'Its doctrines, cosmic stories or myths, and ethical directives are integrally related to the rituals it practices, the sentiments or experience its evokes, the actions it recommends, and the institutional forms it develops'.[22] Lindbeck is pointing to one of the realities that this work has attempted to engage with, which is precisely that doctrine and practice are fundamentally related, but that identity is formed through practice itself (as it embodies doctrinal rules or grammar). Lindbeck suggests that 'Some doctrines, such as the *sola graita* or the *sola fide* in Christianity, are explicit statements of general regulative principles, but most doctrines illustrate correct usage rather than define it'. Doctrine is, like linguistic rules of grammar, that which enables us to formulate something correctly and meaningfully, but does not automatically provide the full content of that which is said. Therefore, 'Faithfulness to such doctrines does not necessarily mean repeating them; rather it requires, in the making of any new formulations, adherence to the same directives that were involved in their first formulation'.[23] Lindbeck sees this functioning in the way in which doctrine itself is reformulated, while remaining constant. He sees the creeds as regulative statements, that themselves are utilizing post-biblical language to form doctrine, but doctrine that points, as linguistic rules or grammar do, to the correct way in which theological statements must be formulated, rather than always to the direct content. So 'It seems that from the very beginning this religion has been committed to the possibility of expressing the same faith, the same teaching, and the same doctrine in diverse ways'.[24]

This work illustrates, in many ways, Lindbeck's understanding of how doctrine functions and helps us delineate the role of theology as a practice of the church that itself is one of the reformatory practices of the church. If one thinks about the shape and content of the historic creeds, they have shaped and formed this work considerably. The Trinitarian confession of God as Father, Son and Spirit shapes all that has been said; parts of the creedal

---

[21] Lindbeck, *Nature of Doctrine*, p. 33.
[22] Ibid., p. 22.
[23] Ibid., p. 81.
[24] Ibid., p. 92.

confession in terms of God as creator underlie the understanding of covenant community and its relationship to the world that has been developed; the fact that the creed subsumes its statements about the church under the confession of the personhood of the Spirit equally has formed the way in which we have examined ecclesiology. At times, we have used some of these foundational 'rules' of the construction of Christian life to urge the reformulation of what we might term secondary doctrinal 'rules'. For example, in urging a move away from the language of the invisible church in the light of thinking about the nature of election and the relationship of time and eternity, this work has suggested the need for revision of the doctrinal rules within which the life of the church is conducted.

This work also suggests that the practice of theology is itself foundational to the reform and renewal of the church. Theology is the activity where the church (often through the vocation of individual theologians who are members of the church, but ultimately as the church gathers in council and engages theologically) reflects upon its own practices and measures them against the narrative of the faith, and the rules and grammar of the faith that we confess to be the essence of what it is to be the church. This work has functioned in this way when it has returned to scripture (the key source for theological engagement), and in the light of the 'grammar' of the faith (its doctrines), has challenged the church to think again about the nature of the practices of covenantal renewal, and indeed the significance of practice as a whole. In this, it has taken doctrinal 'rules' such as *sola gratia*, the confession of the full humanity and divinity of Christ, and the regulative nature of scripture, and urged the church to understand how this regulates the relationship between the church and the world, meaning the church can never simply be understood as an in-group of the saved. In this sense, this work is also a call for a more ecclesially self-aware theological engagement which precisely understands itself as one of the reformatory practices of the church. Theology can never be, in this understanding, either merely playing with grammatical constructions or reflection after the event upon the concrete historical life of the church in simply descriptive terms. It is, rather, a complex and multilayered engagement with the perpetual reformulation of the practice of the church, and the self-identity of the church in the midst of the world, in the light of the 'grammar' of the historic faith.

Perpetual reformation

It is easy in times of drastic cultural change, such as it would appear we are living in globally at present, to resort to a form of conservatism that seeks to do the old thing with yet greater intensity in a bid to hold on to that which matters. Holding onto the church for the sake of its institutions, structures and even perhaps those inside of it is not the vocation of the church. The church in the present context simply must stop worrying about its survival. It is not there to survive. It is there to be for the world. The church has always been a movement that has been constantly reforming and renewing itself. This reality is something that Rowan Williams has reflected upon in the theological '*postscript*', he offers at the end of his work on *Arius*.[25] In reflecting upon the fourth-century debates about Christology, Williams presents a picture in which the realization was that in repeating what it was the church had always said, it was in danger of no longer saying the same thing at all, 'By the 360's – as Athanasius had seen – it had become necessary to choose what *kind* of innovation would best serve the integrity of the faith handed down: to reject all innovation was simply not a real option; and thus the rejection of *Homoousios* purely and simply as unscriptural or untraditional could no longer be sustained'.[26] In the context of neoPlatonisms, it was impossible to simply keep using the traditional language about the son of God without it taking on a meaning and expression that was simply not the original intention. This is characterized as a 'move from a 'theology of repetition' to something more exploratory and constructive. Athanasius' task is to show how the break in continuity generally felt to be involved in the creedal *Homoousios* is a necessary moment in the deeper understanding and securing of tradition'.[27] This is the task of theology, as Williams sees it, because 'The loyal and uncritical repetition of formulae is seen to be inadequate as a means of securing continuity at anything more than a formal level'.[28] To put it in other words, to keep saying the old thing, ultimately in the midst of a changed and changing context, is no longer to be saying the old thing at all, but to be saying a new and different thing. To keep saying the old thing requires the church to find a new way to say it.

---

[25] Rowan Williams, *Arius* (Second edition, London: SCM, 2001).
[26] Williams, *Arius*, p. 235.
[27] Ibid.
[28] Ibid., p. 236.

What Williams argues about the nature of the theological task of the church in its proclamation is, this work contends, equally true of the practices of church life. It is the practices of church life that embody our faith. Our faith is primarily a social and embodied one. It is not to sign up to a set of propositional statements, but to be incorporated into a social reality that is elected and becomes a covenant people for the sake of the world. What forms and reforms it are its practices. Just as with doctrinal formulations, to simply keep repeating the same practices over and over again ultimately means that the old thing is no longer being formed. To be in continuity requires the reform and renewal of the forms and practices of the life of the church, just as it requires reform and renewal of the language of doctrine if continuity is actually to be maintained. Williams notes that, 'It is a particularly thankless task in any period when the Church faces an apparently unmanageable and menacing array of changes'[29] – this, I fear, encapsulates the difficulty of the task of finding the appropriate way in which the forms and practices of church life are required to be renewed in the immediate context of contemporary life at the start of the twenty-first century in the western world.

It is hoped that this book has provided some food for thought for those whose vocation is to lead the practice of the life of the church and to find some orientations within which our life together might continue to be renewed and reformed. These are indeed challenging times for the church. If our society is no longer one that forms identity through collective and cultural memory in the way that it previously has, and this is a central part of the formation of the identity of the church, we need to think deeply and carefully about how we respond to this challenge. Equally, if social bonds are not formed through kinship groups and within a specific locus any longer, this poses a massive challenge to the church, which primarily is a social reality. To return to some of the responses that the church is beginning to make to this context, we must strongly affirm the desire of those involved in Emerging Church and Fresh Expressions movements to engage with the questions that our immediate context of life in God's world poses to us. These are not questions that can be avoided. Equally, with those who are more sceptical of such moves, such as Davison and Milbank, we must uphold their concern that the forms and practices of church life are absolutely central to the formation of the identity

---

[29] Ibid.

of the church. The faith is not a set of propositional statements that can be made manifest in different cultural forms, but rather, is inclusion within the sociality of Christ's body. What we do matters. We have seen that at a basic level that is about how we engage with scripture, reading and rereading it in ways that reform us, and how we engage in the sacramental life of the church. Our practices, though, cannot simply be repeated. Covenantal renewal in a scriptural sense is not about the repetition of practices, but the renewal of practice – repetition with variation. Otherwise, through our very desire to remain in continuity through the repetition of practice, we end up embodying something entirely different.

So where, in the midst of the context of God's world today, might the church begin to explore how it renews its practice as it gathers around the Word and the sacraments? In Giddens' account of the consequences of modernity, it is interesting that some of the issues he points to find resources within our Christian tradition that we might draw upon in response. We have commented above on the shifting patterns in social relationships away from kinship relations to personal intimate relationships. What is not different is the essentially social nature of human beings. Giddens states that

> . . . the world "out there" – the world that shades off into indefinite time-space from the familiarity of the home and the local neighbourhood – is not at all a purely impersonal one. On the contrary, intimate relationships can be sustained at distance . . . and personal ties are continually forged with others with whom one was previously unacquainted. We live in a *peopled* world. . .[30]

The New Testament church, as we explored above, understood some kind of shift from one sociality that gave the individual identity (biological, cultural, ethnic, etc.) to another: being in the body of Christ. What we noted was that this does not destroy the other identity, but radically relativizes it. We now live in a world where it is not simply the biological, cultural, ethnic and social distinctions which form our identity (although I would maintain these are still crucial), but our active self-determination in terms of our decision to locate trust in personal relationships of friendship and sexual encounter. Perhaps the church needs to consider more carefully what it means for these newer roots

---

[30] Giddens, *Consequences of Modernity*, p. 143.

of individual identity to be radically relativized in membership of the body of Christ. This too, does not result in the destruction of these other identities. Just as one was still a Jewish slave woman, but in Christ (although this has political consequences for the way the church engages with social institutions such as slavery), so in our present world, one remains in one's identity forming personal relationships and networks, though in Christ (this too may have political consequences for the churches relationships to some of these social forms). It is impossible to explore here what that might mean in reality, but the question seems pressing and urgent: what practices of church life form the social identity of the church in a social world formed by personal relationships, not kinship relationships? What might these new practices look like, and how will they genuinely form Christian sociality, while radically relativizing, but not destroying, the individual's social identity within the structures of life in the world?

If the above reflection offers some key questions for the church to be asking about its practices of social identity formation, there are also perhaps some hints of key questions that we might ask in terms of the way the church functions as a community of memory. According to Connerton, Giddens and Hervieu-Léger, we no longer live in a world where tradition and cultural memory function in the way in which they previously did. Here, I would note two things that might possibly point us in constructive directions in terms of how we are called to be the People of God in the midst of this new world. First, the issue of the new media in which collective memory is carried, and secondly the way in which the church responds to what Giddens has identified as the 'future-orientated' nature of late modern societies.

Aleida Assmann in her work on cultural memory spends a considerable proportion of her work examining the 'media' of memory. The headings under which she examines these in terms of western culture are writing, image, body and places. All of these she identifies as the media which carry and communicate the inhabited memory that she identifies as forming social identity.[31] In her conclusions, she notes that these media of memory are now shifting in new directions which are rapidly overtaking the media that have previously been significant throughout western civilization. Just as the printing press radicalized the way in which writing as a media carried cultural memory

---

[31] Assmann, *Cultural Memory*, pp. 137–26.

within society, the digital age is another revolutionary moment. 'With the dawn of the digital age, not only is the unchallenged reign of the book coming to an end, but so too is that of material writing in general. . . This revolution signals a radical structural change in the arts of memory'.[32] Assmann fears that this may ultimately bring to an end the age of memory as that which forms identity, but this may not necessarily be so. Information, and therefore memory, has always been communicated and stored in different forms. The church had to learn what the development of the printing press meant for the expression of the faith (and it radicalized it beyond recognition: most Protestants still find it hard to believe that for three quarters of the history of the church, individual bible reading simply was not and could not be a central act of devotion!). We need to learn what the shifts in media presently occurring mean. How do we locate and find practices that orientate us to the past, the world and the future within our present media? Connerton perhaps suggests one line of enquiry when he states that, 'we now live in such an 'over-informed' culture that cleverness will consist, not in accumulating information, which today can be done by any child on the internet, but in rejecting information'.[33] Does the church need to consider what practices might actually uphold a community that needs to be able to reject information, as much as maintain it? Do we need, to be able to hear the things that really matter, to develop practices of forgetfulness?

Similar to our engagement with the new media of memory, there may be significance in Giddens' observation about the future orientation of modernity. Historically, the church has found its vision of the future in the practices that call to mind the memories of God's past activity. Past and future unite in the present moment. Is there, perhaps, a way in which this becomes reversed in our present world but to the same effect? Is it our eschatological vision (which perhaps correlates with what Giddens sees as the necessity for 'utopian realism'[34]) which will enable us to draw the memory of the past from our anticipation of the future? What practices of church life might orientate us to the future in a way that enables the church to be for the world, and in such a way that connects that future orientation with the foundational memory of God's saving activity within history?

---

[32] Ibid., p. 399.
[33] Connerton, *How Modernity Forgets*, p. 146.
[34] Giddens, *Consequences of Modernity*, pp. 151–3.

Taking seriously the election of the church to be the body of Christ for the world in the power of the Spirit is, in our immediate context in the west, a deeply challenging vocation. There will be no easy answers, and no quick fixes. Faithfulness will not result in success in worldly terms. It is hoped, that in the reflections that have been offered in this book, some resources may be found to aid the church in its quest for the reform and renewal of its patterns of life and its practices that may enable the church to respond faithfully to our vocation to be for the world. That process will always reengage us with our scriptures, it will always call us to take seriously God's world as we live in it; it will always call us to take seriously our practices. To do that, we will need to keep focused on God's past activity within history, which has been for the sake of the whole of creation, the places within life in the world where God's Spirit is presently 'blowing where it wills', and the future kingdom of God which prophetically challenges all the structure of life in the world. In short, in our perpetual re-reading of scripture and celebrating of the sacraments, our practices will be faithfully continually reformed and renewed when we maintain the orientation offered to us in the words of Eucharistic acclamation: Christ has died, Christ is risen, Christ will come again.

Bibliography

Assmann, Aleida. *Cultural Memory and Western Civilization: Functions, Media, Archives* (Cambridge/New York: Cambridge University Press, 2011).

Assmann, Jan. *Cultural Memory and Early Civilization: Writing, Remembrance, and Political Imagination* (New York: Cambridge University Press, 2010).

Augustine. *City of God* (Henry Bettenson (trans.), London: Penguin Books, 1984).

— *On Baptism, Against the Donatists* (Dodds, M. (ed.), Edinburgh: T&T Clark, 1872).

Badcock, Gary D. *The House Where God Lives: Renewing the Doctrine of the Church for Today* (Grand Rapids/Cambridge: Eerdmans, 2009).

Barth, Karl. *The Theology of the Reformed Confessions* (Louisville/London: Westminster John Knox Press, 2002).

— *Church Dogmatics* (Edinburgh: T&T Clark, in 4 volumes, 1936–77).

Berger, Peter, Davie, Grace and Fokas, Effie. *Religious America, Secular Europe? A Theme and Variations* (Farnham/Burlington: Ashgate, 2008).

Bockmuehl, Markus and Thompson, Michael B. *A Vision for the Church: Studies in Early Christian Ecclesiology* (Edinburgh: T&T Clark, 1997).

Bonhoeffer, Dietrich. *Living Together* (London: SCM Press, 1954).

— *Sacntorum Communio: A Theological Study of the Sociology of the Church* (Clifford J. Green (ed.), Reinhard Krauss and Nancy Lukens (trans.), Dietrich Bonhoeffer Works, Volume 1, Minneapolis: Fortress Press, 1996).

Braaten, Carl E. and Jenson, Robert W. *Jews and Christians: People of God* (Grand Rapids: Eerdmans, 2003).

Brent, Allen (ed.). *On the Church: Select Treatises* (Popular Patristics Series, Nr. 32, Crestwood, New York: St. Vladimir's Seminary Press, 2006).

Brierley, Peter. *Pulling out of the Nose Dive: A Contemporary Picture of Churchgoing: What the 2005 English Church Census Reveals* (London: Christian Research, 2006).

Brown, Peter. *Augustine of Hippo: A Biography* (Berkeley and Los Angeles: University of California Press, 1969).

Bruce, Steve. *God is Dead: Secularization in the West* (Oxford: Blackwell, 2002).

— *Secularization: In Defence of an Unfashionable Theory* (Oxford: Oxford University Press, 2011).

Calvin, John. *Institutes of the Christian Religion, 1536 Edition* (Battles, Ford Lewis (trans.), Grand Rapids: Eerdmans, 1995).

— *Institutes of the Christian Religion,1559 Edition* (McNeill, John T. (ed.), Philadelphia: The Westminster Press, 1960).

— *Calvin's Commentaries: The Epistles of Paul the Apostle to the Romans and to the Thessalonians* (David W. Torrance and Thomas F. Torrance (eds), Ross Mackenzie (trans.), Grand Rapids: Eerdmans, 1960).

Cartledge, Mark J. and Mills, David. *Covenant Theology: Contemporary Approaches* (Carlisle: Paternoster Press, 2001).

Chadwick, Henry. *Augustine* (Oxford: Oxford University Press, 1986).

Childs, Brevard S. *Memory and Tradition in Israel* (London: SCM, 1967).

Church of England. *Mission-Shaped Church: Church Planting and Fresh Expressions of Church in a Changing Context* (London: Church House Publishing, 2004).

Church of Scotland. *Book of Common Order* (Edinburgh: Saint Andrew Press, 1994).

Community of Protestant Churches in Europe. *Ecclesia semper reformanda* (Draft, unadopted, unpublished paper).

Connerton, Paul. *How Societies Remember* (Cambridge: Cambridge University Press, 1989).

— *How Modernity Forgets* (Cambridge, Cambridge University Press, 2009).

Cornick, David. *Under God's Good Hand: A History of the Traditions which have Come Together in the United Reformed Church in the United Kingdom* (London: The United Reformed Church, 1998).

Curruthers, Mary. *The Book of Memory* (Cambridge, Cambridge University Press, 1990).

Davie, Grace. *Religion in Modern Europe: A Memory Mutates* (Oxford: Oxford University Press, 2000).

— *Europe: The Exceptional Case: Parameters of Faith in the Modern World* (London: Darton, Longman and Todd, 2002).

Davies, Philip R. *In Search of 'Ancient Israel'* (Sheffield: JSOTS, 1992).

Davison, Andrew and Milbank, Alison. *For the Parish: A Critique of Fresh Expressions* (London: SCM, 2010).

DeVries, Simon J. *Yesterday, Today, and Tomorrow: Time and History in the Old Testament* (London: S.P.C.K, 1975).

Dumbrell, William J. *Covenant & Creation: An Old Testament Covenantal Theology* (New South Wales: Paternoster Press, 1984).

Fergusson, David and Sarot, Marcel (eds). *The Future as God's Gift: Explorations in Christian Eschatology* (Edinburgh: T&T Clark, 2000).

Fiddes, Paul. *The Promised End: Eschatology in Theology and Literature* (Oxford: Blackwell, 2000).

Flannery O. P., Austin. *The Basic Sixteen Documents: Vatican Council II. Constitutions, Decrees, Declarations* (Northport, New York/Dublin: Costello Publishing Company and Dominican Publications, 1966).

Frymer-Kensky, Tikva, et al. (eds). *Christianity in Jewish Terms* (Colorado: Westview Press, 2000).

Gibbs, Eddie and Bolger, Ryan K. *Emerging Churches: Creating Christian Community in Postmodern Cultures* (London: SPCK, 2006).

Giddens, Anthony. *The Consequences of Modernity* (Cambridge: Polity Press, 1990).

Glasson, Barbara. *I Am Somewhere Else: A Gospel Reflection on an Emerging Church* (London: DLT, 2005).

Gockel, Matthias. *Barth & Schleiermacher on the Doctrine of Election: A Systematic-Theological Comparison* (Oxford: Oxford University Press, 2006).

Green, Laurie. *Let's Do Theology* (London: Mowbray, 1990).

Greggs, Tom. *Barth, Origen and Universal Salvation: Restoring Particularity* (Oxford: Oxford University Press, 2009).

— *Theology Against Religion* (London: T&T Clark, 2011).

Gunton, Colin. *The Promise of Trinitarian Theology* (Edinburgh: T&T Clark, 2003).

Haight S. J., Roger. *Christian Community in History: Historical Ecclesiology, Volume One* (New York/London: Continuum, 2004).

— *Christian Community in History: Comparative Ecclesiology, Volume Two* (New York/London: Continuum, 2005).

— *Ecclesial Existence: Christian Community in History, Volume Three* (New York/London: Continuum, 2008).

Halbwachs, Maurice. *On Collective Memory* (Lewis A. Coser (ed.), Chicago, IL: University of Chicago Press, 1992).

Harris, Richard. *After the Evil: Christianity and Judaism in the Shadow of the Holocaust* (Oxford: Oxford University Press, 2003).

Healy, Nicholas M. *Church, World and the Christian Life: Practical-Prophetic Ecclesiology* (Cambridge: Cambridge University Press, 2000).

Hervieu-Léger, Daniéle. *Religion as a Chain of Memory* (Cambridge: Polity Press, 2000).

Hill, Craig C. *In God's Time: The Bible and the Future* (Grand Rapids/Cambridge: Eerdmans, 2002).

Hull, John M. *Mission-Shaped Church: A Theological Response* (London: SCM, 2006).

Hunsinger, George (ed.), *For the Sake of the World: Karl Barth and the Future of Ecclesial Theology* (Grand Rapids/Cambridge: Eerdmans, 2004).

Huss, John. *De Ecclesia* (New York: Charles Scribner's Sons, 1915).

Jinkins, Michael. *The Church Faces Death: Ecclesiology in a Post-Modern Context* (New York/Oxford: Oxford University Press, 1999).

John Knox Series. *The Church in Reformed Perspective: A European Reflection* (Geneva: John Knox Series, 2002).

Kimball, Dan. *The Emerging Church: Vintage Christianity for New Generations* (Grand Rapids: Zondervan, 2003).

Kirwan, Christopher. *Augustine* (London: Routledge, 1989).

Lemche, Niels Peter. *The Israelites in History and Tradition* (London: SPCK, 1998).

Leuenberg Church Fellowship. *Church and Israel: A Contribution from the Reformation Churches in Europe to the Relationship between Christians and Jews* (Frankfurt am Main: Lembeck, 1992).

— *The Church of Jesus Christ: The Contribution of the Reformation towards Ecumenical Dialogue on Church Unity* (Frankfurt am Main: Lembeck, 1995).

Levinson, Bernard M. *Legal Revision and Religious Renewal in Ancient Israel* (New York: Cambridge University Press, 2008).

Lohse, Bernhard. *Martin Luther's Theology* (Edinburgh: T&T Clark, 1999).

Luther, Martin. *Luther's Works, American Edition* (Lehmann, Helmut T. (ed.), 55 volumes, Philadelphia: Fortress Press, 1958–1983).

McDonald, Suzanne. *Re-Imaging Election: Divine Election as Representing God to Other and Others to God* (Grand Rapids: Eerdmans, 2010).

McKim, Donald K. *Introducing the Reformed Faith: Biblical Revelation, Christian Tradition, Contemporary Significance* (Louisville: Westminster John Knox, 2001).

McLaren, Brain D. *Church on the Other Side: Exploring the Radical Future of the Local Congregation* (Grand Rapids: Zondervan, 2006).

— *Everything Must Change: Jesus, Global Crises, and a Revolution of Hope* (Nashville: Thomas Nelson, 2007).

McNutt, Paula. *Reconstructing the Society of Ancient Israel* (London: SPCK, 1999).

McPake, John L. *How do We Understand Our Present Reformed Identity?* (Unpublished, 2002).

Minear, Paul S. *Images of the Church in the New Testament* (London: Lutterworth Press, 1960).

Moltmann, Jürgen. *Theology of Hope: On the Ground and Implication of a Christian Eschatology* (London: SCM, 1967).

— *The Coming of God: Christian Eschatology* (London: SCM, 1996).

Novak, David. *The Image of the Non-Jew in Judaism* (New York and Toronto: Edwin Mellen Press, 1983).

— *The Election of Israel: The Idea of the Chosen People* (Cambridge: Cambridge University Press, 1995).

Osten-Sacken and Peter von der. *Christian-Jewish Dialogue: Theological Foundations* (Philadelphia: Fortress Press, 1986).

Pannenberg, Wolfhart. *Systematic Theology, Volume 3* (Grand Rapids: Eerdmans, 1989).

Presbyterian Church in the United States of America. *Book of Confessions* (Louisville: PCUSA, 1999).

— *Our Confessional Heritage: Confessions of the Reformed Tradition with a Contemporary Declaration of Faith* (Presbyterian Church in the United States, 1978).

Rahner, Karl. *The Trinity* (London: Burns and Oates, 1970).

Remaud, Michel. *Israel, Servant of God* (London/New York: T&T Clark, 2003).

Rendtorff, Rolf. *The Covenant Formula: An Exegetical and Theological Investigation* (Edinburgh: T&T Clark, 1998).

— *The Canonical Hebrew Bible: A Theology of the Old Testament* (David E. Orton (trans.), Leiderdorp: Deo Publishing, 2005).

Lindbeck, George A. *The Nature of Doctrine: Religion and Theology in a Postliberal Age* (London: SPCK, 1984).

Roberts, Richard H. *A Theology on its Way?* (Edinburgh: T&T Clark, 1991).

Rogers, Jr., Eugene F. *Sexuality and the Christian Body* (Oxford: Blackwell, 1999).

Rohls, Jan. *Reformed Confessions: Theology from Zurich to Barmen* (Louisville: Westminster John Knox Press, 1998).

Schlabach, Gerald W. *Unlearning Protestantism: Sustaining Christian Community in an Unstable Age* (Grand Rapids: Brazos Press, 2010).

Spinks, Bryan D. and Torrance, Iain R. *To Glorify God: Essays on Modern Reformed Liturgy* (Edinburgh: T&T Clark, 1999).

Steinmetz, David. *Calvin in Context* (New York/Oxford: Oxford University Press, 2010).

Stringer, Martin D. *A Sociological History of Christian Worship* (Cambridge, Cambridge University Press, 2005).

Taylor, Charles. *A Secular Age* (Cambridge, MA and London, England: The Belknap Press of Harvard University Press, 2007).

Thompson, David. *Stating the Faith: Formulations and Declarations of Faith from the Heritage of the United Reformed Church* (Edinburgh: T&T Clark, 1990).

United Reformed Church. *Year Book 1973/4* (London: United Reformed Church, 1974).

— *The Manual* (Sixth Edition, London: United Reformed Church, 2000).

— *Conversations on the Way to Unity 1999-2001: The Report of the Informal Conversations between the Church of England, the Methodist Church and the United Reformed Church* (London: United Reformed Church, 2001).

— *Worship: From the United Reformed Church* (London: United Reformed Church, 2003)

— *Year Book 2012* (London: United Reformed Church, 2012).

van Buren, Paul M. *A Christian Theology of the People Israel* (3 volumes, New York: Seabury Press, 1980 & 1983 and San Francisco: Harper and Row, 1988).

Vischer, Lukas (ed.). *Reformed Witness Today: A Collection of Confessions and Statements of Faith Issued by Reformed Churches* (Bern: Evangelische Arbeitsstellle Oekumene Schweiz, 1982).

Watson, Gerard. *Greek Philosophy and the Christian Notion of God* (Blackrock: The Columbia Press, 1994).

Weatherhead, James L. *The Constitution and Laws of the Church of Scotland* (Edinburgh: Church of Scotland, 1997).

Weinfeld, Moshe. *The Promise of the Land: The Inheritance of the Land of Canaan by the Israelite* (Berkeley/Los Angeles/Oxford: University of California Press, 1993).

Welker, Michael. *God the Spirit* (Minneapolis: Fortress Press, 1994).

Whitelam, Keith W. *The Invention of Ancient Israel: The Silencing of Palestinian History* (London: Routledge, 1996).

Williams, Rowan. *On Christian Theology* (Oxford: Blackwell, 2000).

— *Arius* (Second Edition, London: SCM, 2001).

Willis, David and Welker, Michael (eds).

Toward the Future of Reformed Theology (Grand Rapids, Eerdmans, 1999).

World Council of Churches. *The Theology of the Churches and the Jewish People: Statements by the World Council of Churches and its Member Churches* (Geneva: WCC, 1988).

Wright, Nicholas T. *The Climax of the Covenant: Christ and the Law in Pauline Theology* (Edinburgh: T&T Clark, 1991).

Wyschogrod, Michael. *The Body of Faith: God in the People Israel* (San Francisco: Harper and Row, 1983).

Yates, Frances. *The Art of Memory* (London: ARK Paperbacks, 1966/84).

Zachman, Randall C. *Reconsidering John Calvin* (Cambridge: Cambridge University Press, 2012).

Bible Index

Author Index

CPSIA information can be obtained
at www.ICGtesting.com
Printed in the USA
LVOW10s2307270617

539620LV00002B/18/P